The Concept of Authority

Joon-Seok Park

景仁文化社

PREFACE

This book aims to elucidate the positivist grounds of the normativity of a legal system by concentrating on the notion of authority of law.

Philosophers have long grappled with the problem of obligation to obey the law, either as the problem of the normativity of law or as the problem of the authority of state. The two problems have been dealt with separately, and the issue of relationship between them was until quite recently dismissed. However, considering that law is characterized by its 'so-called' *authoritativeness*, the notion of authority closely relates to the problem of the normativity of law.

The most remarkable attempts to articulate the grounds of the normativity of law are made by Hans Kelsen and H.L.A. Hart. They both regard two notions as essential to the explanation of the normativity of law: ultimate rule and systemic validity. These two notions play central role in their theories of the normativity of law.

This book shows, however, that Kelsen and Hart have failed for several reasons, and that it is impossible for them, without contradicting themselves, to invest legal norms with the property of neutral obligatoriness before resorting to the notion of authority of law.

Here, it is necessary to examine the notion of authority carefully. For 'authority' has traditionally been construed as the authority of *person*, but not of *law* itself. Actually, there is no consensus among theorists about the concept of authority. It has been understood either (*a*) as the justified power, or (*b*) as the right — either a liberty or a claim-right — to rule, or (*c*) as the normative capacity to impose duty.

Whichever notion above theorists may pick out to unpack the concept of authority, they conceive of it as *positional*, i.e. as an "ability" to do something. Authority is, for them, always the positional authority of a *person* or a body of persons involved in an authority relationship with subjects, but not of *law*.

However, we should conceive of the concept of authority not as positional but as *dispositional*, i.e. as respectable properties. For the notion of positional authority is (1) not sensitive enough to reflect a typical way to balance private interests among members of modern societies, and (2) unable to reproduce what Hart calls "the salient features of law", since it is embedded in a simple reductivist model of a legal system. The notion of rule or its internal aspects are unlikely to feature in any models of a legal system unless and until the notion of positional authority gives way to its dispositional counterpart.

The authority of law is not construed, in this book, as constituting a test of validity of any theories of the nature (or concept) of law. The theory of authority is, thus, regarded as the 'thin' theory which conceives of the authority (of law) simply as necessary for the law to exist as a system. In this respect, I object to Raz's conviction to the effect that the theory of authority provides support for the sources thesis. The critical analysis of Raz's argument done by employing 'the argument from falsity' and 'the nature thesis' shows that he fails to give sufficient support to his argument.

The central tenet underlying this book is that the notion of authority relates directly to the analysis of the structure of legal system, and therefore has an influence on the theory of (the nature of) law but only indirectly. What constitutes a test of validity of any theories of the nature of law is not the authority (of law) but the system of rules itself. And the authority (of law) is necessary for the law to exist as a system of rules. Therefore, not only exclusive but also inclusive and anti-positivism can resort to the concept of authority (of law) in the course of playing around with rules of a legal system.

I would like to thank my dissertation advisors at Seoul National University, Hun Sup Shim, Do kyun Kim, who are both respected scholars and distinguished teachers. They have encouraged me ever since I met them and chose to study philosophy of law. Moreover, they taught me how to lead a single-hearted life. Without their care, this book would never have been born and finished. My special thank must also go to Hyeon-Cheol Kim who has been my mentor. His invaluable comments on this book really helped.

I would also like to thank the selection board of SNU law series. Byoung Jo Che, the former director of SNU Law Research Institute, and In Seop Chung, the present director, also deserve my sincere thanks for their help. I really enjoyed several seasons with them at SNU Law Research Institute. Paul Shepherd, my australian friend and colleague at SNU Graduate School of Law, read the whole manuscript of this book and corrected my poor English. I am grateful for his incredible generosity.

My deepest gratitude must go to my father and mother, who set an example of responsible parents. With all my love and respect, I dedicate this small book to them. Finally, I would like to say I love you to my wife and my pretty baby.

contents

Ⅲ. Concepts of Authority • 75

Ⅳ. The Authority of Law • 129

Ⅴ. Conclusion • 151

I. Normative Foundations of a Legal System

1. Scope and Strategy

Philosophy of law is a branch of practical philosophy the main problem of which can be suggested in brief as finding the answer to the question of 'what one should do.' It does not help, of course, to answer the question by saying that 'one should do what ought to be done.' What must be sought is the basis on which we can guide our behaviour and, therefore, establish the standards of behaviour to which we can validly require ourselves to conform. Thus, the problem of practical philosophy comprises standards of human behaviour and their justificatory grounds.

Philosophers have long grappled with the practical problem as such in a specific form, namely, the problem of an obligation to obey the law. Are there any obligations to obey the law? Should we be bound to respect law? If so, under what conditions? Should we obey the law simply because it is a valid law (in the positivist sense), or only when it satisfies certain criteria of social justice?

This problem of obligation to obey the law cuts across moral, political and legal philosophies. Moral and political philosophers, on the one hand, have regarded it as (at least being a part of) the problem of the authority of state. Many, though not all, of those philosophers have supposed that these two are both sides of the coin. If state has a legitimate authority over its subjects, then, they believe, its subjects have an obligation to obey its law.

On the other hand, legal philosophers have dealt with it as a part of the problem of normativity of law.[1] What is the difference between an armed robber's order to turn over your wallet and the law levying tax on your properties?[2] How can the coercive order given by state, courts or police officials be interpreted as an objectively valid normative order? And more specifically, those who define the concept of the validity of law as its 'binding force' suggest that one has an obligation to obey the law regulating one's behaviour and therefore ought to behave as it provides, when it is valid. Some may raise an objection to interlocking problems of validity and authority in this way on the grounds that validity as 'binding force' concerns a *legal* obligation, whereas authority con-

---

1) I agree with Joseph Raz in stipulating that the law is normative "because its function is to guide human behaviour" or "in that it serves, and is meant to serve, as a guide for human behaviour." Joseph Raz, *The Concept of a Legal System: An Introduction to the Theory of Legal System*, Clarendon Press, Oxford, 1978 (1970), p.3, pp.168-9.

2) According to Hans Kelsen, this question can trace its history back to St. Augustine's *Civitas Dei*. Hans Kelsen, *Pure Theory of Law*, 2nd Edition, translated by Max Knight, University of California Press, Berkeley and Los Angeles, 1970 (1960), p.48; H.L.A. Hart, *The Concept of Law*, 2nd Edition, Clarendon Press, Oxford, 1994 (1961), p.82.

cerns a *moral* obligation. This objection is, however, misguided. For, as we shall see later, obligation to obey the law is, in both cases, a moral obligation. As Alf Ross rightly concludes, "[t]o assert that a legal system possesses validity or binding force is not to say anything about legal obligations or facts, but is to express our moral obligations."[3]

1) Authority and Validity

The problem of obligation to obey the law is, thus, a meeting place of branches of practical philosophy. However, in spite of this fact, there have been few discourses on the relationship between the problem of authority or legitimacy and the problem of normativity or validity, other than on each of the isolated problems. It seems that there are several reasons for philosophers to dismiss the issue of relationship between them from their mind. The most evident one of those reasons may be that moral and political philosophers have directed their attention to a possibility of rendering certain 'political' justification of authority, whereas many legal philosophers either have committed themselves to, or have at least been influenced by, the prevailing positivist doctrine of separation of law and morality, and of the existence of law and its political

---

3) Alf Ross, "Validity and the Conflict between Positivism and Natural Law", in Stanley L. Paulson and Bonnie Litschewski Paulson (eds.), *Normativity and Norms: Critical Perspectives on Kelsenian Themes*, Clarendon Press, Oxford, 1998, pp.153-4.

(and moral) justification. Of course, it may be the case that philosophers have simply been inspired by individual judgment of themselves, that is, not by doctrinal generalization, to the effect that the issue of relationship between them is a matter of little significance.

Whatever reasons they were actually motivated by, however, such a judgment of non-significance itself seems to be groundless. For one reason, the subject of authority is not exhausted by the issue of its justification and, in that result, may shed light along other passages on the problem of the nature of law, or more directly on the problem of its normativity. The theme of authority in contemporary practical philosophy concerns at least three different but related problems, which are a problem of concept, a problem of function and a problem of justification. Roughly speaking, the first is on the nature and conceptual structure of authority and has features that make it distinguishable from, though sometimes confused with, others, especially the third. Such confused explanations found in philosophical writings might feel unbearably misguided for some analytical theorists of philosophy of law.[4] As Joseph Raz

---

4) While it is required to discern the first from the third, it is often, but not always, the case that last two problems invite theorists to connect them. Understandably, certain entity or an institution may be justified by recourse to its function or benefits brought into by it. But supposedly, in the case of deontologist justification, functional benefits might be ignored since it is supposed to be *ipso facto* right to obey the authority. Cf. Hyo Chong Park, *State and Authority* (in Korean), Pakyoungsa, Seoul, 2001, p.22. However, it is worth mentioning here that in spite of deep disagreement over their

reasonably says, discussion of the nature of authority would not be exhausted by explaining the way in which people come to accept or recognize the authority of someone.[5] This view, however, does not have an implication that the legitimacy of authority can be established without questioning the nature of authority.

For another reason, the characteristics of law seem to make it necessary for us to consider the problem of authority, or authoritativeness. Admittedly, both the laws and the legal materials, which should be distinguished from each other, are characterized by their so-called authoritativeness.[6] It is a natural result of this fact that, though different from the traditional way in which the problem of authority has been dealt with, we need recognize the problem of authority not merely as that of *state* but also as that of *law* itself[7] and that, as Ross points out when he criticizes Alfred Verdross and Karl Bergbohm, the relationship between the problem of authority and the problem of validity is not simply interpreted to the effect

---

fundamental moral beliefs, both consequentialist and deontologist justifications of authority share the same inferential structure which is namely 'syllogistic', otherwise they would have failed to avoid the naturalistic fallacy. Each of the major premises of those syllogisms must be a norm ('keep your words', 'do fair and square', etc. for instance) under which some facts are considered to be subsumed.

5) Joseph Raz, *The Authority of Law: Essays on Law and Morality*, Clarendon Press, Oxford, 1983 (1979), pp.5-7.

6) H.L.A. Hart, "Definition and Theory in Jurisprudence", *Essays in Jurisprudence and Philosophy*, Clarendon Press, Oxford, 1983, p.28; Raz (1978a), p.38, p.71.

7) Raz (1983), p.29.

that "positive law possesses 'validity', derived from the authority of the state."[8]

What implications, then, does it convey for a law to be authoritative, or to have an authority over people whose behaviour it regulates? What is the conceptual difference, or relationship, between the validity regarded as binding force and the (legitimate) authority which, supposedly, entails an obligation to which one should be bound?[9] And, more basically, why is the authority of law expected to be legitimate, or to have legitimacy: either for moral and political justification of its authority, or for its being valid, or for something else?

A great many questions, including those mentioned above, that seem to be crucial for understanding the nature of law require us to take authority seriously. Philip Soper exhibits his interpretation of this issue in a similar tone. He claims that the assumption that

---

8) Ross (1998), p.157. Ross criticizes each of them for different reasons. He criticizes Verdross, "an ardent defender of natural law", for his using the word 'positivism' to denote too many, and Bergbohm for his employing a doctrine of validity which in fact contradicts with his own positivist commitment.

9) The same question is raised by Ernesto Garzón Valdés but remains unresolved. Valdés suggests that 'duty to obey' is, at least partially, used as a "synonym" for 'validity' both in Kelsen and Suárez, and that the two terms are "analytically interdependent." Ernesto Garzón Valdés, "Two Models of Legal Validity: Hans Kelsen and Francisco Suárez", translated by Ruth Zimmerling, in Stanley L. Paulson and Bonnie Litschewski Paulson (eds.), *Normativity and Norms: Critical Perspectives on Kelsenian Themes* (1998), p.265, p.271.

one does not need to decide what law is before deciding whether there is an obligation to obey it is unwarranted.[10] Raz also claims that the concept of authority plays a part in our understanding of the nature of law as well as in determining our obligation to the law.[11] Moreover, he attempts to employ his analysis of the concept of authority in evaluating theories of the nature of law.[12] As H.L.A. Hart has already pointed out, the concept of authority "bestrides both law and political theory."[13]

2) Authority and Neutrality

It may be said that there are various ways in which we can establish the normativity of a legal system. Hans Kelsen examines some candidates for the way and rejects all of them but one.[14] The only one that has survived is the so-called 'pure theoretical way', or more generally, a legal positivist way.

What should be noted here is that, according to Kelsen, such candidates are indiscriminate in their presupposing a hypothetical

---

10) Philip Soper, "Legal Theory and the Obligation to Obey", *Georgia Law Review* 18 (Summer 1984), p.891.

11) Raz (1983), pp.29-30.

12) Joseph Raz, *Ethics in the Public Domain: Essays in the Morality of Law and Politics*, Clarendon Press, Oxford, 1994, p.195.

13) Hart (1994), p.98.

14) Hans Kelsen, "Why Should the Law be Obeyed?", *What is Justice?*, University of California Press, Berkeley and Los Angeles, 1957, p.257 ff. He examines and rejects doctrines of natural law (including doctrine of justice) and Christian theology.

basic norm as the ultimate reason for the validity of law. The only criterion that can help us discriminate between them is acceptability of them as the *foundations*[15] of law from the point of view of a science of law the function of which is "not the evaluation of its subject but its value-free description."[16] The foundations of law can be neither "an animistic superstition" that "men ought to obey the commands of nature"[17] nor "a meta-physical assumption" that "men ought to obey the commands of God."[18]

But then, is there not any possibility to accept as the foundations of law certain moral and political principles which are by and large sound, that is, which are neither animistic nor metaphysical? Tony Honoré offers an adequate explanation of Kelsen's position on this question to us.

He declines to look for an ethical or political justification for the binding character of legal norms. Why so? His refusal to entertain

---

15) The German words 'Grundlage' and 'Grundordnung' are both translated as 'foundation'. In this *book*, and both in Kelsen and Hart as well, I think, the term 'foundation' is used in the sense of 'Grundlage'. Cf. Hans Kelsen, "Die Grundlage der Naturrechtslehre", translated by Carmen G. Mayer, in John Finnis (ed.), *Natural Law Vol. 1*, New York University Press, New York, 1991, p.125 ff. (Peter Heath's translation is also available. See Hans Kelsen, *Essays in Legal and Moral Philosophy*, translated by Peter Heath, D. Reidel Publishing Company, Dordrecht, 1973, p.114 ff.); Robert Alexy, "Postscript", *A Theory of Constitutional Rights*, translated by Julian Rivers, Oxford University Press, New York, 2002 (1986), pp.390-4.
16) Kelsen (1970), p.68.
17) Kelsen (1957a), p.258.
18) Kelsen (1957a), p.261.

the idea that moral or political principles make laws binding is dictated, I think, by an aspiration which is at the core of his concern. He wants to show that, given that it is impossible to secure agreement on moral and political principles, law can be regarded as an autonomous system of social control, independent of morals and politics. If it is to be so regarded, it must possess its own justification, based on its own ideology. It cannot parade in borrowed finery.[19)]

Kelsen thinks that the foundations of law must be objective and that any moral and political principles cannot be accepted as the objective foundations of that law, for such principles are inevitably biased and thus lack even the possibility that those who are regulated by a law which belongs to a certain legal system would reach an agreement on the contents of them. Kelsen's criteria of acceptability as the foundations of law can be regarded, though full investigation of this is beyond the purpose of this book, as at least including the possibility of consensus. He says that "[i]t is paramount and cannot be emphasized enough to understand that not only one moral order exists, but many different and even conflicting ones; that a positive legal order may on the whole conform with the moral views of a certain group of the population (especially the ruling one), yet may conflict with the moral views of an-

---

19) Tony Honoré, "The Basic Norm of a Society", *Making Law Bind: Essays Legal and Philosophical*, Clarendon Press, Oxford, 1987, p.94. [Footnote omitted.]

other group."[20] Therefore, we can rewrite the main question of Kelsen as 'are there foundations independent of moral and political values, or any *neutral* foundations on which we can establish the normativity of a legal system?'[21]

Now we can ask him what would happen if there were cases in which certain human necessity conflicts with his *neutrality thesis*[22] by obliging someone, for example, to disregard the requirement of consensus itself or to override what has already been agreed to.[23] First, such human necessity may be reflected in the law whose na-

---

20) Kelsen (1970), p.68.
21) Hubert Rottleuthner uses instead an expression "internal foundation", noticing "internalists" emphasizing the self-generating character of a legal order. But he classifies Lon Fuller, with Kelsen and Niklas Luhmann, as internalists. Hubert Rottleuthner, *Foundations of Law*, Springer, Dordrecht, 2005, p.161 ff. Cf. Kelsen refers to grounding validity of law on neutral (or internal) foundations as "self-grounding (Selbstbegründung)" of law. Hans Kelsen, "Die Selbstbes-timmung des Recht", translated (in Korean) and edited by Hun Sup Shim, *Schriften zur Rechtstheorie*, Bub Moon Sa, Seoul, 1990, p.95.
22) This reflects his cause of the unbridgeable gap between the 'ought' and the 'is' as well as law's independence from moral and political value. Therefore, it comprehends theses that Raz calls the contingent connection thesis and the sources thesis, and is not identical with the principle of the autonomy of norms. Raz (1983), p.125; Joseph Raz, "The Purity of the Pure Theory", in Richard Tur and William Twining (eds.), *Essays on Kelsen*, Clarendon Press, Oxford, 1986, pp.81-2.
23) The word 'necessity' means, here, what Kelsen calls "the motivating effect" (the psychological sense) the confusion of which with another meaning of it, "the binding character of an obligation" (the normative sense), should be avoided. Hans Kelsen, "A 'Dynamic' Theory of Natural Law", *What is Justice?* (1957), p.191.

ture can be explained in various ways. Some philosophers may regard it as guaranteeing someone mere immunity from that requirement, while others go further, claiming that it confers on him the
power to have the final word. And still others may prefer the conception of duty-imposing law as an explanation of it, that is, their
preferred explanation is that someone should be under a certain
duty to balance those two needs: to free a society of, or to bind it
with, the requirement of consensus in specific cases. Second, it may
also be possible for any society to have no such law, in spite of
the existence of such human necessity: "Necessity knows no law."

It is a matter of course that in both cases the problem of conflict
between that human necessity and Kelsen's neutrality thesis can
arise. It is worth mentioning here that such human necessity is
basically *the necessity for authority* or, to put it in G.E.M. Anscombe's words, 'the necessity of a task' from which authority a-
rises.[24] This is the central tenet of the theory of the social contract. And John Rawls also shares it although he identifies the original contract not as one to set up a particular form of governmental authority, but as one to draw the principles of justice.[25]
The same point as mine is made by A. John Simmons. He puts it
thus:

---

24) G.E.M. Anscombe, "On the Source of the Authority of the State", Ratio 20
    (1978). Reprinted in Joseph Raz (ed.), *Authority*, New York University
    Press, New York, 1990, p.147. [References are to the reprint.]
25) John Rawls, *A Theory of Justice*, 2nd Edition, Harvard University Press,
    Cambridge, 2003 (1971), p.10.

> Rawls seems relatively unconcerned with justifying the state (or
> a kind of state) in a way designed to rebut the (real or imagined)
> objections of anarchists or others who favor nonstate forms of co-
> operation. Rawlsian justification is principally a justification of co-
> ercion offered to those who already accept the necessity of living
> in some kind of state. The only real justificatory question is: what
> kind of state? ··· They select, in short, the best form for a state to
> take, not the state itself. The moral necessity of a large-scale poli-
> tical / economic institutional structure seems to be a background as-
> sumption of, not a demonstrated step in, the project of political jus-
> tification in Rawlsian political philosophy.[26]

Therefore, it is the case that the question at issue takes its rise from the conflict between authority and consensus. Now, it might be thought that the conflict between authority and consensus des-cribed above is translated into the conflict between authorities[27] for the following grounds. First, modern democratic countries insti-tutionalize, either customarily or by enactment, division of powers. Second, decisions of a certain ('authoritative') body of persons are regarded, in those countries, as representing national consensus. How-ever, the conception of conflict between authorities fails to reflect the (common) undemocratic nature of authority, which enables Plato in *Republic* to embrace, for the guidance of men, 'coercion through

---

26) A. John Simmons, "Justification and Legitimacy", *Ethics* 109 (July 1999), p.758.

27) Cf. This is what a plurality of the Supreme Court of U.S. said in *Goldwater v. Carter*, which shall be discussed below.

reason' for which he later in *Laws* substitutes rule of law.[28)]

The following case for which I am much indebted to In-Seop Chung[29)] shows that the problem of conflict between authority and consensus is neither confined to a political area[30)] nor always represented as a case of discrepancies between what is law and what is not, and that therefore not only neutrality but also authority should be considered, in order for us to articulate normative foundations of law.

The Constitution of the Republic of Korea provides that the President, who is the Head of State and represents the State vis-à-vis foreign states, has the power to conclude and ratify treaties, and that the National Assembly has the right to consent to the conclusion and ratification of treaties which fall into the categories specified in the Constitution.[31)] And Art.6 para.1 of the Constitu-

---

28) Hannah Arendt, "What is Authority?", *Between Past and Future: Eight Exercises in Political Thought*, Penguin Books, New York, 1977, pp.107-8.
29) In-Seop Chung, "Termination of Treaties and Legislative Approval" (in Korean), *Seoul International Law Journal* 11 (2004), p.139 ff.
30) In Korea, the following case has never been taken into court, but has been in United States. *Goldwater v. Carter* is highly cited as that case. However, in *Goldwater v. Carter*, Justice Rehnquist said that the case posed a non-justiciable political question. (This was the plurality opinion.) 444 U.S. 996 (1979), at 1002. As to brief criticism contending that the Court's approach is problematic, see Erwin Chemerinsky, *Constitutional Law: Principles and Policies*, 2nd Edition, Aspen Publishers, New York, 2002, p.277, p.363.
31) Art.60 para.1 "The National Assembly shall have the right to consent to the conclusion and ratification of treaties pertaining to mutual assistance or mutual security; treaties concerning important international organizations; treaties of friendship, trade and navigation; treaties pertaining to any restriction

tion reads as follows: "Treaties duly concluded and promulgated under the Constitution ⋯ shall have the same effect as the domestic laws of the Republic of Korea." However, there is no single provision in the Constitution or other domestic laws of ROK to control the procedure of treaty termination.[32] The question is who has the power to terminate treaties on what conditions. The crucial problem, here, is whether or not treaties of categories specified in Art.60 para.1 concluded with the consent of the National Assembly shall be terminated, in return, with the consent of the National Assembly.[33] For those treaties "have the same effect" as domestic laws and ordinary domestic laws are always terminated by the actions of the National Assembly designed to create another laws conflicting with the first. (The first laws are either substituted or simply repealed by the second laws. And both the cases involve law-

---

in sovereignty; peace treaties; treaties which will burden the State or people with an important financial obligation; or treaties related to legislative matters"; Art.66 para.1 "The President shall be the Head of State and represent the State vis-à-vis foreign states"; Art.73 "The President shall conclude and ratify treaties; accredit, receive or dispatch diplomatic envoys; and declare war and conclude peace."

32) Chung (2004), p.141. Things are not different in United States. Art. Ⅱ §2 cl. 2 of the Constitution of the United States of America provides only that the President "shall have Power, by and with the Advice and Consent of the Senate, to make Treaties, provided two thirds of the Senators present concur", without mentioning the power to terminate treaties.

33) It also was the very point at issue in *Goldwater v. Carter*, where Senator Goldwater contended "that just as the president cannot unilaterally repeal a law, neither is it constitutional for the president to rescind a treaty without the Senate's consent." See Chemerinsky (2002), p.139.

creating actions of the National Assembly.) Therefore, it is beyond powers of the President to terminate ordinary domestic laws, unless the State were "in time of internal turmoil, external menace, natural calamity or a grave financial or economic crisis."[34] And even when the State were in crises as such, termination of laws would be completed by the post-factum approval of the National Assembly.[35]

Are treaties also terminated by the actions of the National Assembly? Or can the President unilaterally terminate treaties which derive their validity, at least partially, from the congressional actions?[36] It is, of course, quite important to answer this question and, therefore, to bridge a gap in the law prescribing the treaty-terminating procedure. Actually, Chung devotes major sections of

---

34) Art.76 para.1 "In time of internal turmoil, external menace, natural calamity or a grave financial or economic crisis, the President may take in respect to them the minimum necessary financial and economic actions or issue orders having the effect of Act, only when it is required to take urgent measures for the maintenance of national security or public peace and order, and there is no time to await the convocation of the National Assembly"; Art.76 para.2 "In case of major hostilities affecting national security, the President may issue orders having the effect of Act, only when it is required to preserve the integrity of the nation, and it is impossible to convene the National Assembly."

35) Art.76 para.3 "In case actions are taken or orders are issued under paragraphs (1) and (2), the President shall promptly notify it to the National Assembly and obtain its approval"; Art.76 para.4 "In case no approval is obtained, the actions or orders shall lose effect forthwith. In such case, the Acts which were amended or abolished by the orders in question shall automatically regain their original effect at the moment the orders fail to obtain approval."

36) As to pros and cons on this question, see Chung (2004), p.149 n.35.

his article which was referred to above to coping with this question. But what this book concerns itself with is the underlying cause of the gap, i.e. the fact that at the root of this gap lies the conflict between authority and consensus. Should the foundations of the normativity of a legal system be always neutral, or comply with the requirement of consensus, even though there exists no positive law relevant to given cases at the constitutional level?

2. Overview

Two main concepts involved in this study are authority and validity of law; through these concepts inquiry into the normativity of law will be made in the following chapters. Chapter 2 will review Kelsen and Hart's positions on the problem of the normativity of law, focusing on their notions of ultimate rule and systemic validity. Although it is evident that these two notions do not exhaust their theoretical devices of reasoning, we will address only these two notions since they allow us to sketch out general positions of those philosophers. Therefore, the notions other than the two, the major instances of which are 'the point of view of a science of law' (Kelsen) and 'the internal point of view' (Hart), will be touched on briefly.

There are significant similarities between Kelsen and Hart's approaches to the problem. Nevertheless, as is occasionally pointed out, each of them holds a different view of the nature of ultimate rule, validity and thus normativity of law. Both approaches, however, are problematic, since they fail to eliminate at least three different but related theoretical defects, let alone the ambiguity of the word 'validity' itself. Chapter 2 will outline different meanings of the word and examine such problematic topics as 'validity of ultimate rule', 'validity and conflicts between norms', and 'validity and justification of legal system' and also show that, to eliminate those defects, it is necessary to introduce the notion of authority of *law*.

Exploring the notion of authority of law, chapter 3 also examines the notion of political authority, which is more familiar to us. At first, ideas of practical and theoretical authority will be addressed. Many theorists regard political authority as practical, but some others stand on the opposite site.

Then, an investigation into three competing models of the nature of political authority, i.e. an 'influence' model, a 'normative capacity to impose duties' model and a 'right to rule' model, will be made. These models, however, are on the common assumption that every practical authority, including the authority of law, is subjective or *positional*. Such an assumption will be thoroughly examined. Also I shall suggest that the authority of law is a rather *dispositional* than positional concept.

Chapter 4 is devoted to speculating about the relationship between the authority of law and the nature of law. First, it will be shown that the notion of positional authority is deeply embedded in a simple reductivist model of a legal system, and that therefore it cannot reproduce what Hart calls the salient features of law: the continuity of legislative authority, the persistence of law and the self-binding force of legislation. Second, it will be examined whether the authority of law constitutes a genuine test of validity of any theories of the nature (or concept) of law. This issue connects to the Razian thesis, which Wilfrid Waluchow calls "Raz's most powerful argument",[37] to the effect that "a proper understanding of the concept of authority commits us to exclusive positivism."[38]

In the later part of chapter 4, the critical analysis of Raz's argument for the thesis will be done by employing 'the argument from falsity' and 'the nature thesis', and it shows that Raz fails to give sufficient support to his argument.

According to many legal theorists, including Raz, law claims legitimate authority. What do they mean by this cliché? *How* such claims to authority are laid by law? Are they assuming what law claims is nothing more than what the courts say that it claims?[39] From this question should we sharply divide the question of conceivability of the authority of law. Even though it is possible to

---

37) Wilfrid Waluchow, *Inclusive Legal Positivism*, Clarendon Press, Oxford, 1994, p.123. Tim Dare calls it the "argument from authority." Tim Dare, "Wilfrid Waluchow and the Argument from Authority", in Tom D. Campbell (ed.), *Legal Positivism*, Ashgate / Dartmouth, Aldershot, 1999, p.350.
38) Dare (1999), p.350.
39) Cf. Joseph Raz, *The Morality of Freedom*, Clarendon Press, Oxford, 1990 (1986), p.70; Raz (1983), p.236.

talk directly of the authority of law itself rather than talk of a person in authority,[40] it is unwarranted that the nature of authority in the first context is simply the same as that in the latter context. As has already been mentioned, the authority of law is objective and dispositional conception while political authority has been understood to be subjective and positional.

When those theorists say that a single law, or a legal system presents itself as legitimate, they anticipate the following two questions. First, is the legitimacy of law 'an objective feature' of valid law?[41] Second, does it not matter whether or not law is telling the truth?[42] And 'the argument from falsity' also concerns these questions.

In conclusion, the central tenet underlying this book is that the notion of authority relates directly to the analysis of the structure of legal system, and therefore has an influence on the theory of

---

40) Raz (1983), p.29.
41) Ota Weinberger, "Legal Validity, Acceptance of Law, Legitimacy. Some Critical Comments and Constructive Proposals", *Ratio Juris* 12 (December 1999), p.347; William A. Edmundson, "Legitimate Authority without Political Obligation", *Law and Philosophy* 17 (1998), p.56; Robert Alexy, *Begriff und Geltung des Rechts*, Verlag Karl Alber, Freiburg and München, 1992, pp.108-9.
42) Larry Alexander and Emily Sherwin, "Deception in Morality and Law", *Law and Philosophy* 22 (2003), pp.427-30; Patric Durning, "Joseph Raz and the Instrumental Justification of a Duty to Obey the Law", *Law and Philosophy* 22 (2003), p.620; Edmundson (1998), p.60; R. Ladenson, "In Defense of a Hobbesian Conception of Law", *Philosophy and Public Affairs* 9 (Winter 1980). Reprinted in Raz (ed.), *Authority* (1990), p.37. [References are to the reprint.]

(the nature of) law but only indirectly. If this is correct, we can say that the authority of law does not constitute a genuine test of validity of any theories of the nature of law, and is necessary for the law to exist as a system of rules. Therefore, not only exclusive but also inclusive and anti-positivism can resort to the authority (of law) in the course of playing around with rules of a legal system.

II. Kelsen and Hart on Normativity of Law

Undoubtedly, Hans Kelsen and H.L.A. Hart were two of the most remarkable philosophers of law in the last century. Their prodigious influence on modern jurisprudence has not declined for decades. On the contrary, their themes have continuously been accompanied by voluminous books and essays written by both admirers and critics. Of all their valuable contributions to legal theories, this chapter examines what they both regard as essential to the explanation of the normativity of a legal system: ultimate rule and systemic validity.

As has already been said, discussion of the subject of the normative foundations of a legal system would not be exhausted by exploring these two notions. What Kelsen calls "the basic norm of a positive legal order" is the basic norm "seen from the point of view of a science of positive law."[1]

> [T]he validity of this constitution [: the historically first constitution] must be presupposed *if we want to interpret* (1) the acts performed according to it as the creation or application of valid

---

1) Kelsen (1957a), p.262.

general legal norms; and (2) the acts performed in application of these general norms as the creation or application of valid individual legal norms. Since the reason for the validity of a norm can only be another norm, the presupposition must be a norm.[2]

Such an interpretation means "derivation" of legal meaning of a certain act from "a norm whose content refers to the act." The norm presupposed to make the historically first constitution objectively valid is nothing other than what he calls the basic norm. According to him, only and all those norms are "the objects of the science of law."[3] To put it in Honoré's words will render us a clearer picture of "the point of view of a science of law" which is of critical importance in Kelsen's theory of the normative foundations of a legal system.

No particular law can be shown to be good. All that can be shown is that from the point of view of this or that person or group — X or Y or lawyers or Christians or utilitarians — it ought to be obeyed. But this is enough to make the norm, in Kelsen's terms, objectively valid: that is, binding and justified *from the chosen point of view.*

··· The most that is possible is a more modest project. We can study the implications of the assumption, which this or that person or group may entertain, that laws create obligations. We can

---

2) Kelsen (1970), p.200. [Those in brackets are mine. Original emphasis omitted and mine added.]
3) Kelsen (1970), p.4.

try to find out if there is a point of view from which laws which are effective can also be held to impose binding obligations.

A person who, instead of taking for granted that laws create obligations, asks on what assumptions it could be true that they do so, adopts a distinctive point of view. It is not the point of view of any particular person who may think laws binding. The appropriate point of view is rather that of legal science or theory, that is, of the theorist who has a professional concern with the whole legal system and, indeed, with legal systems in general.[4]

Kelsen says that the legal-scientific interpretation of the acts of will of someone about the behaviour of others as the norm-creating acts, i.e. the legal-scientific interpretation of the subjective meaning of the acts as their objective meaning,[5] is "conditional upon" the presupposition of the basic norm.[6]

Hart's theory of the normative foundations of a legal system is

---

4) Honoré (1987), p.93. [Footnote omitted.]

5) Kelsen says that it is necessary to distinguish between the subjective and the objective meaning of an act. He puts it, "'Ought' is the subjective meaning of every act of will directed at the behaviour of another. But not every such act has also the objectively this meaning; and only if the act of will has also the objective meaning of an 'ought', is this 'ought' called a 'norm'. If the 'ought' is also the objective meaning of the act, the behavior at which the act is directed is regarded as something that *ought* to be not only from the point of view of the individual who has performed the act, but also from the point of view of the individual at whose behavior the act is directed, and of a third individual not involved in the relation between the two." Kelsen (1970), p.7.

6) Hans Kelsen, *General Theory of Norms*, translated by Michael Hartney, Clarendon Press, Oxford, 1991 (1979), p.256.

directed, like that of Kelsen, against reductivism.[7] Hart shows that the doctrine which "insists that habitual obedience to orders backed by threats is the foundation of a legal system"[8] fails to account for "some of the salient features of a legal system."[9] According to the reductivist theorists, to have an obligation to do something means nothing more than that there is a chance or likelihood for the person under the obligation to suffer an unpleasant experience, e.g. a punishment, in the event of disobedience. However, "the statement that someone has or is under an obligation does indeed imply the existence of a rule."[10] Hart insists that duty or obligation is a "rule-dependent" notion,[11] but that the reductivist doctrine has no resources to feed the concept of a 'rule' properly. To put it in his own words,

> The root cause of failure is that the elements out of which the theory was constructed, viz. the ideas of orders, obedience, habits,

---

7) Raz (1986), pp.81-5.
8) Hart (1994), p.61.
9) Hart (1994), p.79.
10) Hart (1994), p.85. In a different place, Hart calls this feature of statements of legal obligation "the 'normativity' of such statements and statements *of the law* or the legal position of individuals under the law." And he rejects the idea of reducing statement of the law to statement about the law. "To say that a man has a legal obligation to do a certain act is not, though it may imply, a statement about the law or a statement that a law exists requiring him to behave in a certain way." H.L.A. Hart, "Legal Duty and Obligation", *Essays on Bentham: Studies in Jurisprudence and Political Theory*, Clarendon Press, Oxford, 1982, p.144.
11) Hart (1994), p.89.

and threats, do not include, and cannot by their combination yield, the idea of a rule, without which we cannot hope to elucidate even the most elementary forms of law.[12]

A single rule or a set of rules (one specific instance of which a legal system is) cannot be reduced to 'the habitual obedience to orders backed by threats' since a social rule has a feature which he calls "the internal aspect of rules." According to Hart, it is the key to explaining the normativity of law. For the problem of the normativity of law is, for Hart, nothing other than "explaining the e-valuative dimension of legal language while remaining true to the separation thesis."[13] He believes that it is one of the crucial features which distinguish social rules from mere habits that have an external aspect, 'the regular uniform behaviour' of members of a social group, only.

> How does a habit differ from a rule? What is the difference between saying of a group that they have the habit, e.g. of going to the cinema on Saturday nights, and saying that it is the rule with them that the male head is to be bared on entering a church?[14]

The internal aspect of rules can be captured by considering "the *social* dimension of rules, namely the manner in which members of

---

12) Hart (1994), p.80.
13) Dennis Patterson, "Explicating the Internal Point of View", *SMU Law Review* 52 (Winter 1999), p.69.
14) Hart (1994), p.55.

a society *perceive* the rule in question, their *attitude* towards it",[15] since it is manifested in a "reflective critical attitude" of members of the group to certain patterns of behaviour.[16]

The point of view of a science of law and the internal point of view are of great importance in understanding Kelsen and Hart on the issue of the normativity of law. Nonetheless, we can grasp the structure of their theories of a legal system as the two most venerable models of the positivist, and foundationalist[17] as well, approach to the task of articulating the grounds of law by concentrating on their notions of ultimate rule and systemic validity. Therefore, it will suffice to explore those two notions below.

---

15) Raymond Wacks, *Understanding Jurisprudence: An Introduction to Legal Theory*, Oxford University Press, New York, 2005, p.76.

16) Hart (1994), p.57. Although there are not a few of similarities between their views of legal statements, Kelsen and Hart do not concur. Raz indicates that "Kelsen advances a cognitivist interpretation of all normative discourse. He rejects expressive explanations such as Hart's. For him a normative statement, be it legal, moral, or other, expresses a practical attitude only in that it expresses a belief in the existence of a valid norm, and a norm constitutes a value. Hence the normative aspect of legal statements is not to be explained by their illocutionary force nor by the fact, taken by itself, that they express an acceptance of a standard of behaviour. It has to be explained by the fact that such statements state or presuppose the existence of a value or a norm, that is, a normatively binding standard and not merely a social practice." Raz (1986), pp.86-7. [Footnote omitted.]

17) For a brief description of 'epistemological foundationalism' or 'the foundationalist picture of the structure of a body of knowledge', see the following section of this book.

1. Ultimate Rule and Systemic Validity

1) Ultimate Rule of a Legal System

Kelsen and Hart embark on the task of articulating the grounds of law, concerning themselves among others with the issue of legal cognition, which would be crystallized by explaining the criteria of identification of law. Definitely, they are not legal sceptics. As Sean Coyle points out, legal sceptics are those who deny "that there is any recognisable feature or set of features that could be used to mark off legal norms from other normative kinds or, at a wider level, legal systems from any other frame-work that is the object of practical discourse."[18] The views upheld by Kelsen and Hart can be called the legal version of foundationalism. To do justice to this understanding of their views, it is helpful to remind ourselves of some notions used in modern epistemology.[19]

In epistemology, there exist questions about the structure of a body of knowledge as there exist, in jurisprudence, questions about

---

18) Sean Coyle, "Hart, Raz and the Concept of a Legal System", *Law and Philosophy* 21 (2002), p.276.

19) Edmund Gettier has convincingly disproved a traditional thesis that knowledge is "justified, true belief." Edmund Gettier, "Is Justified True Belief Knowledge?", *Analysis* 23 (1963), p.121 ff. But this does not stop one, I think, from following the traditional way in order to draw an analogy between epistemological foundationalism and, namely, legal foundationalism. Thus, 'knowledge' and 'justified (true) belief' will be used interchangeably in this book.

the structure of a body of law.[20]

> The natural picture, prominent in the history of philosophy ⋯,
> is that a body of knowledge consists of a foundation of noninfer-
> ential knowledge and a superstructure of knowledge that is in some
> sense inferentially based on the foundations.[21]

This picture is foundationalism. It has traditionally been sup-
ported by the following argument, the purpose of which is to es-
cape from what Michael Williams calls "Agrippa's Trilemma."[22]
He names it after the ancient sceptic who, he thinks, is the first
man that articulated it.[23]

> **AT**: How can someone's claim that he knows something
> be justified? He will try to justify his claim by suggesting
> another thing in support of it. But such an 'evidence' in

---

20) According to Raz, the problem of structure ("Is there a structure common
    to all legal systems, or to certain types of legal system?") is one of the
    four problems the solutions to which "a complete theory of legal system"
    seeks to find. Raz (1978a), p.2.
21) Robert Audi, "Introduction: A Narrow Survey of Classical and Contem-
    porary Positions in Epistemology", in Michael Huemer (ed.), *Epistemology:*
    Contemporary Readings, Routledge, London, 2002, p.15.
22) Michael Williams, "Skepticism", in John Greco and Ernest Sosa (eds.),
    The Blackwell Guide to Epistemology, Blackwell Publishers, Malden, 1999,
    p.38 ff.
23) Another name "Münchhausen-Trilemma", which goes back to Hans Albert,
    attains widespread publicity. Kurt Seelmann, *Rechtsphilosophie*, C.H. Beck,
    München, 1994, p.154 ff.

turn demands its own justification. For, in order for him to convince sceptical challengers that he know something, he cannot cite another thing that he just believes to be true. Now, he tries to show that he is justified in believing the second thing to be true, and thus in suggesting it as the evidence, by citing the third thing. But that new evidence also needs to be justified. Then, there remains a set of options:

"First, keep trying to think of something new to say, i.e. embark on an *infinite regress*. Second, at some point, refuse to answer, i.e. make a dogmatic assumption. Third, at some point, repeat something he has already said, i.e. reason in a circle."[24]

With none of the three have epistemologists been satisfied. They find a way out. The foundationalist way is to classify knowledge into two groups of a different nature: foundation and superstructure. Knowledge of the latter sort finds its justification from knowledge of the first sort, which needs no justification of its own. If there is the availability of knowledge of the first sort, "Agrippa's Trilemma" can be avoided. For one can stop at some point without 'refusing' to justify since no one is urged to justify what does not need justifying.

There is a structural similarity between transforming a mere belief into *knowledge* and transforming a mere expression of will into

---

24) Williams (1999), p.39.

law. Kelsen and Hart claim that there is an ultimate rule "which, in the last resort, is used to identify the law"[25] in a given system of rules, or which, as a norm validly presupposed in the foundation of a given system of norms, has "only an *epistemological* function." That is, it has the function "to interpret the *subjective* meaning of the acts of human beings by which the norms of an effective coercive order are created, as their *objective* meaning."[26] The following passages from Kelsen are the conclusive evidence of the foundationalist legal thinking.

> The norm which represents the reason for the validity of another norm is called, as we have said, the "higher" norm. But the search for the reason of a norm's validity *cannot go on indefinitely* like the search for the cause of an effect. It *must end* with a norm which, as the last and highest, is presupposed.[27]

> The quest for the reason of validity of a norm is not — like the quest for the cause of an effect — *a regressus ad infinitum*.[28]

---

25) Hart (1994), p.111.
26) Kelsen (1970), p.202. At the same place, he writes: "'How is it possible to interpret without recourse to meta-legal authorities, like God or nature, the subjective meaning of certain facts as a system of objectively valid legal norms describable in rules of law?' The *epistemological* answer of the Pure Theory of Law is: 'By presupposing the basic norm that one ought to behave in accordance with the subjective meaning of the constitution-creating act of will — according to the prescriptions of the authority creating the constitution.'" [Emphasis added.]
27) Kelsen (1970), p.194. [Emphasis added.]
28) Hans Kelsen, *General Theory of Law and State*, translated by Anders Wedberg, Harvard University Press, Cambridge, 1949, p.111.

The main function of "the point of view of a science of law" is to explain nothing else but that to *presuppose* the highest norm is not "making a dogmatic assumption", but doing what is legitimately required.

(1) Basic Norm

Kelsen thinks that the legal system[29] consists of legal norms,[30] which are valid not because they have certain (moral) content but because they are created in a way determined, not always directly but ultimately, by the basic norm of the system. At first, he asks why someone's act of killing another can be interpreted as the execution of punishment, and is not murder. It may be answered, he continues, that the act can be interpreted as such "only if it was prescribed by an individual legal norm, namely as an act that 'ought' to be performed, by a norm that presents itself as a judi-

---

29) As to the notions of normative "system" and "order", see Se-Hyuk Oh, "Normenkonflikte und ihre Lösungsmethoden − unter Einbeziehung von Einheit des Normensystems" (in Korean), unpublished PhD dissertation, Seoul National University, 2000, pp.40-3.

30) Kelsen (1970), p.218. Kelsen views the legal system as a system of norms, whereas Hart views it as a system of rules. To know the difference between the two concepts of norm and rule, it is of good use to note the following remark made by Kelsen: "··· a rule *pre*scribing a definite behavior of entities, that is, a norm." Kelsen (1957b), p.177. According to Raz, there are rules which are not norms as well as norms which are not rules (nor principles), although 'rule' is the nearest equivalent of 'norm' in English. Joseph Raz, *Practical Reason and Norms*, Princeton University Press, Princeton, 1990 (1975), p.9, p.49 and p.208; Raz (1978a), pp.168-86.

cial decision."[31] But then, under what conditions is someone, i.e. a judge, authorized to create such an individual (legal) norm? An answer to the effect that there is "a criminal law that contains a general norm"[32] according to which a law-breaker can be sentenced to death by a judge may be given. It is of a matter of course that the reason why legislators' expression of will—that is a mere fact that cannot itself be the reason for the validity of a certain norm[33]—about someone else's conduct can be interpreted, in this case, as a criminal law should also be given. And the reason may be that a body of legislators, or simply the legislature, is authorized by the constitution to create the general norm.[34]

In this way, Kelsen inquires further into the problem of the authority of authors of the constitution. He sees it as the problem of the validity of the constitution, which is subdivided into the constitutions of the present and the past.[35] He says that the validity of the existing constitution can be traced back to the validity of the historically first constitution that, taken literally, cannot invoke the

---

31) Kelsen (1970), p.199.
32) Kelsen (1970), p.200. And as regards the differentiation between Rechtssatz and Rechtsnorm, see the same book, p.71 ff.; Oh (2000), p.17; Raz (1983), p.148.
33) Kelsen (1970), p.193.
34) Kelsen (1970), p.200.
35) As we shall see later, however, he is mistaken in believing that the problem of the authority of authors of the existing constitution can be properly dealt with by considering the problem of the validity of the historically first constitution. See Ⅱ. 2. 3) - (2) and Ⅳ. 1. 1) of this book.

validity of its (positive) predecessor. What remains, thus, in question is the reason for the validity of the historically first constitution.

> [I]f we ask for the reason of the validity of the historically first constitution, then the answer can only be (if we leave aside God or "nature") that the validity of this constitution — the assumption that it is a binding norm — *must be* presupposed⋯ Since the reason for the validity of a norm can only be another norm, the presupposition must be a norm. ⋯ Since it is the basic norm of a legal order (that is, an order prescribing coercive acts), therefore this norm, namely the basic norm of the legal order concerned, must be formulated as follows: Coercive acts ought to be performed under the conditions and in the manner which the historically first constitution, and the norms created according to it, prescribe. (In short: One ought to behave as the constitution prescribes.)[36]

He suggests that there "must be" a presupposed basic norm according to which the "fathers" of the historically first constitution ought to be obeyed. This is, in Kelsen's view, the ultimate rule that the foundations of a legal system consist in. As we have already seen, the basic norm *must be* presupposed *only if* we are concerned

---

36) Kelsen (1970), pp.200-1. [Original emphasis omitted and mine added.] A different formulation of the basic norm is presented at p.208: "the basic norm prescribes: 'Force ought to be exerted under the constitutions and in the manner prescribed by the by and large effective constitution and by the by and large effective general and effective individual norms created according to the constitution.'"

with "juristic thinking", i.e. take the point of view of a science of law. Therefore, it can be said that "the basic norm can be presupposed, but it need not be."[37]

(2) Rule of Recognition

Hart asserts that there are two different though related types of rules in a developed legal system. Rules of one type, which he calls "primary rules", are *duty-imposing* rules under which people "are required to do or abstain from certain actions." ("rules of obligation") Rules of the other type, which he calls "secondary rules", are *power-conferring* rules by which an individual (or body of persons) is authorized "to introduce new primary rules and to eliminate old ones" ("rules of change"), "to make authoritative determinations of the question whether, on a particular occasion, a primary rule has been broken" ("rules of adjudication"), or to justify ultimately his (or its) law-identifying and law-applying activities ("a rule of recognition").[38]

---

37) Kelsen (1991), p.255. He has clung to the same idea since, at least, the first edition of *The Pure Theory of Law*. "The pure theory of law is well aware that the specifically normative meaning of certain material facts, the meaning characterized as 'law', is the result not of a necessary interpretation but of a possible interpretation, possible only given a certain basic presupposition···" Hans Kelsen, *Introduction to the Problems of Legal Theory*, 1st Edition of *The Pure Theory of Law*, translated by Bonnie Litschewski Paulson and Stanley L. Paulson, Clarendon Press, Oxford, 1992 (1934), p.34.

38) Hart (1994), pp.94-7. It should be noted here that Hart himself does not

According to Hart, the rule of recognition to the effect that "certain criteria of validity are to be used in identifying the law" is the ultimate rule that the foundations of a legal system consist in.[39] Hart suggests, therefore, that it is a "needless reduplication" to presuppose a basic norm to the effect that the constitution in the clauses of which "a supreme criterion of validity" is contained ought to be obeyed.[40] The rule of recognition is not a presupposed norm or "the ultimate hypothesis",[41] but exists only as "a practice of the courts, officials, and private persons in identifying the law by reference to certain criteria." He concludes that "its existence is a *matter of fact*."[42] As Gerald J. Postema points out, Hart thinks that "law rests, at its foundations, on a special and complex custom or convention."[43] However, the statement that the rule of recognition

---

explain the rule of recognition in this way. He describes it as providing 'the ultimate criteria used by courts in identifying valid rules of law.' But some theorists raise questions about the coherence of his ideas, claiming that such a description leads to logical "circularity" by presenting the rule of recognition, unlike the other secondary rules, as imposing a duty to follow it on judges. Neil MacCormick, *H.L.A. Hart*, Stanford University Press, Stanford, 1981, pp.108-9. Raz also says that "it must be concluded that the rule of recognition is a duty-imposing law." Raz (1978a), p.199.

39) Hart (1994), p.100, p.105.

40) Hart (1994), p.106, p.293. Graham Hughes also expresses the same opinion as Hart: "It is not at all necessary to assert the proposition that an effective constitution ought to be complied with; this appears analytically as a *superfluous* attempt⋯" Graham Hughes, "Validity and the Basic Norm", *California Law Review* 59 (1971), p.703. [Original emphasis omitted and mine added.]

41) Kelsen (1949), p.116.

42) Hart (1994), p.110.

exists as, or rests on, a practice or convention does not entail a wrong statement that it *is* a mere practice or convention. Hart says that "the ultimate rule of recognition may be regarded from two points of view: one is expressed in the *external statement* of fact that the rule exists in the actual practice of the system; the other is expressed in the *internal statements* of validity made by those who use it in identifying the law."[44]

Hart suggests that by structuring a legal system as "the combination of primary rules of obligation with the secondary rules of recognition, change and adjudication", we would be well-equipped to handle the problem of authority as well as the problem of validity.

> Not only are the specifically legal concepts with which the lawyer is professionally concerned, such as those of obligation and rights, validity and source of law, legislation and jurisdiction, and sanction, best elucidated in terms of this combination of elements. The concepts (which bestride both law and political theory) of the state, of authority, and of an official require a similar analysis if the obscurity which still lingers about them is to be dissipated.[45]

2) Systemic Validity

It is well-known that, in Kelsen's project, the neutrality of legal

---

43) Gerald J. Postema, "Coordination and Convention at the Foundations of Law", *Journal of Legal Studies* 11 (January 1982), p.166.
44) Hart (1994), p.112. [Emphasis added.]
45) Hart (1994), p.98.

norms is secured by what is called "chains of validity." Kelsen says that "the reason for the validity of a norm can only be the validity of another norm",[46] and that the ultimate reason for the validity of norms in a legal system is the presupposed validity of the basic norm.

According to Carlos Santiago Nino, two different though related chains of "derivation" are implicit in so-called "chains of validity." One is the chain of derivation of *rules*, and the other is the chain of derivation of *judgments of validity*. Nino claims that "the basic norm is not a norm that belongs to the chain of derivation of rules, but is part of the chain of derivation of judgments of validity. In other words, the basic norm *is* a judgment of validity."[47] It appears that the judgment of validity is what Jerzy Wróblewski calls a *metanorm*.[48]

However, the fact that the ultimate reason for the validity of other rules of a system is construed as a norm is called into question by neither of them. Hence we shall not draw here such a (dimensional) distinction. Now, the following description of chains of

---

46) Kelsen (1970), p.193.
47) Carlos Santiago Nino, "Confusions surrounding Kelsen's Concept of Validity", in Stanley L. Paulson and Bonnie Litschewski Paulson (eds.), *Normativity and Norms: Critical Perspectives on Kelsenian Themes* (1998), pp.257-8.
48) "In practical legal language the expression 'legal rule *R* is valid' means 'one ought to apply *R*.' It is, thus, a *metanorm* in relation to the rules of valid law." Jerzy Wróblewski, *The Judicial Application of Law*, Kluwer Academic Publishers, Dordrecht, 1992, p.76. [Emphasis added.]

validity given by Raz is brief and to the point.

> The unity of the legal system consists in the fact that all its laws belong to one chain of validity and all the laws of a chain of validity are part of the same system. The normativity of laws is assured by the fact that each of the laws in a chain derives its validity from the one before it. The basic norm is essential to the solution of both problems. It provides the non-factual starting point essential to the explanation of normativity, and it guarantees that all the laws of one system belong to the same chain of validity.[49]

Similarly, Hart employs a notion of "chains of legal reasoning", which seems to be the cognitive counterpart of chains of validity. And the idea of legal validity figures prominently in such reasoning, as well.

> If the question is raised whether some suggested rule is legally valid, we must, in order to answer the question, use a criterion of validity provided by some other rule. Is this purported by-law of the Oxfordshire County Council valid? Yes: because it was made in exercise of the powers conferred, and in accordance with the procedure specified, by a statutory order made by the Minister of Health. ⋯ We may query the validity of the statutory order and assess its validity in terms of the statute empowering the minister to make such orders. Finally, when the validity of the statute has been queried and assessed by reference to the rule that what the Queen in Parliament enacts is law, we are brought to a stop in

---

49) Raz (1983), p.126.

inquiries concerning validity: for we have reached a rule which, like the intermediate statutory order and statute, provides criteria for the assessment of the validity of other rules; but it is also unlike them in that there is no rule providing criteria for the assessment of its own legal validity.[50]

As is usual with him, Hart tries putting a semantic interpretation on the concept of validity. He says that "to say that a given rule is valid is to recognize it as passing all the tests provided by the rule of recognition."[51] Rules which pass the tests do not exist haphazardly but as a system. Accordingly, the legal validity is characterized as a systemic notion by him.[52]

It may be the case that we should exercise extra caution so that we might not overlook the subtle difference between 'being the reason for validity' and 'providing criteria of validity'. Nevertheless, for the present purpose, it will suffice to point out the fact that both Kelsen and Hart rely heavily on the systemic notion of (legal) validity.[53]

The idea of validity plays a crucial role in their foundationalist schemes. Just as the foundationalist picture of *knowledge* is secured

---

50) Hart (1994), p.107.
51) Hart (1994), p.103.
52) It should be noted here that both Kelsen and Hart describe a legal system as a hierarchical system either of norms, or of rules.
53) Dick W.P. Ruiter, "Legal Powers", in Stanley L. Paulson and Bonnie Litschewski Paulson (eds.), *Normativity and Norms: Critical Perspectives on Kelsenian Themes* (1998), p.472.

by the notion of epistemic *justification* which renders superstructure affixed to its foundations, the foundationalist picture of *law* is assured by the legal *validity* which, in the course of systematizing rules of law, plays the same role as justification in epistemic foundationalism.

2. Normativity and Validity

1) Concepts of Validity

As we have already seen, the legal validity is basically characterized as a systemic notion by Kelsen and Hart. And it plays, together with the ultimate rule, a central role in their theories of the normativity of a legal system. Now, our concerns are problems unrelieved or even aggravated by the concept of validity. As long as the operative word is 'validity', a rule which is neither valid nor invalid, or a rule which is valid but at the same time conflicts with another, and even higher, rule which is also valid must be problematic. Those problems may threaten the notion of legal *system* itself.

However, we need first to make the meaning of the term 'validity' clear. In spite of the fact that Kelsen and Hart rely heavily on the notion of validity in articulating the grounds of law and its normativity, the meaning of 'validity' is still elusive. Many theorists, including Kelsen and Hart, use the term 'validity' quite differently and, what is worse, they occasionally enjoy a plurality of meanings of this term.[54] As Eugenio Bulygin says, there is no consensus among them about its exact meaning.[55]

Under the circumstances, the categorization of usage seems to be unavoidable. Hun Sup Shim mainly distinguishes between factual and normative meanings of the term 'validity' in jurisprudential use, while catering for its logical and ontological usage together.[56] Here, it is noteworthy that he does not mean by 'logical usage' how the term 'validity' is used *in logic*. In logic, 'validity' is an attribute of an argument, but not of a single statement. If premises are true in a 'valid' argument, then conclusion is always true.[57] Nino also contrasts factual validity with normative validity. However, when he thinks of the first, he is considering membership, but not efficacy.[58] Quite differently, Se-Hyuk Oh suggests that the notion of membership, together with the notion of binding force, falls into the category of normative validity.[59]

Robert Alexy classifies concepts of validity into three categories:

---

54) Oh (2000), p.23.

55) Eugenio Bulygin, "An Antinomy in Kelsen's Pure Theory of Law", in Stanley L. Paulson and Bonnie Litschewski Paulson (eds.), *Normativity and Norms: Critical Perspectives on Kelsenian Themes* (1998), p.297.

56) Hun Sup Shim, *Rechtsphilosophische Untersuchungen I — Recht · Moral · Macht* (in Korean), Bub Moon Sa, Seoul, 1982, p.61 ff.

57) Wesley C. Salmon, *Logic*, 3rd Edition, translated (into Korean) by Kang Jae Kwak, Pakyoungsa, Seoul, 2004, p.39.

58) Nino (1998), p.261.

59) He appears to regard membership and binding force not as *meanings* of the term 'validity' but as competing *criteria* of it. Oh (2000), p.22.

sociological, ethical and juridical.[60] He defines each of the three in corresponding terms of efficacy (Wirksamkeit), moral correctness (Richtigkeit) and authoritative enactment (autoritative Gesetzteit).[61] Wróblewski also divides the concepts of validity into three groups. They are factual, axiological and systemic validity of law. He treats systemic validity as a basic notion, and the first two as correctives to it.[62] Similarly, Bulygin suggests three different concepts for which the terms 'valid' and 'validity' can be used. He refers to each concept as efficacy, binding force and membership.[63]

Ross likewise points out that there are three different ways in which the word 'valid' is used. It is used to indicate the *actual existence* of a norm or a system of norms (*gælende / geltend*), being in accordance with a system of norms (*gyldig / gültig*) and the binding force.[64] Here, we should not confuse the first of the three with what Kelsen calls the *specific existence* of norms.[65] For the first is equated with efficacy, i.e. factual validity, by Ross, whereas the specific existence of norms is identified with their binding force, i.e. normative validity, by Kelsen.[66] Bulygin, thus, even renames

---

60) Alexy (1992), p.139 ff.
61) On the whole, Alexy uses the word "autoritative" as a synonym for "ordnungsgemäße". Alexy (1992), p.16 n.3.
62) Wróblewski (1992), p.76.
63) Eugenio Bulygin, "Valid Law and Law in Force", unpublished proceedings of Alf Ross's 100 Years Birthday Conference, Copenhagen, 1999, p.35 ff.
64) Ross (1998), pp.158-9. Cf. Ross expresses, at p.162, regret about having translated *gælende* as valid in *On Law and Justice*.
65) Kelsen (1970), p.10.
66) Ross (1998), p.159; Kelsen (1970), pp.7-8.

the first "norms *in force.*"[67]

In order not to bring about confusion, in the following pages we shall examine meanings of the word 'validity' within the Alexy — Wróblewski — Bulygin framework.

(1) Membership

Hart regards rules which pass the tests provided by the rule of recognition as being valid. Provided the rule of recognition determines whether certain rules belong to a given legal system, the systemic validity of a given rule means nothing else but its membership. Kelsen also uses, though not always, the term 'validity' in this sense. A norm which has been created "ultimately in a way determined by a presupposed basic norm" is valid. Provided that "only a competent authority can create valid norm"[68] and that "the validity of an already valid norm" can be repealed by another, i.e. *derogating*, norm,[69] a norm which has been created by a competent authority and has not been derogated by another norm can be regarded as belonging to a legal system.

Bulygin puts it simply as "a norm is valid in a legal system if

---

67) Bulygin (1999), p.50. Raz and Inés Weyland also say that a legal system is in force if it is effectively followed. But Kelsen uses the terms 'valid norm' and 'norm in force' interchangeably. Raz (1983), p.151; Inés Weyland, "Idealism and Realism in Kelsen's Treatment of Norm Conflicts", in Richard Tur and William Twining (eds.), *Essays on Kelsen*, Clarendon Press, Oxford, 1986, p.268; Kelsen (1949), p.117.
68) Kelsen (1970), p.194.
69) Kelsen (1991), p.106.

and only if it belongs to or is a member of this system."[70] A more detailed version of the definition of systemic validity is suggested by Wróblewski. He writes as follows.

> [A] rule R is valid in legal system LS if the following conditions are fulfilled: (a) R is enacted according to the rules valid in LS and thus has come into force; or (b) R is an acknowledged consequence of the rules valid in LS; (c) R has not been formally repealed ("derogated"); (d) R is not inconsistent with the rules valid in LS; (e) if R is inconsistent with any rule valid in LS then (ea) R is not treated as invalid according to the rules about conflict between legal rules or (eb) R is interpreted in such a way as to eliminate the inconsistency in question.[71]

Raz also says that a rule *of law* is legally valid if and only if it is systemically valid.[72] But he does not think that the terms 'legal validity' and 'membership' are identical in their meaning. For, under certain conditions (e.g. those established by private international law), most legal systems recognize and enforce many rules which do not belong to the system, that is, which are not rules *of law*.[73] Only in the case of rules of law, legal validity and membership overlap perfectly.

---

70) Bulygin (1999), p.36.
71) Wróblewski (1992), p.77.
72) Raz (1983), p.153.
73) Raz (1983), p.149.

(2) Efficacy

Validity has been construed as efficacy by sociologists of law and legal realists, but philosophers of law at large discriminate between the two.[74] Kelsen defines efficacy of law as the conformity of actual human behaviour with legal norms. To put it into his own words, "[e]fficacy of law means that men actually behave as, according to the legal norms, they ought to behave, that the norms are actually applied and obeyed."[75] He claims that the efficacy is not an attribute of law, whereas the validity (regarded as the binding force) is a quality of law.[76] Despite ordinary language, he says, efficacy is a quality *of the actual behaviour* of men, but not *of law* itself.[77] Efficacy is an *is*, whereas validity is an *ought*.[78]

Ross and Raz suggest that Hart *uses*, apart from *mentioning*, the term 'validity' only in the sense of membership.[79] And Bulygin contends further that efficacy is not a *meaning* of the term 'vali-

---

74) Shim (1982), pp.64-7.
75) Kelsen (1949), p.39.
76) Kelsen (1949), pp.39-40. But this statement appears vitiated because he later says that "truth and falsity are properties of a statement, whereas validity is *not* the property of a norm, but is its existence, its specific ideal existence." Hans Kelsen, "Law and Logic", *Essays in Legal and Moral Philosophy*, translated by Peter Heath, D. Reidel Publishing Company, Dordrecht, 1973, p.230. [Emphasis added.]
77) Kelsen (1949), p.40. Cf. Bulygin has an idea to the contrary. He proposes that efficacy is a dispositional property of (customary) norms. Bulygin (1999), p.43, p.50.
78) Kelsen (1991), p.4; Kelsen (1970), p.10.
79) Ross (1998), p.162; Raz (1986), p.96.

dity' but a *criterion* of it, and that to distinguish between the two is of great importance. He thinks, like Kelsen and Hart, that the legal validity is characterized, *inter alia*, as a systemic notion.[80] And a norm belongs to a system either because it is enacted by a competent authority ("enacted norm"), or because it is efficacious ("customary norm"). Those reasons are two *criteria* of membership, the systemic validity of norms.[81] Similarly, Wróblewski regards factual validity as adding a new condition to the conditions of systemic validity which we have already seen:[82]

(f) *R* is not derogated by *desuetudo*.[83]

(3) Binding Force

As has already been mentioned, Raz rejects the view that legal validity simply means membership, since the first has broader extension than the latter. He turns his attention to the linguistic phenomenon where "legally valid" is used interchangeably with "legally binding", and states that "[a] legally valid rule is one which has the normative effects (in law) which it claims to have."[84] However, it seems far form indisputable whether such a statement reaches the *central core* of meaning which the term 'legally valid

---

80) Bulygin (1998), p.310.
81) Bulygin (1999), p.50.
82) See Ⅱ. 2. 1) - (1) of this book.
83) Wróblewski (1992), p.79.
84) Raz (1983), p.149.

(binding)' has. This is partly because Raz upholds the view that the normativity of law is one thing, the obligation to obey the law is quite another.[85] But we are now considering under the heading of 'binding force' normative or axiological validity (of law), which consists of the obligation to obey the law.[86] Moreover, the statement cannot be construed as simply describing the situation where men behave in conformity with a rule, or are sanctioned by legal authorities when a breach of it happens. For that statement is not about efficacy but about normative or axiological validity.

Nino, who I think gets to the core, suggests that there are three features of the notion of validity. First, to say that a rule is valid is to say that it has binding force and that its prescriptions constitute conclusive reasons for action. Second, the lack of validity implies that a rule does not have the normative consequences that it claims to have. Third, the meaning of the term 'validity' is not descriptive but normative.[87]

To sum up, legal validity in this sense, thus, refers to the (legally) binding force. And to say that a rule is valid is to say that it

---

85) Raz maintains that normativity is one of the most important features of the law, and at the same time that there is no obligation or duty to obey the law. Raz (1978a), p.3, p.170; Raz (1983), p.233. As we shall see later, his view as such is to conceive of the normativity as "social normativity."

86) Kelsen makes this point clear. He says that "[b]y 'validity', the binding force of the law — the idea that it ought to be obeyed by the people whose behavior it regulates — is understood. The question is why these people ought to obey the law." Kelsen (1957a), p.257.

87) Nino (1998), p.254.

ought to be obeyed. As is well-known, Kelsen has recurrently elucidated the same point.

> A norm referring to the behavior of a human being is "valid" means that it is binding — that an individual ought to behave in the manner determined by the norm.[88]

Ross suggests that axiological validity should be eliminated from Kelsen's theory,[89] while Nino insists that, in Kelsen's theory, systemic validity should give way to axiological validity.[90] However, though it is of importance to consider how to reconcile two pictures of "validity" underpinned by Kelsen's theory, i.e. systemic and axiological ones, it seems imprudent to make one collapse into the other. As Wróblewski and Alexy demonstrate, issues surrounding axiological validity are intimately connected with the competing theories of law, e.g. natural law theory, (inclusive and exclusive) legal positivism and legal realism, etc.[91]

2) Two Conceptions of the Normativity of Law

As we have already described, Kelsen and Hart share the foun-

---

88) Kelsen (1970), p.193.
89) Ross (1998), pp.159-61. Ross maintains that "[t]he normative notion of validity is an ideological instrument supporting the authority of the state."
90) Nino (1998), pp.256-61.
91) On the contrary, the *authority* of law does not relate to the nature (or concept) of law in direct way. As to this claim, see Ⅳ. 2. 2) and Ⅳ. 2. 3) of this book.

dationalist scheme in structuring a legal system, and they both rely heavily on the notion of validity in articulating the grounds of
law and its normativity. Nevertheless, they do not use the term
'validity' in the same way. Hart uses this term only in the sense of
membership, whereas Kelsen attaches more to it.

According to Raz, different conceptions of the normativity of
law give birth to different notions of legal validity. He distinguishes between two conceptions of the normativity of law, and explains how Kelsen and Hart come to conceive of the legal validity
differently.

> Two conceptions of the normativity of law are current. I will
> call them justified and social normativity. According to the one
> view legal standards of behaviour are norms only if and in so far
> as they are justified. They may be justified by some objective and
> universally valid reasons. They may be intuitively perceived as
> binding or they may be accepted as justified by personal commit-
> ment. On the other view standards of behaviour can be considered
> as norms regardless of their merit. They are social norms in so far
> as they are socially upheld as binding standards and in so far as
> the society involved exerts pressure on people to whom the stand-
> ards apply to conform to them.[92]

The concept of *justified normativity* gives rise to the notion of
axiological validity. In this view, to say of the law that it exists as

---

92) Raz (1983), p.134.

a norm, i.e. that it has a normative feature, is to say that it has binding force. And, as I have already mentioned, axiological validity or binding force of law consists in the obligation to obey the law.[93] Hence, the problem of normativity of law is 'analytically' tied to the problem of the obligation to obey the law.[94]

However, the concept of *social normativity* does not need to be accompanied by the notion of axiological validity. In this view, the law has a normative feature because it is socially recognized as a binding rule,[95] and the normativity of law does not entail the existence of the obligation to obey, or to recognize as binding, the law.[96] It may be objected that Hart affirms the existence of the obligation to obey the rules of community, while at the same time conceiving of the normativity (of law) as social normativity. Such an objection is, however, imprudent and therefore misguided. For his affirmation of the obligation as such is a provisional one. The obligation as such is justified by Hart on condition that "there are any moral rights at all."[97]

Raz claims that Kelsen conceives of the normativity (of law) as

---

93) Ross (1998), pp.153-5; Nino (1998), p.259.

94) Raz (1983), p.137.

95) Cf. Kelsen sharply distinguishes his doctrine of the basic norm from what he calls a doctrine of *recognition*. Kelsen (1970), p.218 n.83.

96) Raz (1983), p.137.

97) H.L.A. Hart, "Are There Any Natural Rights?", *Philosophical Review* 64 (1955). Reprinted in Carl Wellman (ed.), *Rights and Duties Vol. 4: Human Rights and Universal Duties*, Routledge, New York, 2002, pp.1-2. [References are to the reprint.]

justified normativity, whereas Hart endorses the view that the law
is fundamentally a social norm. Hart thinks that the concept of
social normativity can account for the normative feature of law, but
Kelsen does not think so. He instead firmly believes that "the concept of social normativity is not a concept of normativity at all."[98]
Accordingly, viewed through Kelsenian glasses, Hart appears to
have failed to differentiate himself from the reductivist theorists
who characteristically replace normativity with regularity.[99] On the
contrary, seen from the Hartian viewpoint, Kelsen seems unsuccess-
ful in discriminating between himself and the natural lawyers who
are characterized by adherence to the concepts of justified normativity and axiological validity.[100]

Hart and Kelsen would reply that the internal point of view and
the point of view of a science of law, respectively, can meet the
challenges. First, the reductivist theorists have misleadingly dis-
regarded the internal aspect of rules, which Hart takes into account.
Second, the natural lawyers have assumed that legislators' expression of will about someone else's conduct can be interpreted as
valid norm, if and only if it conforms to the natural law (the ultimate rule of) which is self-evident and thus unconditionally or ab-
solutely valid.[101] But Kelsen rejects the possibility of legal norms

---

98) Raz (1983), p.136.
99) "It has been argued that Hart, like the classical positivists, has in fact
    failed adequately to account for the normativity of law, giving too much
    prominence to the social thesis." Postema (1982), p.166.
100) Ross (1998), pp.151-2; Raz (1983), p.134.

with unconditional, absolute validity.

> A norm is "directly evident" means that it is immanent in, or emanates from, reason. The concept of a directly evident norm presupposes the concept of a practical reason, that is, a norm-creating reason; but this concept is untenable.[102]

According to Kelsen, legislators' expression of will can be interpreted as a valid norm on condition that the basic norm, the validity of which is neither self-evident nor unconditional, is presupposed (*as valid*)[103] from the point of view of a science of law.[104]

Now, it seems quite natural and even necessary for theorists to ask which of the two *competing* conceptions of the normativity of law is better to retain. But no way is it of necessity the case. For what this book concerns itself with is, as I have already mentioned,[105] the fact that both Kelsenian and Hartian approaches are problematic and therefore untenable until modified by introducing the notion of authority of law.

3) The Necessity for Authority

We have seen, in earlier parts of this chapter, that Kelsen and

---

101) Kelsen (1970), pp.220-1.
102) Kelsen (1970), p.196.
103) Kelsen (1949), p.111.
104) Kelsen (1991), p.256; Kelsen (1970), p.200; Kelsen (1957a), p.262.
105) See I. 3. of this book.

Hart regard the notions of ultimate rule and legal validity which is characterized as a systemic notion as essential to the explanation of the normativity of a legal system. In modern civilized countries, they believe, rules of law do not exist as a disordered heap of 'separate rules', but form a well-organized system.[106] And those two notions play crucial parts in "making a system out of a multitude of rules."[107] However, it is doubtful whether those notions can fulfill the tasks they have before them. Actually, a series of questions has been raised by many theorists about their *systemic* malfunction.

According to Hart and Raz, what distinguishes the law from other normative standards, e.g. rules of etiquette, is its systemic characteristics.[108] And many writers today regard as central, though not unique, to positivist jurisprudence its representation of law as a system of rules and standards.[109] Kelsen has already put this idea explicitly.[110] In *General Theory of Law and State*, he starts off by saying that,

> Law is an order of human behavior. An "order" is a system of rules. Law is not, as it is sometimes said, a rule. It is a set of rules

---

106) Hart (1994), p.92.
107) Kelsen (1949), p.110.
108) Hart (1994), p.234; Raz (1978a), p.89.
109) Coyle (2002), p.276; Postema (1982), p.167 n.3 and accompanied text by this note.
110) According to Raz, Kelsen was the first who appreciated the significance of the notion of a legal system. Raz (1978a), p.2.

having the kind of unity we understand by a system. It is impossible to grasp the nature of law if we limit our attention to the single isolated rule.[111]

Raz develops this idea much further and asserts that "[t]he explanation of the normativity of the law, ⋯ [is] based on the concept of a legal system rather than on the concept of a law."[112] Here, despite some disagreement among such analytical jurists as Kelsen, Hart and Raz, and the fact that "the meaning of the common assertion that laws belong to or constitute a *system* of laws" still needs clarifying,[113] it seems indisputable that problems threatening the notion of legal *system* itself should be resolved.

(1) The Validity Problematic

The whole basis of foundationalist schemes have been called into question by many theorists. Some have given their attention to the concept of the ultimate rule that is of a different nature from any other rules belonging to a certain legal system. Other theorists have focused on the notion of the legal validity which determines whether any rule belongs to a certain legal system.

However, none of them has denied that both the notions are tightly interlocked. The ultimate rule is, by definition, the final rea-

---

111) Kelsen (1949), p.3.
112) Raz (1978a), pp.169-70.
113) H.L.A. Hart, "Kelsen's Doctrine of the Unity of Law", *Essays in Jurisprudence and Philosophy* (1983), p.310, p.335.

son for, or the source of the supreme criterion of, validity of all the rules other than itself that constitute one legal system. On the other hand, whether the ultimate rule itself is, or even can be thought to be, valid is also a controversial issue. Normally, the problems concerning one lead to the problems concerning the other.

Now, we will concentrate our minds on the notion of legal validity and examine below three issues which are in turn 'validity of ultimate rule', 'validity and conflicts between norms' and 'validity and justification of legal system'. The task of this thesis is to show that the notion of validity alone cannot render a set of rules, including the ultimate rule, systemically organized, and that it should be accompanied by the notion of authority of *law*. My view is not, as Raz audaciously has it, that the concept of authority of law upholds a particular view on the nature of law,[114] but simply that the authority (of law) is necessary for the law to exist as a system.

(a) Validity of Ultimate Rule

Kelsen makes it clear that the ultimate rule whose validity "cannot be derived from a higher norm"[115] is presupposed "as valid"[116] in itself for the following reason.

---

114) Raz (1994), p.202. Raz's view as such will be closely examined in chapter 4 of this book.
115) Kelsen (1970), p.195.
116) Kelsen (1949), p.111.

> The basic norm is not created in a legal procedure by a law-creating organ. It is not — as a positive legal norm is — valid because it is created in a certain way by a legal act, but is valid because it is presupposed to be valid; and it is presupposed to be valid because without this presupposition no human act could be interpreted as a legal, especially as a norm-creating, act.[117]

To put it differently, the ultimate rule is seen, from the point of view of a science of law, as unquestionably valid. Indeed, Kelsen asserts that "the *reason* for its validity *cannot be questioned*."[118] Valdés calls this assertion into question, quoting Bulygin as saying, "[w]hat meaning can the word 'validity' have when it is applied to the norm that allows us to speak of validity in the first place?"[119] Hart objects to the view that the ultimate rule is presupposed as valid. He contends that what is really presupposed is not the validity of the ultimate rule, but "the normal background or context of statements of legal validity" of rules other than the ultimate rule.[120] A similar, though not identical, criticism is given by Hughes. The gist of his criticism is phrased as follows: "It would, therefore, be correct to say that *the statement* that a particular norm of the system is valid *presupposes* that there is a valid (generally accepted) basic norm, but it would be misleading to say that *the validity of the basic norm* resides in a presupposition."[121] Hughes thinks that

---

117) Kelsen (1949), p.116.
118) Kelsen (1970), p.195. [Emphasis added.]
119) Valdés (1998), p.269.
120) Hart (1994), p.108.

there exists "the possibility of an independent criterion" of the validity of the ultimate rule. But Hart rejects it. Hart goes further, claiming that the ultimate rule itself "can neither be valid nor invalid"[122] since the criteria of its validity cannot *ex hypothesi* be questioned.

> We only need the word 'validity', and commonly only use it, to answer questions which arise *within* a system of rules where the status of a rule as a member of the system depends on its satisfying certain criteria provided by the rule of recognition. *No such question can arise* as to the validity of the very rule of recognition which provides the criteria; it can neither be valid nor invalid but is simply accepted as appropriate for use in this way.[123]

However, as Alexy rightly says, the case is that questions arise occasionally as to the validity of the constitution in the clauses of which a supreme criterion of validity is contained.[124] Shim likewise regards those questions as questions about the validity of the sys-

---

121) Hughes (1971), p.700.
122) Shim shows that an idea of the ultimate rule that is neither valid nor invalid can be traced, at least, back to Karl Engisch and Walther Burckhardt. Shim (1982), p.79 n.70.
123) Hart (1994), pp.108-9. [Emphasis added.] In this passage, Hart seems to say that we cannot ask questions about the validity of the whole legal system to which the rule of recognition belongs. But many theorists think that it is legitimate to ask questions not about the validity of a particular rule of a system, but about the validity of the system as a whole. See Shim (1982), p.69; Alexy (1992), p.144 ff.
124) Alexy (1992), p.162, p.165.

tem as a whole, and thereby as questions which we can and do raise.[125] And when Raz assumes that all rules are either legally valid or legally invalid,[126] he is opposing the Hartian conception of the ultimate *rule* that is neither valid nor invalid.[127] It is largely due to the fact that Raz has doubts about Hart's doctrine of the rule of recognition. Raz writes that "[i]t seems to me that to answer the question whether a certain suggested law exists as a law in a certain legal system one must ultimately refer not to a *law* but to a *jurisprudential criterion*."

Despite these criticisms of their theories, and the difference between their own conceptions of the ultimate rule as well, Kelsen and Hart concur that the reason for, or the criteria of, its validity cannot be questioned. Such a dubious thesis is, in fact, already implicit in the definition of the term 'foundation'. The ultimate rule, as the *foundational* one, is devised to have the property of a *"prima causa"*,[128] an "axiom" of Euclidean geometry[129] or a "singularity" of the Big Bang Theory.[130]

(b) Validity and Conflicts between Norms

Is it possible that two norms which belong to the same (momen-

---

125) Shim (1982), p.69.
126) Raz (1983), p.146 n.1.
127) Raz (1978a), p.200. [Emphasis added.]
128) Kelsen (1949), p.383.
129) Hughes (1971), pp.702-3.
130) Honoré (1987), p.102.

tary) legal system, and each of which is legally valid are in conflict? Kelsen underwent a drastic change in his position on this matter.[131] When he first dealt with this problem of 'norm conflicts (within the same legal order)' he denied that a conflict between two valid norms is possible. A conflict of norms was regarded as a logical contradiction.[132]

> Hence it is by no means absurd to say that two legal norms "contradict" each other. And therefore only one of the two can be regarded as objectively valid. To say that *a* ought to be and at the same time ought not to be is just as meaningless as to say that *a* is and at the same time that it is not. A conflict of norms is just as meaningless as a logical contradiction.[133]

He mistakenly believed that conflicts between norms are one of the three horns of certain trilemma in a legal science. I shall call such an alleged *impossible trinity* 'Kelsen's Trilemma'.

KT: It is impossible for any legal system to satisfy all

---

131) As to the change in Kelsen's position on the matter of 'norm conflicts', see J.W. Harris, "Kelsen and Normative Consistency", in Richard Tur and William Twining (eds.), *Essays on Kelsen* (1986), p.201 ff.; Weyland (1986), p.261. Harris contends that "the principal reason for Kelsen changing his views on derogation, non-contradiction and deduction concerns the retification of norms", and prefers Kelsen's earlier view, considering the necessity of normative consistency. Harris (1986), p.213.
132) Hart (1983b), p.327; Oh (2000), p.66.
133) Kelsen (1970), p.206.

the following three conditions simultaneously.

(1) If two norms belonging to the same legal system are in conflict, both cannot be valid. (one of the two conflicting norms is valid and the other is invalid.)

(2) A norm whose content is incompatible with the content of another norm is in conflict with that norm. Nevertheless,

(3) A norm is valid, despite another, even higher, valid norm whose content is incompatible with its content.

Kelsen came to the conclusion that "no conflict between a higher norm and a lower norm is possible",[134] using *modus tollens*. First, he assumed that (1) is true.[135] Second, he denied the consequent of (1), that is, affirmed (3).[136] Hence, he denied the antecedent of (1), that is, concluded that (2) is not true.

Kelsen also drew his own conclusion that conflicts between norms of the same level can always be solved by inter pretation,[137] and that, therefore, no 'lasting' conflict between them is possible, em-

---

134) Kelsen (1934), p.72; Kelsen (1970), p.208; Hans Kelsen, "Der Begriff der Rechtsordnung", in Hun Sup Shim (ed.), *Schriften zur Rechtstheorie* (1990), p.59.
135) Kelsen (1970), p.206; Kelsen (1990b), p.59.
136) Kelsen (1934), pp.72-5; Kelsen (1970), pp.267-76; Kelsen (1990b), pp.59-62. Here, Kelsen developed a doctrine of "normative alternatives" to circumvent problems of so-called "unconstitutional" statutes and "unlawful" judicial decisions (or the "norm contrary to a norm" in general).
137) Kelsen (1970), pp.206-8; Kelsen (1990b), p.59.

ploying *modus ponens*. First, he assumed that (1) is true. Second, he affirmed the antecedent of (1), that is, (provisionally) affirmed (2).[138] Hence, he affirmed the consequent of (1), that is, concluded that (3) is not true.

Needless to say, this argument is untenable. The form *modus tollens* can be converted into the form *modus ponens*, since the major premise of the latter is immediately inferred by conversion from the major premise of the first, and *vice versa*. But Kelsen arbitrarily affirmed (3), and denied (2) in *modus tollens*, while denying (3), and affirming (2) in *modus ponens*.

Kelsen later changes his position on this problem of 'norm conflicts', renouncing the above major premise (1): the logical contradiction thesis.

> There is no doubt that such conflicts between norms exist. ⋯ The conflict between norms presupposes that both norms are valid. The assertions concerning the validity of both conflicting norms are true. Therefore, a conflict between norms is not a logical contradiction and cannot even be compared to a logical contradiction.[139]
>
> Even within one and the same legal system, moreover, conflicts of norms are possible and by no means rare: conflicts between norms of higher and lower order, ⋯ ; conflicts between norms of

---

138) Kelsen (1970), p.205, p.207; Kelsen (1990b), p.59.
139) Hans Kelsen, "Derogation", *Essays in Legal and Moral Philosophy*, translated by Peter Heath, D. Reidel Publishing Company, Dordrecht, 1973, p.271.

the same order, ⋯ There can even be conflicts, indeed, between norms of one and the same law. What is essential to all of them is that *both* the conflicting norms are valid, so that if one is o-beyed the other must be violated; and it can only be violated if it, too, remains valid.[140]

This later view is nothing more than Hart's position on the problem of 'norm conflicts'. Hart, like many theorists,[141] understands conflicts between norms in terms of "the logical impossibility of joint conformity."[142] This definition of a conflict between norms, however, "leaves entirely open" the question of their coexistence as valid norms of the same legal system.[143] For Hart, therefore, it is possible to say, 'two norms belonging to the same legal system are actually in conflict. Nevertheless, both of them are valid.'

[i]t is worth noting that logicians of repute in constructing systems of deontic logic have allowed for the possibility of conflicting obligations ('one ought to do *A*' and 'one ought not to do *A*'). There seems no formal inconsistency in such a notion, and a logi-

---

140) Kelsen (1973b), p.233. [Footnote omitted.]
141) For a brief list of the theorists of this view, see Se-Hyuk Oh, "Hans Kelsens Gedanken über das verfassungswidrige Gesetz: In Bezug auf den Normenkonflikt und Derogation" (in Korean), *Korean Journal of Legal Philosophy* 1 (1998), p.125, n.81.
142) Hart (1983b), pp.325-7. "So if one rule prohibits and another rule permits the same action by the same person at the same time, joint conformity will be logically impossible and the two rules will conflict." [Footnote omitted.]
143) Hart (1983b), pp.325-6.

cal calculus which is out to catch the logical properties of actual human codes of behaviour should not rule out such possibilities of conflict in advance by taking it as an axiom that 'one ought to do A' entails that it is not the case that 'one ought not to do A'.[144]

However, if 'unlawful' judicial decisions and 'unconstitutional' statutes (or rules against the ultimate rule in general) are, like 'unjust' laws, nonetheless *valid*, what does (the reason for, or criterion of) validity serve? Talking to the validity of law is getting us nowhere.

(c) Validity and Justification of Legal System

If Kelsen had given, in the course of a lengthy discourse on 'norm conflicts', his attention to the *dynamic* nature of the legal system, he would not have suffered self-contradiction. As is well-known, Kelsen himself distinguishes between *static* and *dynamic* normative systems, explaining how a norm comes into existence, i.e. "takes on validity."[145] The first is the system whose norms are *deduced* from the content of the basic norm by way of a logical operation which he calls "subsumption."[146] In that system, a norm is valid "because its content is logically deducible from [the] basic norm"[147] that has "a *substantive, static* character."[148]

---

144) Hart (1983b), p.331. [Footnote omitted.]
145) Kelsen says that "truth and falsity are properties of a statement, whereas validity is not the *property* of a norm, but is its *existence*, its specific ideal existence." Kelsen (1973b), p.230. [Emphasis added.]
146) Kelsen (1949), p.112; Kelsen (1970), p.195.
147) Kelsen (1970), p.198.

In case of the latter, however, norms belonging to the system cannot be deduced from, but are *created* according to, the basic norm.[149] And a norm is valid "because it is created in a constitutional way",[150] i.e. "in a way determined by [the] basic norm"[151] that has "a thoroughly *formal, dynamic* character."[152] He suggests that systems of *legal* norms are dynamic ones, whereas systems of *moral* norms are static. Therefore, the basic norm of a legal system can and does "supply only the reason for the validity, not the content of the norms based on it."[153]

Kelsen also took account of the dynamic *abrogation* (as well as *creation*) of legal norms, when the loss of validity occurs irrespective of 'norm conflicts'.[154] But he did not, mistakenly, distinguish between static and dynamic systems while explaining how a norm *in conflict with another norm* goes out of existence, i.e. loses its validity. No sooner had he realized it than there was a change in his view on the problem of 'norm conflicts', or *vice versa*.

---

148) Kelsen (1934), p.56. [Emphasis added.]
149) Kelsen (1949), p.113; Kelsen (1970), p.197.
150) Kelsen (1949), p.119.
151) Kelsen (1970), p.198.
152) Kelsen (1934), p.56. [Emphasis added.]
153) Kelsen (1970), p.196, p.197.
154) "These norms are valid ⋯ because they are created in a constitutional way. ⋯ ; they cease to be valid ⋯ when they are annulled in a constitutional way, ⋯" Kelsen (1949), p.119.

Derogation, ⋯ plays an important part in the sphere of a positive *legal* order but can also arise within the sphere of a positive
moral order where, however, it will hardly be taken into consideration because of the much greater stability of this normative order. Within a positive *moral* order, a norm ordinarily does not lose
its validity by derogation, ⋯155)

As we have already seen, in his article "Derogation" (1962) Kelsen renounces the first condition of **KT**: the logical contradiction
thesis. It will be useful to recall the remaining conditions.

(2) A norm whose content is incompatible with the content of another norm is in conflict with that norm. Nevertheless,

(3) A norm is valid, despite another, even higher, valid
norm whose content is incompatible with its content.

Condition (2) indicates that whether two norms are in conflict
depends on the *static* principle which Hart calls "the logical impossibility of joint conformity."156) And condition (3) shows that
the static principle of 'norm conflicts' does not dictate that at least
one of the two conflicting norms loses its validity.157) To put it in

---

155) Kelsen (1973a), p.261. [Emphasis added.]
156) Hart (1983b), p.327. It should be noted here that the static principle of
    "the logical impossibility of joint conformity" is a common logical crite-
    rion of conflicts between *legal* norms, between *moral* norms, and between
    legal and *moral* norms.

Kelsen's own words, "a conflict of norms cannot be a logical contradiction, or anything analogous to such a thing; and hence it cannot be resolved either according to the logical principle of non-contradiction, or by any principle analogous to this."[158] Then, whether a norm *in conflict with another norm* goes out of existence is subject to the *dynamic* principle: A norm is deprived of its validity when it is "annulled in a constitutional way",[159] i.e. either by "*desuetsudo*" or by a derogating norm which is, in turn, created in a constitutional way.[160] So I object to Oh's conviction to the effect that "Kelsen's theory of the 'unconstitutional' statute would be consistent with his idea of the legal system as a hierarchy of norms (*Stufenbau*), if it regarded the 'unconstitutional' statute not as being voidable but as being void."[161]

Ultimately, Kelsen's later view on the problem of 'norm conflicts' can trace its origin back to the difference between *static* and *dynamic justifications* of a normative system.[162] However, it should be distinguished from an erroneous statement that "[a] prescription may be regarded as authoritative either *because* it is subsumable under a higher rule, or *because* it is made by someone occupying an institutional role",[163] or that Kelsen "works with two types of

---

157) Oh says that "a conflict between norms itself makes, in principle, no difference!" Oh (2000), p.106.
158) Kelsen (1973b), p.233.
159) Kelsen (1949), p.119.
160) Kelsen (1973b), p.234.
161) Oh (1998), p.120.
162) I borrow these terms from Oh's dissertation. Oh (2000), p.46.

authorisation"[164] on the relation of a higher norm to a lower norm within a *legal* system. The case is that Kelsen just upholds two independent principles: a *static* principle of 'norm conflicts' and a *dynamic* principle of 'norm validation'. To put it differently, a static and a dynamic justification (of a normative system) respectively.[165] A static justification validates only norms of a static type, while a dynamic justification validates only norms of a dynamic type. However, as I have already mentioned, a static justification identifies conflicts between norms of both types.

But a dynamic justification, or a dynamic principle of 'norm validation', fails to recognize the difference between a norm and a "norm contrary to a norm" since both of them are *valid*.[166] Once

---

163) J.W. Harris, "Kelsen's Conception of Authority", *Cambridge Law Journal* 36 (November 1977), p.359. [Emphasis added.]

164) Stanley L. Paulson, "Material and Formal Authorisation in Kelsen's Pure Theory", *Cambridge Law Journal* 39 (April 1980), p.172.

165) Cf. Joel Feinberg and Raz distinguish between validity and justification of law, whereas Honoré and Weinberger do not. Joel Feinberg, "The Nature and Value of Rights", *Journal of Value Inquiry* 4 (1970). Reprinted in Carl Wellman (ed.), *Rights and Duties Vol.1: Conceptual Analyses of Rights and Duties*, Routledge, New York, 2002, p.87. [References are to the reprint.]; Raz (1983), p.150; Honoré (1987), p.91 n.3; Ota Weinberger, "Introduction: Hans Kelsen as Philosopher", in Hans Kelsen, *Essays in Legal and Moral Philosophy* (1973), p.XVIII.

166) Despite the fact that the validity of individual norms is *provisional* when they are created by courts of first instance, while being *definitive* when created by courts of last instance, it is not the case that there exist two *types* of validity. Similarly, what Stanley L. Paulson calls "presumptive legal validity (vermutungsweise Gültigkeit)" is not regarded as an independent type of validity. Kelsen (1970), p.269; Oh (2000), p.25 n.65, p.70

again, talking only to the validity of law is getting us nowhere.

(2) Between Validity and Authority Approaches

The natural lawyers have fixed those problems by conceiving of the normativity of law as 'statically' justified normativity, thereby upholding the notion of axiological validity.[167] First, for them, the validity of rules of positive law derives ultimately from natural law whose validity *is* self-evident. There is no such problem as the validity of the ultimate rule because natural law is neither *pre-supposed* as valid nor beyond the usage of term 'validity'. Second, the natural lawyers uphold *static* principles of 'norm conflicts' and of 'norm validation'. So there is no such problem as norm conflicts between valid norms. Third, they renounce the last condition of **KT**, i.e. a *dynamic* principle of 'norm validation' which cannot afford the opportunity to differentiate between a norm and a "norm contrary to a norm".[168]

But Kelsen and Hart cannot endorse this solution formulated by

---

n.242; Paulson (1980), p.191 n.60.

167) See Ⅱ. 2. 2) of this book.

168) As to the important recent writers in natural law theory, see Brian H. Bix, "Natural law: The Modern Tradition", in Jules Coleman and Scott Shapiro (eds.), *The Oxford Handbook of Jurisprudence and Philosophy of Law*, Oxford University Press, Oxford, 2002, p.75 ff. Bix classifies as natural lawyers the following theorists: Jacques Maritain, Lon Fuller, Ronald Dworkin, John Finnis, Michael Moore, Robert P. George, Lloyd Weinreb, Ernest J. Weinrib, Randy E. Barnett, Deryck Beyleveld, Roger Brownsword, Richard Dien Winfield, Alan Brudner, etc.

natural lawyers without contradicting themselves. Hart conceives of the normativity of law as social normativity, thereby upholding only the systemic notion of validity. Things are not so different in Kelsen's scheme. Despite the fact that he adheres to the view according to which legal validity refers to the (legally) 'binding force', he thinks of a legal system as a dynamic system, thereby conceiving of its normativity as 'dynamically' justified normativity. Actually, even the fact that Kelsen employs the notion of axiological validity is not a solution but a *source* of another theoretical problem, since the concept of axiological validity itself appears incongruous with his commitment to the positivist cause of the separation of law and morality.[169] Moreover, both Kelsen and Hart affirm the last condition of **KT**, while renouncing its first condition.

They must, then, seek to find a solution to those problems without recourse to the notion of static validation or axiological validity. However, it is still the case that the sense of 'obligatoriness' is embedded in the term 'normativity' of law. How can Kelsen and Hart ensure the neutrality of legal norms and, at the same time, their quality of being obligatory? Neither neutrality nor obligatoriness of legal norms is successfully captured by the notion of systemic validity, which fails to guarantee the first by rendering the system precarious, and fails to incorporate the latter by confining

---

169) Ross (1998), pp.159-60; Bulygin (1998), pp.308-10; Valdés (1998), p.270; Raz (1983), p.137.

itself to the identification of norms as belonging to a legal system.

As I have already suggested, it is impossible for them to invest legal norms with the neutral obligatoriness before resort to the notion of authority of law. This solution can be expressed by the following theses:

(1) If a norm is legally valid and, at the same time, its content is compatible with the contents of other norms (of the system) which are also legally valid, it has authority to guide people's behaviour.

(2) Even though any norm has authority to guide people's behaviour, it does not follow that the norm is legally valid.

(3) A norm is legally valid when it belongs to a given system of legal norms, while it has authority when people to whom the system applies are bound to respect it in the course of practical reasoning.

(4) The foundations of a legal system do not consist in the validity of the ultimate rule but consist in its authority.

The "question of the authority of law" is, according to Raz, concerned with "the way in which the fact that a certain action has some legal consequences should affect practical deliberation generally and moral considerations in particular."[170] And the fact that a certain action has the legal consequences entails the legal validity of that action. For not only rules but also certain actions are valid "if and only if they have the normative consequences they purport to have."[171] Hence, the question of the authority of law is concerned with the way in which the legal validity of a certain action should affect practical deliberation generally and moral considerations in particular. Here, we can draw a line between the question of the authority of law and the related question of the validity of law or certain actions ruled by the law. The first is a matter of practical reasoning, while the latter is ultimately a matter of judicial recognition:[172] *the thesis (3)*. So we can say that Kelsen obscures the issue of a legal system when he sees the problem of the 'authority' of creators of *lower* norms as the problem of the 'validity' of *higher* norms. If a judge is authorized to create a certain individual norm, according to him, it is because there exists a valid general norm which confers norm-creating authority on a judge.

Now, from the mere fact that a norm belongs to a given system of legal norms, that is, that a norm is legally valid, it does not follow that the norm has authority to guide people's behaviour. To be authoritative, a norm which is legally valid ought not to fall into the category of the "norm contrary to a norm". None of the two (or more) norms in conflict with each other can have authority, despite

---

170) Raz (1983), p.vi.
171) Raz (1983), p.150.
172) H.L.A. Hart, "Scandinavian Realism", *Essays in Jurisprudence and Philosophy* (1983), p.165.

the fact that all of them are legally valid: *the thesis (1)*.

From the theses (1) and (3), we can infer that where the *dynamic* justification of a norm obtains, it is not sufficient for the authority of that norm. J.W. Harris can be considered, I think, to be committed to the similar idea when he says that "*subsumption is a sufficient condition for authority*."[173] And Harris goes further, claiming that "subsumption is not a necessary condition for normative authority."[174] In cases of *original norms*, i.e. "norms the creation conditions of which do not include the existence of other norms",[175] it is a matter of course that a norm is subsumable under no other norm that is valid. To that extent Harris' second claim is right. But in cases of *derivative norms*, i.e. norms the creation conditions of which consist of "the existence of a certain norm" and "the occurrence of certain events",[176] a valid norm which is, at the same time, subsumable under another norm which is also valid has authority. This is what the thesis (1) indicates.

All things considered, the legal validity of a norm is not always required for its authority. Original norms can, irrespective of their

---

173) Harris (1977), p.358. [Emphasis added.] Cf. He distinguishes between two *static* principles of "norm validation": practical inference (or deduction) and subsumption. But I think that S.L. Paulson is right, at least in understanding Kelsen, to say that "subsumption is a mongrel category, used as shorthand for the syllogism, for the argument from *modus ponens*, and so on." Paulson (1980), pp.175-6.
174) Harris (1977), p.358.
175) Raz (1978a), p.61 n.1.
176) Raz (1978a), p.61.

validity, be authoritative. From the thesis (3), it follows that the ultimate rule that falls within original norms is authoritative if people are bound to respect it. However, the ultimate rule is, by definition, neither deduced from nor created according to some further rule. It does not, therefore, exist as a "valid rule" whose validity is "identified by some further rule of validity."[177] The ultimate rule serves as the foundation of a legal system, being the final reason for, or the source of the supreme criterion of, validity of all the rules other than itself that constitute one legal system. But it does so authoritatively rather than validly: *the thesis (2) and (4)*. Hence, although Hart shows extreme reluctance to say of the 'validity' of the rule of recognition, we can work in safety with the 'authority' of the rule of recognition.[178]

---

177) Postema (1982), p.166.
178) e.g. Postema (1982), p.168.

III. Concepts of Authority

It has been established that the authority of law as well as its (systemic) validity is indispensable to guarantee the normativity of a legal system without recourse to the notion of static validation of a legal system or axiological validity of law, which the natural lawyers characteristically endorse. However, nothing has been suggested so far about the nature, or rather the concept, of the authority (of law). In this chapter we will turn our attention to that issue.

1. Basic Ideas of Practical Authority

1) Disagreement

Most legal and political theorists irrespective of their conclusions on the matter of justifiability of political authority think that political authority is of the practical sort.[1] These theorists maintain that the directives issued by political authorities provide their reci-

---

1) Tom Christiano, "Authority", *The Stanford Encyclopedia of Philosophy* (Fall 2004 Edition), Edward N. Zalta (ed.), URL = <http://plato.stanford.edu/archives/fall2004/entries/authority/>, section 1.1; Heidi M. Hurd, "Challenging Authority", *Yale Law Journal* 100 (April 1991), p.1619.

pients with reasons for action, which guide people's behaviour.[2] According to this traditional view, the utterances of a political authority are best understood by drawing an analogy with command rather than advice. The first requires recipients to obey it, whereas the latter provides mere reasons for belief.

> Surely what counts, from the point of view of the person in authority, is not what the subject thinks but how he acts. I do all that the law requires of me if my actions comply with it. There is nothing wrong with my considering the merits of the law or of action in accord with it. Reflection on the merits of actions required by authority is not automatically prohibited by any authoritative directive, though possibly it could be prohibited by a special directive to that effect.[3]

At one end of this theoretical spectrum are those theorists who claim that the authority of a state is exercised by issuing the laws which have the power to command and that, therefore, people resident in its territory have the obligation to obey its law. The opposite end is occupied by those who claim that state's claim to authority cannot be conceptually justified, and that people have no

---

2) It does not lead to a false conclusion that guidance is the only function of reasons for action. "Reasons are referred to in explaining, in evaluating, and in guiding people's behaviour. The concept of a reason is used for various other purposes as well, but these three are primary and the rest are derived from or dependent on them." [Footnote omitted.] Raz (1990a), pp.15-16.
3) Raz (1990b), p.39.

such an obligation. But a traditional presumption that political authority is of the practical sort remains unchanged in all positions from across this spectrum.

Strictly speaking, however, there is no agreement among theorists on this issue. Some theorists against the traditionalist approach view the (claimed) authority of state as a theoretical authority.[4] According to them, the utterances of political authority provide mere reasons for belief, not reasons for action.

(1) Authority: Practical or Theoretical

Theorists who regard political authority as providing reasons for belief argue that the theory of political authority will be conceptually incoherent if understood as a practical authority, and that the only alternative available for us to overcome anarchist challenges is the idea of political authority as a theoretical authority. Heidi M. Hurd, one of the most steadfast claimants along this line, argues as follows:

> We began by considering the traditional view of legal authority
> —the theory of practical authority. This theory was found to be
> conceptually incoherent: despite Raz's sophisticated attempt to res-
> cue it from incoherence, the concept of practical authority foun-
> dered upon the paradoxical demand that we act contrary to the ba-

---

4) As to a brief list of theorists who join such camp, see Hurd (1991), p.1667 n.91.

lance of reasons when commanded to do so ⋯ But there remains a final theory of authority, one which stands a chance of vindicating our deeply felt conviction that laws possess a special status and are worthy of our most serious consideration: the theory of theoretical authority.[5]

Her argument is very convincing to the extent that it refutes Joseph Raz and his followers' arguments which are enjoying high reputation,[6] though sharing with them the same fallacious assumption, of which a full-fledged investigation will be made later. For the present section, we just focus our attention on her argument against Razian reasoning.

(a) Theory of Practical Authority: J. Raz

According to Raz, reasons for action have dimensions of strength and level, which must be distinguished. First, Some reasons for action are logically "stronger or more weighty [*sic*] than others."[7] If there is a reason for certain action, and there is another reason for contradictory action, then these two reasons are conflicting. And

---

5) Hurd (1991), pp.1666-1667. [Footnote omitted.]

6) Razian argument "has become perhaps the most celebrated of attempts to explain both the source of and the solution to that paradox. ⋯ Raz's appeal to a so-called sophisticated view of practical reasoning has been hailed by many contemporary legal theorists as the definitive means of escaping, once and for all, the difficulties that have long been thought to plague the traditional view of legal authority and obligation." Hurd (1991), pp.1620-1621. [Footnote omitted.]

7) Raz (1990a), p.25.

the stronger reason "overrides" the weaker when they conflict. In other words, conflicts of reasons for and against an action are resolved by their relative strength or weight, and this way of resolving conflicts of reasons can be called 'overriding'. Second, Some reasons for action are on a different level with others. A reason of a higher order or level "prevails over" reasons of a lower level when they conflict. Raz claims that we should distinguish reasons for action into first-order and second-order reasons, the latter of which is at a higher level than the first.[8] To put it in another way, conflicts between first-order and second-order reasons are resolved not by their relative strength but by "kind" or hierarchy. He defines a second-order reason as "any reason to act for a reason or to refrain from acting for a reason." The first category of second-order reason is called positive second-order reasons and the latter category negative second-order reasons.[9] And "a second-order reason to refrain from acting for some reason" or a negative second-order reason is named an exclusionary reason.[10] Therefore, the way of resolving conflict between a first-order reason and a second-order exclusionary reason is referred to as 'excluding'. To sum up, "there are two ways in which reasons can be defeated. They can be overridden by strictly conflicting reasons or excluded by exclusionary reasons."[11]

---

8) Raz (1990a), p.36.
9) Raz (1983), p.17.
10) Raz (1990a), p.39; Raz (1983), p.17.
11) Raz (1990a), p.40. Cf. As to explanation of the features characteristic of

Sometimes a reason for an action is, at the same time, an exclusionary reason to refrain from acting on the basis of reasons against it. Raz calls such reasons protected reasons for an action.[12] And then, he explicates the essential feature of practical authority by recourse to this concept of protected reason. Practical authority is thought involving the normative power which is defined as an ability to change protected reasons.[13] To exercise practical authority, in his thought, is to exercise its normative power to change protected reasons. And one way in which protected reasons can be changed is by issuing an exclusionary instruction, which is itself a protected reason and instances of which are command and order given by person entitled to do so.[14]

Raz's theory of practical reasoning, see Louis E. Feldman, "Originalism through Raz-colored Glasses", *University of Pennsylvania Law Review* 140 (April 1992), p.1393 ff. We can see the same, though unfledged, idea of practical reasoning in I. Kant. Kant says that "[o]nly what is connected my will merely as ground and never as effect, what does not serve my inclination but *outweighs* it or at least *excludes* it altogether from calculations in making a choice—hence the mere law for itself—can be an object of respect and so a command." I. Kant, *Groundwork of the Metaphysics of Morals*, 4:400 in Mary J. Gregor (trans. and ed.), *Immanuel Kant — Practical Philosophy*, Cambridge University Press, Cambridge, 1999 (1996), p.55. [Hereinafter *Groundwork*. Footnote omitted and emphasis added.]

12) Raz (1983), p.18.

13) Raz (1983), p.18; Raz (1990b), p.24, p.38.

14) Raz specifies three ways in which practical authority can change protected reasons. First, practical authority can issue an exclusionary instruction which is itself a protected reason. Second, it can grant permission to perform an action which had hitherto been prohibited by an exclusionary instruction. Third, it can confer its power on another. See Raz (1983), p.18.

Unlike cases of advice or request, he claims, command and order are thought to be given with an intention that they shall be taken as protected reasons. To explain in detail, commands or orders are issued not only to tip the balance of first-order reasons for an action but also to exclude action on the basis of such a balance.[15] This is what Raz exactly means by issuing protected reasons.

To summarize, if one is entitled to command, i.e. to change protected reasons by issuing another protected reason, for instance, then it is logically true that one has practical authority over the addressee of the command.[16] And the addressee is justified in not acting on the basis of the balance of first-order reasons since there is a prevalent reason not to do so. Therefore, to follow the commands of practical authority is far from abandoning reason or forfeiting one's autonomy.[17]

(b) Theory of Theoretical Authority: Heidi M. Hurd

Raz argues that there is no actual paradox between rationality and authority, and that, therefore, those who endorse the traditional concept of practical authority are not guilty of misunderstanding. Hurd illustrates this as follows:

These points shall be revisited later. (See Ⅲ. 1. 2) - (3) of this book.)
15) Raz (1983), pp.21-3.
16) Raz (1983), p.15.
17) Raz (1983), p.25.

According to those within Razian camp, one who thinks that the exercise of practical authority is inconsistent with rational choice-making wrongly assumes that there are no valid protected reasons for action—that is, that one is never justified in not doing what ought to be done on the balance of first-order reasons. One wrongly assumes, that is, that there are no second-order exclusionary reasons for action. If there is an example which makes intelligible the manner in which one might refuse to act on the balance of first-order reasons for action, then one must admit the existence and force of second-order exclusionary reasons. And with such an admission the dilemma of practical authority is rendered illusory and the traditional theory of legal obligation is vindicated.[18]

Hurd, however, discloses that such an ambitious attempt to account for the compatibility between the concept of practical authority and the concept of rationality turns out to be a failure. There, she explains, are two related problems which frustrate it. The first problem is poor exemplification. She claims that the examples employed by Raz to show the exclusionary features of the protected reasons for action which laws are supposed to provide are either irrelevant or exposed to the very matter in dispute, i.e. the paradox between rationality and authority or the dilemma of practical authority. The second is, what she calls, "conceptual incoherence." Here, Hurd claims further that the concept of protected reason itself is conceptually problematic and thus it is impossible to reconcile prac-

---

18) Hurd (1991), p.1622.

tical authority with rationality, and that this problem gives birth to the first problem and explains the difficulty of giving relevant examples.

Two main examples Raz employs are the case of incapacity and the case of promise.[19] To suggest these in abridged versions,

> **C1**: Ann has had a long and strenuous day to be flat out. In that late evening, she is presented with an investment proposition, which must be answered until the midnight, by her friend. She tells her friend that it is impossible for her to take a rational decision on the merits of the case since she is too tired and upset to trust her own judgement.

> **C2**: Colin promised his wife that in all decisions affecting the education of his son he will act only for his son's interests and disregard all other reasons. Now, he has to decide whether or not to send his son to Eton. He decides to do so because of his promise, disregarding all other considerations, for instance sound finance, unless they affect his son's welfare even indirectly.

According to Hurd, in the case of **C1**, "that one is tired is not a

---

19) Joseph Raz, "Reasons for Action, Decisions and Norms", in Joseph Raz (ed.), *Practical Reasoning*, Oxford University Press, Oxford, 1978, pp.130-1. The same examples are also exhibited, with the third one, in Raz (1990a), pp.37-9.

reason to refrain from acting on the balance of first-order reasons. Indeed it is not a reason for action at all."[20] Physical and, at the same time, psychological exhaustion gives Ann *a reason to believe* that there are other reasons for rejecting the proposition, "which are at the present elusive, but which, if added to the balance, would result in one's finding the [investment] an unwise proposition."[21] However, Raz tries to explain it in terms of *a reason not to act*.

> She insists that though she is taking a decision against the offer, she can rationally do so not on the ground that on the merits the offer ought to be rejected but because she has *a reason not to act* on the merits of the case.[22]

In the case of **C2**, Raz claims that Colin's promise gave him a first-order reason for considering his son's interests and an exclusionary reason for disregarding other reasons against it. To put it in other way, Colin's promise gave him a protected reason to consider his son's interests only. Speaking strictly, such reasons for *considering* and for *disregarding* are reasons for belief or judgment, but not action. This reveals the reason that Hurd does not simply adopt **C2** but employs a new case of promise in which one gave his sister a promise to assist his mother. A reason for *assi-*

---

20) Hurd (1991), p.1623.
21) Hurd (1991), p.1623.
22) Raz (1978b), p.131. [Emphasis added.]

sting his mother is, of course, a reason for action.[23]

Then, Hurd counterclaims, if rightly understood, that we need *stronger reason* to believe that it is rational to act as instructed by laws against the balance of reasons to act otherwise, whereas promises are *no more rational* than laws. Therefore promises cannot satisfy such a need.

She asserts that "in all such cases [as **C1**, **C2** for examples] in which we have a reason to doubt our ability ⋯ to balance the first-order reasons for and against action, that doubt functions only as a reason for belief concerning the validity of those reasons, not as a reason for action."[24] Raz struggles to save himself from this attack by saying,

> [The notion of exclusionary reasons] is easily confused with several similar but distinct ideas. First, it can be confused with a reason to avoid thinking, considering, or attending to certain matters. I contributed to that confusion myself by giving some examples in which it appeared that the need to avoid anxiety or mistakes likely to occur if one were to consider certain matters, is the reason for an exclusionary reason. But in all these cases my assumption was that the anxiety and so forth are caused not by at-

---

23) As to such an inconsistency in works of Raz, see Hurd (1991), p.1626 n.27. Some theorists also note that Raz's example of promise is contingent on such a fact as the content of a promise and thus cannot be generalized. See Michael S. Moore, "Authority, Law, and Razian Reasons", *Southern California Law Review* 62 (March/May 1989), p.856 n.96 and accompanying text, p.858.

24) Hurd (1991), p.1625.

tending to or thinking about certain matters, but by the fact that one does so because certain reasons should guide one's behaviour, and that is why one has to establish what they are. If one ought not to act for these reasons, one would be relieved of the pressure which brings the undesirable side effects in its wake. So that while the good to be achieved has to do with one's thinking, the reason it provides is a reason not to act for certain reasons.[25]

But Raz's argument seems somewhat inadequate. What he should have met is not an objection that **C1** concerns a reason to avoid thinking, but an objection that it concerns a reason to think (that there are other reasons for action of which one is then unaware).

More significantly, Hurd suggests that the concept of protected reason itself is conceptually incoherent, reminding us that the dilemma of practical authority[26] is similar to the old-fashioned riddle of the source of ultimate justice.[27] She summarizes the dilemma in the following form:[28]

---

25) Raz (1990a), p.184. [Footnote omitted.]

26) "Is what makes such action rational the sheer fact that one has been commanded to pursue it, or does the rationality of a commanded act depend upon something further?" Hurd (1991), p.1627.

27) "Is what God says right because God says it; or does God say it because it is right?" Hurd (1991), p.1627. This question was raised by Plato in the following form: "[i]s what is holy holy because the gods approve it, or do they approve it because it is holy?" Plato, *Euthyphro*, 10a in Edith Hamilton and Huntington Cairns (eds.), *The Collected Dialogues of Plato Including the Letters*, Princeton University Press, Princeton, 1961, p.178.

28) Hurd (1991), p.1628.

(1) If the exclusionary reason generated by a command bars action in accord with first-order reasons against the commanded action, then it (pragmatically) bars the consideration of those reasons.[29]

(2) If the exclusionary reason generated by a command (pragmatically) bars the consideration of those reasons, then it (pragmatically) bars the consideration of any reasons for the commanded action beyond that provided by the fact that the command has been issued.

(3) HENCE: Upon the receipt of a command, the only reason for action that one should consider is the fact that some action has been commanded.[30]

---

29) Premise (1) is what Raz exactly objects to. He persistently asserts that exclusionary reasons do not bar the consideration of excluded reasons. As to his objection, see Joseph Raz, "Facing Up: A Reply", *Southern California Law Review* 62 (March/May 1989), p.1156 ff. But he still fails to defeat premise (1) without discarding **C1**. He argues that "[t]here may be cases where, given that one's judgment is unreliable, there is reason for one not to contemplate the pros and cons if doing so may lead one to act on one's judgment. But given that one's decision or rule puts an end to this danger, once it is adopted there is no longer a reason not to reflect, idly, on the merits." Raz (1989), p.1157 n.8. His argument, however, is invalidated since in **C1** the exclusionary reason, if any, is not provided by Ann's decision or rule of thumb to reject the proposition when too tired. As Raz himself admits, such a decision or rule is a reason to *reject* rather than *accept* it, whereas the exclusionary reason is simply a reason not to act on the merits of it and, if any, provided by the very fact that Ann is too tired. Raz (1990a), pp.37-8.

30) Actually, the same conclusion can also be drawn from the functional analysis of authority by Raz. As to this, Louis E. Feldman says that "[a]s a consequence of the Preemptive Thesis, subjects faced with an authoritative command from legal authority are precluded from considering the justification values that, according to the Dependence Thesis, underlie the com-

(4) But, if an action is rational solely because it has been commanded, then any action that is commanded is rational.

(5) If, alternatively, an action is rational only if it comports with other requirements, then the sheer fact that an action has been commanded cannot rationally justify the performance of the act.

(6) Since the consequent of (4) is false, the antecedent of (4) must be false.

(7) Since the antecedent of (4) must be false, then the antecedent of (5) must be true.

(8) If (5) is true, then to act rationally, one must act for reasons other than the fact that one has been so commanded.

(9) HENCE: Action pursed on the basis of an exclusionary reason is irrational.

She explicates further that there are various attempts to save Razian legacy from bankruptcy, but in vain. In brief, there are two categories of arguments in favor of Razians: attempts to defeat premise (4) and attempts to soften premise (3).[31] Attempts to modify premise (4) by restricting right to command to legitimate authority or by restricting actions to be commanded within authority's proper jurisdiction are rebutted by the argument that in order to judge whether indeed an authority is legitimate and within its jurisdiction one ought not to be prohibited from that judgment.[32] The other attempts to modify premise (3) by acknowledging com-

---

mand." Feldman (1992), p.1400.
31) Hurd (1991), p.1628.
32) Hurd (1991), pp.1633-4.

plementary judgments by addressees necessary are also rebutted by the argument that "practical authority requires what it simultaneously prevents, and is thus incoherent."[33]

Then, if a command requires the same result as the balance of reasons, the command is useless. On the other hand, if a command requires the different result from the balance of reasons, the command is irrational.[34] Therefore, to be rational, people must follow their balance of reasons, but not commands of practical authority. And this amounts to the conclusion that protected reasons which prohibit people from following their balance of reasons are conceptually incoherent, and that the concept of practical authority which assumes the ability to issue protected reasons is also incoherent.[35]

(2) Political Authority as a Practical Authority

Though Hurd convincingly defeats Raz and his followers in their elaborate speculation that political authority is of the practical sort, her whole theory of theoretical authority is not indisputable. First, it seems that she is confused about the concept of obligation to obey the law which is generally, though not universally,[36] deemed

---

33) Hurd (1991), p.1637.
34) As to similar description of the paradox between rationality and authority, see Scott J. Shapiro, "Authority" in Jules Coleman and Scott Shapiro (eds.), *The Oxford Handbook of Jurisprudence and Philosophy of Law* (2002), p.391.
35) Hurd (1991), p.1641.
36) Leslie Green, "Legal Obligation and Authority", *The Stanford Encyclopedia*

correlated with political authority.

> So where does this leave us? Have we backed ourselves into a
> theoretical corner from which we can only escape by embracing a
> philosophy of anarchy? Our situation, I think, is not this desperate
> ⋯ Does all this necessitate the view that there is no such thing as
> legal obligation as it has long been conceived? The answer seems
> quite clear: Yes. But while there may be nothing that obligates us
> legally, there may be much that obligates us morally.[37]

She regards obligation to obey the law as a *legal* obligation.
Traditionally, however, obligation to obey the law has been conceived to be a *moral* obligation. In this respect, her so-called alternative idea of what 'obligates us morally' is, in fact, not a virgin
peak, rather a well-trodden path. To return, she examines H.L.A.
Hart's attempt, for instance, to establish an obligation to take rules
as sources of reasons for action, while mistakenly regarding his
concept of obligation to obey the rules as a legal obligation.[38] But,

---

of Philosophy (Fall 2004 Edition), Edward N. Zalta (ed.), URL = <http://
plato.stanford.edu/archives/fall2004/entries/legal-obligation/>, section 2.

37) Hurd (1991), p.1666. [Footnote omitted.]
38) Hurd (1991), p.1649 ff. As for additional evidence, "At stake throughout
    this discussion is the very concept of our duty to obey the law. If I am
    right and the theories of practical and influential authority fail to provide
    a foundation for the law's authority, then it follows that *legal* obligation,
    as it has been traditionally conceived, is an illusion." (p.1614), "I think that
    this theory of 'as if' obligation more closely approximates what most le-
    gal theorists in fact think about the dynamics of *legal* obligation." (p.1642),
    "A theory of influential authority, supplemented by a theory of why such

as we know, Hart himself articulates it to the contrary.

> The rules may provide that officials should have authority to enforce obedience and make further rules, and this will create a structure of legal rights and duties, but the *moral* obligation to obey the rules in such circumstances is due to the co-operating members of the society, and they have the correlative moral right to obedience.[39]

She confuses, in my view, obligation in the law with obligation to the law.[40] The first is a "legal requirement with which law's subjects are bound to conform",[41] whereas the latter is a moral requirement to obey the mandatory norms issued by political authority. Needless to say, obligation to obey the law entails such a moral requirement. As he clearly puts it, "[h]istorically, most philosophers agreed that [obligations to the law] include a *moral* obli-

---

influence is weighty, may thus be expected to produce behavior generally comporting with the commands of law, and so may be thought to explain what has long been thought of under the guise of the traditional concept of *legal* obligation. Moreover, such a theory allows for behavior that on occasion conflicts with such commands and so explains what has long been thought to require a theory of the limits of *legal* obligation." (p.1644), "As such, the traditional concept of *legal* obligation is indefensible⋯ For if I am right, the law cannot generate unique *legal* obligations. Rather, if the law is to possess any authority at all it must be by virtue of accurately reflecting other obligations−those *moral* obligations which exist antecedent to the enactment and enforcement of the law." (p.1677). [Emphasis added.]

39) H.L.A. Hart (1955). p.11. [Original emphasis omitted and mine added.]
40) Green (2004), introduction, section 1 and 3.
41) Green (2004), section 1.

gation to obey, or what is usually called political obligation."[42)]

Alf Ross, as has already been mentioned in chapter 1, even proves that obligation to obey the law cannot but be a moral obligation. He puts it,

> It seems obvious that the duty to obey the law cannot mean, here, a legal duty or obligation in the same sense in which these terms are used to describe the legal situation arising in certain circumstances governed by a legal norm — for example, the obligation of the debtor to pay a contracted debt. An obligation in this technical sense means that the debtor runs the risk that legal sanctions will be carried out against him. For the act of 'not obeying the law', however, there is and can be no sanction different from the sanction for not paying the debt.
>
> I can put it another way. A duty is always a duty to behave in a certain way. In this case, the required behaviour is 'to obey the law.' How do we obey the law? By fulfilling our legal obligations — for example, by paying our debts. It follows that the obligation to obey the law does not prescribe any behaviour that is not already prescribed by the law itself. And it follows in turn that if the duty to obey the prescriptions of a legal system is to mean something different from the obligation prescribed directly by this system, then the difference cannot consist in the *required behaviour — what* we are bound to do — but must consist exclusively in *how* we are bound. The meaning of the binding force inherent in a legal system is that the legal obligations corresponding to the rules of the system — for example, the obligation to pay a debt — are

---

42) Green (2004), introduction. [Original emphasis omitted and mine added.]

not merely legal duties deriving from the threat of legal sanctions. They are also *moral duties* in the *a priori* sense of true moral obligations deriving from the natural law principles that endow the legal system with its validity or binding force.[43]

Second, she mistakenly disregards the difference between the conceptual coherence of practical authority and the compatibility of the concept of practical authority with the concept of practical rationality. 'The round square' or 'the prime number smaller than 2' is an example of the idea which is conceptually incoherent.[44] There, however, is no incoherence as such in obligating people not to act in accordance with the balance of reasons that they previously had but to act as commanded simply because they are told to do so.[45] What appears problematic is just that such claim of practical authority as this sounds paradoxical in relation to another concept (the concept of practical rationality). But if one of the two concepts thought to be contradictory to each other is conceptually incoherent, then no genuine room would be left for the word 'paradox' or 'dilemma'. If she makes the concept of authority conditional upon

---

43) Ross (1998), pp.153-4.

44) Even the same example as mine is sometimes, and mistakenly, employed in favor of Hurd. "'Legitimate authority' is like the round square: a concept that cannot be exemplified because it contains a contradiction in terms." Govert den Hartogh, *Mutual Expectations: A Conventionalist Theory of Law*, Kluwer Law International, The Hague, 2002, p.128.

45) For the same reason, it is right, I think, of Raz to suggest that "[t]here seems to be no logical incoherence in the idea of ascetic or self-denying reasons." Raz (1990a), pp.183-184.

the principle of practical rationality, it would result in cutting arbitrarily a horn off the dilemma.

Owing to such a mistake, though she impressively undermines the Razian solution to the paradox between authority and rationality, she draws a wrong conclusion that political authority is of the theoretical sort. But it would be misleading to say that she implies that law claims theoretical authority. She just suggests that law must be thought to possess theoretical authority. In this respect, a well-known criticism that the theory of theoretical authority is mistaken about law's claim is somewhat pointless.

> [T]he epistemic approach badly misinterprets the claims of political authorities. Political authorities claim that their directives are more than mere reasons to believe — they claim that they are reasons to act. One does not comply with an order simply by believing that the order was justified; one must act on this belief.[46]

It is a matter of course that law claims practical authority,[47] that

---

46) Shapiro (2002), p.400.

47) This must be distinguished from a controversial thesis, which is claimed by Raz, that law necessarily claims (legitimate) practical authority. But it is incontestable that law claims practical authority, not as a matter of concept but as a matter of fact. As to Raz's thesis, see Raz (1994), pp.199-202. In this point William A. Edmundson agrees with him. Edmundson (1998), p.56. And as to the controversy surrounding it, see Kenneth Einar Himma, "Inclusive Legal Positivism", in Jules Coleman and Scott Shapiro (eds.), *The Oxford Handbook of Jurisprudence and Philosophy of Law* (2002), p.147 ff.

is, that law commands, rather than advises or requests. This is what not only defenders of the theory of practical authority suggest, but also Hurd acknowledges by saying that "one who issues a command thus purports to be a practical authority"[48] or that "when one issues a command, ⋯ [o]ne claims ⋯ to possess practical authority."[49] She argues, meanwhile, that such a claim compels people to abandon their rationality and thus is unacceptable.

Be that as it may, what Hurd is entitled to infer from the premise that the concept of practical authority is incompatible with the principle of rationality is that Razians, or defenders of the theory of practical authority in general are still impaled upon the horns of the dilemma, and that they cannot but yield to philosophical anarchists unless they succeed in finding a new solution to this dilemma. She is not logically permitted to go beyond this and conclude that the concept of practical authority is, therefore, conceptually incoherent. Whether or not to employ a different premise exclusive of practical authority is just another story. Raz rightly argues as follows:

> The paradoxes of authority can assume different forms, but all of them concern the alleged incompatibility of authority with reason or autonomy ⋯ Arguments along these lines do not challenge the coherence of the notion of authority nor do they deny that some people are believed to have authority or actually have *de fac-*

---

48) Hurd (1991), p.1618.
49) Hurd (1991), p.1619.

to authority. They challenge the possibility of legitimate, justified, *de jure* authority. Their paradoxical nature derives not from their denial of legitimate authority but from the fact that the denial is alleged to derive from the very nature of morality or from fundamental principles of rationality.[50]

Therefore, we are still justified in regarding political authority as a practical authority, that is, as giving people reasons for action. Hereinafter I shall use 'authority' to refer to practical authority. On this basis, problems of concept, function and justification of authority of law will be tackled below. My point is, as will be shown at the end of this chapter, that what really matters is not whether it is practical or theoretical, but whether it is positional or dispositional.

2) Three Basic Ideas

Now we are in a position to take seriously the varied ideas each of which has been claimed to capture the essential feature of authority. Theorists have not concurred in the conceptual account of authority, notwithstanding the traditional view which was introduced above as the 'theory of practical authority' which they held in common. They have inherited, and have been attached to, a blurred image of legitimate authority. And then, while differently situated and committed, they have devoted themselves to investigating how

---

50) Raz (1983), pp.3-4.

its definite contours should be drawn.

As is well-known, there are varied ideas to which they have, in fact, reduced the concept of legitimate authority.[51] Three of the most familiar or basic are power, right and capacity. First, some theorists regard legitimate authority as power or influence over people that is justified in coercing them into conforming to its law. Secondly, other theorists account for it referring to a concept of the right to exercise power of which a right to rule, or a right to be obeyed, etc. is an example. Thirdly, still others employ as legitimate authority the idea of special normative capacity, other than power or right, to impose duties on people.

In what follows these three ideas will in turn be sketched out. Our attention will be paid, in the first place, to the difference among them. But in the long run, we will focus on a common denominator of them, in the sense of a common shortcoming. In brief, they can neither reflect a typical way to balance private interests among members of modern societies, nor enable a model of a legal system to reproduce what Hart calls the salient features of law.[52]

---

51) Christiano (2004), section 1; Raz (1990b), p.23 ff. It should be noted that Christiano's classifications are not identical to mine. He suggests that "[d]e facto authority, on anyone's account, is distinct from political power." But as we shall see below, some theorists think otherwise. And I doubt whether he can legitimately distinguish (justified) power from (justified) coercion, which is regarded by him as falling under conceptions of authority.

52) Actually, it belongs to the main theme of this thesis to show what this common shortcoming is. See III. 2. 2) and IV. 1. of this book.

(1) Justified Power or Influence

Legitimate authority has sometimes been understood as justified power or influence[53] over people who reside within the territory occupied by that authority. William McBride suggests in his paper that "the term 'authority' denotes nothing further than the idea of possessing the ability ('power') to coerce and of exercising that power when such possession and exercise are considered accepta- ble by some other person."[54] According to him, the difference bet- ween authority, which has long won favour with people, and sheer coercion, to which only the coercive agent has preferred to con- sent, consists in social acceptability. Thus, "the 'authority' of a per- son or an institution is simply a function of the acceptance of his or her or its coercive power."[55]

T. Hobbes and J. Austin are often regarded as standing in with this line. While criticizing the theory of law as coercive order ba- cked by threats, Hart describes Austin's concept of the sovereign,

---

53) "Authority thus appears as a species of the genus 'social control' or 'in- fluence' ⋯ and the main task of analysis thus becomes that of exhibiting the distinctive type of influence involved in the idea of authority." R.B. Friedman, "On the Concept of Authority in Political Philosophy", in R.E. Flathman (ed.), *Concepts in Social and Political Philosophy*, Macmillan, New York, 1973. Reprinted in Raz (ed.), *Authority* (1990), pp.59-60. [Re- ferences are to the reprint. Footnote omitted.]
54) William McBride, "The Fetishism of Illegality and the Mystifications of 'Authority' and 'Legitimacy'", *Georgia Law Review* 18 (Summer 1984), p.874.
55) McBride (1984), p.875.

who and whose subordinates are lawgivers, as "a person or body of persons whose orders the great majority of the society habitually obey and who does not habitually obey any other person or persons."[56] R. Ladenson claims that Hart regards the Austinian and Hobbesian notion of sovereignty as meaning "nothing more than being in a position to issue orders backed by credible threats",[57] and then Ladenson advocates the Hobbesian conception by indicating that actually Hobbes, unlike Austin, distinguishes authority from power. Richard S. Peters also contrasts the Hobbesian conception of authority as "a right to do something" with that of de Jouvenel as "the ability of a man to get his proposals accepted."[58] Ladenson puts it,

> Hobbes defines "the sovereign" not only as someone with substantially more power than anyone else in a given social group, but also as the possessor of governmental authority. One can thus distinguish between Austinian and Hobbesian conceptions of law, only one of which, Austin's, clearly involves a crudely reductionistic account of sovereignty.[59]

---

56) Hart (1994), p.50. For detailed analysis of attributes of Austin's sovereignty, see Raz (1978a), p.6 ff.
57) Ladenson (1980), p.33. [References are to the reprint. Footnote omitted.]
58) Richard S. Peters, "Authority", *Proceedings of The Aristotelian Society* 32 (1958). Reprinted in Richard E. Flathman, *Concepts in Social & Political Philosophy*, Macmillan, New York, 1973, p.147. [References are to the reprint.]
59) Ladenson (1980), p.34.

It may be thought that Hart does not affirm any feature that differentiates Hobbes's position from Austin's. For Hart himself argues that Hobbes might well be interpreted as ironing out flaws of the theory of law as coercive order through providing an "ingenious" remedy to these flaws one of which, according to him, is hardship suffered in the course of explaining the persistence of law, and voices his suspicion that "[it] is not immediately clear, if we dispense with the notion of a rule in favour of the simpler idea of habit, what the 'authority' as distinct from the 'power' of a legislator can be."[60] But the case is that Hart has an idea to the contrary. He actually affirms the characteristic feature that differentiates Hobbes's account of the Sovereign from Austin and Bentham's. To put it in Hart's own words,

> Hobbes, like Bentham, thought that all laws were commands of a Sovereign but, unlike Bentham, thought the commands were laws only if given to those who were under a prior obligation to obey, and his account of this prior obligation was that it arose from the subject's covenant or contract to obey the commander. So on Hobbes's view the Sovereign in giving his commands which are law is exercising a right arising from the subject's contract. Bentham, however, would have none of this prior obligation to obey nor of the social contract alleged to generate it nor of the idea that in making laws the Sovereign was exercising a right or normative power, so ⋯ he defined the Sovereign in flatly descriptive non-normative terms as one who is habitually obeyed by his subjects

---

60) Hart (1994), p.63.

and himself habitually obeys no one.[61]

It is thus unfair for Ladenson to criticize Hart for failing to differentiate the Hobbesian conceptions of law and authority from Austin's.

In spite of Peters, Ladenson and Hart's advocacy, however, Hobbes seems to have thought that the two concepts can be used interchangeably. Hobbes writes as follows:

> In every commonwealth, the *Man* or *Assembly* to whose will individuals have subjected their will (in the manner explained) is said to hold SOVEREIGN AUTHORITY [*SUMMAM POTESTATEM*] or SOVEREIGN POWER [*SUMMUM IMPERIUM*] or DOMINION [*DOMINIUM*].[62]

The word '*potestas*' is normally translated as 'authority', while the latter can be traced back to its proper etymology '*auctoritas*'. And such a convention is worth respecting in reading Hobbes in parti-

---

61) H.L.A. Hart, "Commands and Authoritative Legal Reasons", *Essays on Bentham: Studies in Jurisprudence and Political Theory* (1982), p.253.

62) Thomas Hobbes, *Elementa Philosophica de Cive*, chapter V in Richard Tuck and Michael Silverthorne (eds.), *Hobbes − On the Citizen*, Cambridge University Press, Cambridge, 1998, p.73. [Hereinafter *De Cive.*] Hobbes sometimes uses expressions as 'the Greatest of humane Power' or 'the supreme Authority' in describing the position of one who is called SOVERAIGNE. See Thomas Hobbes, *Leviathan, or the Matter, Forme, & Power of a Common-wealth Ecclesiasticall and Civill*, chapter X in Richard Tuck (ed.), *Hobbes − Leviathan*, Cambridge University Press, Cambridge, 1996, pp.62-65. [Hereinafter *Leviathan.*]

cular, notwithstanding a well-known passage from Cicero which distinguishes *potestas* from *auctoritas*: *cum potestas in populo auctoritas in senatu sit*.[63] There are good reasons for it. In *Leviathan*, originally written in English, Hobbes himself draws an analogy between authority and *dominion*, by suggesting that "as the Right of possession, is called Dominion; so the Right of doing any Action, is called AUTHORITY and sometimes *warrant*. So that by Authority, is always understood a Right of doing any act."[64] And he repeats that a sovereign has "sovereign power."[65]

To some extent, therefore, it is reasonable to say that his concept of authority, even though accompanied by the word "Right [*Jus*]",[66] simply means *justified* power which, of course, has long been thought to be distinguished from *potentia*, the *sheer* power or capacity to do something. And even the distinction between *auctoritas* and *potestas* drawn by Cicero shows, though indirectly, Hobbes to be slanted to the notion of power.[67]

As is implied by Hart and Ladenson, quoted above, the Hobbe-

---

63) Cicero, *De Legibus*, 3.28. "potestas belongs to the people, auctoritas resides in the Senate."
64) *Leviathan*, p.112.
65) *Leviathan*, p.121.
66) For instance, see *Leviathan*, p.112 ff.; *De Cive*, p.75 ff.
67) J.P.V.D. Balsdon and Hannah Arendt translate the word '*potestas*' in the passage from Cicero as 'power'. Arendt adds that "[t]he most conspicuous characteristic of those in authority is that they do not have power." See J.P.V.D. Balsdon, "Auctoritas, Dignitas, Otium", *The Classical Quarterly* 10 (May 1960), p.43; Arendt (1977), p.122.

sian conception of authority is denounced for confusing justified
authority with justified power. R.P. Wolff suggests that "[a]uthority
is the right to command, and correlatively, the right to be obeyed.
It must be distinguished from power, which is the ability to compel
compliance, either through the use or the threat of force."[68] Raz
also claims that "the justified use of power is one thing and authority is another",[69] and that "[a] person needs more than power (as
influence) to have *de facto* authority."[70] That *more* is expressed as
"an appeal for compliance by the person(s) subject to the authority",[71] or as "an appeal not to fear but to respect for authority",[72]
or as a normative "call on its subject beyond the threat."[73]

Even though we could disregard the difference between *de facto* authority and power, the Hobbesian conception of authority is
also criticized for "putting the cart before the horse."[74] According
to Raz, legitimate authority cannot be defined as justified *de facto* authority since "the notion of legitimate authority is presupposed
by that of *de facto* authority"[75] but not *vice versa*.

---

68) R.P. Wolff, *In Defense of Anarchism*, Harper & Row, Publishers, New
    York, 1976 (1970), p.4.
69) Raz (1990b), p.25.
70) Raz (1983), p.9.
71) Raz (1990b), pp.25-6.
72) Hart (1994), p.20.
73) Ronald Dworkin, "The Model of Rules", *University of Chicago Law Re-
    view* 35 (1967). Reprinted in Joel Feinberg and Jules Coleman (eds.),
    Philosophy of Law (7th Edition), Wadsworth, Belmont, 2004, p.86. [Re-
    ferences are to the reprint.]
74) Raz (1983), p.8.

(2) The Right to Rule

Many theorists think that legitimate authority has a right to rule, or right to be obeyed over subjects who owe obedience to the authority. It should be noted here that obedience does not imply existence of an obligation to obey, though this fact sometimes fails to call theorists' attention.[76] It is for this reason that theories of authority as a right to rule diverge. Some theorists think that subjects owe not just obedience but obligation to the authority. According to them, people have a moral obligation to obey, or not to interfere with authority. But other theorists deny all kinds of obligations which are correlatives of rights to rule, and just admit that people do not have a right to resist, so far as legitimate authority is concerned. To put it in another way, they conceive a right to rule or to be obeyed as what is called a *liberty* by Hart,[77] or what is termed a *privilege* by Wesley N. Hohfeld.[78]

---

75) Raz (1983), p.9.

76) Kent Greenawalt and Rolf Sartirious remind us of this matter, quoting Anscombe, who writes, "[a]uthority arises from the necessity of a task whose performance requires a certain sort and extent of obedience on the part of those for whom the task is supposed to be done." Anscombe (1978), p.147. Kent Greenawalt, *Conflicts of Law and Morality*, Oxford University Press, New York, 1987, pp.56-7; Rolf Sartorious, "Political Authority and Political Obligation", *Virginia Law Review* 67 (1981). Reprinted in William A. Edmundson (ed.), *The Duty to Obey the Law: Selected Philosophical Readings*, Rowman & Littlefield Publishers, Lanham, 1999, p.146. [References are to the reprint.]

77) Hart (1955), p.5.

78) "['Liberty'] is by no means so common or definite a word as 'privilege.'"

(a) Authority as a Privilege or Liberty

As is mentioned above, Ladenson, advocating a Hobbesian conception of law, claims that the concept of authority and that of power must be distinguished. According to him, the notion of governmental power is only one of the two "basic elements" constituting the notion of governmental authority.

> The notion of governmental authority involves two basic elements. First, to have such authority is to have governmental power, the exercise of which is effectively uncontested. ··· Second, a plausible conception of governmental authority must incorporate the notion of the right to rule.[79]

The right to rule, here, falls under the kind of rights which are termed privileges or liberties. And he terms this kind of rights "justification-rights",[80] implying that "governmental authority constitutes a moral justification for coercion" and that there is no subjects' obligations or "duties of allegiance to the state or of compliance with the law."[81] Kent Greenawalt also doubts the claimed "linkage" of political authority and the duty to obey its laws and

Wesley N. Hohfeld, "Some Fundamental Legal Conceptions as Applied in Judicial Reasoning", *The Yale Law Journal* 23 (1913). Reprinted in Dennis Patterson (ed.), *Philosophy of Law and Legal Theory*, Blackwell Publishing, Oxford, 2003, p.305. [References are to the reprint.]

79) Ladenson (1980), pp.34-5.
80) Ladenson (1980), p.35.
81) Ladenson (1980), p.37.

suggests that without recourse to an obligation to obey the authority and its laws, we can tell a legitimate governmental authority from a band of robbers.[82] He, then, concludes that it would be "patently false" if someone asserts that acknowledging legitimacy of political authority implies subjects' duties to obey all its directives. He just regards the warrant to issue certain kinds of directives as an undoubtful constituent part of the core of legitimate authority, and the essence of such warrant as justification-right.[83]

Tom Christiano, however, esteems this conception of authority as justification-rights to be "not much more" than the conception of authority as justified coercion.[84] And such an evaluation of it sounds reasonable in the light of constituent parts of legitimate authority in both theories. Ladenson, who writes, "possession of the governmental power and *acceptance* by those one presumes to govern of its exercise jointly constitute as justification for coercive acts which would otherwise be immoral",[85] does not differ with McBride who regards authority as nothing further than the power to coerce, and its moral force as a function of the *acceptance* of that power. Therefore, the conception of authority as justification-rights is exposed to the same objections as to the conception of authority as justified coercion: confusing justified authority with justified power and putting the cart before the horse.

---

82) Greenawalt (1987), p.51.
83) Greenawalt (1987), p.54.
84) Christiano (2004), section 1.
85) Ladenson (1980), p.36. [Emphasis added.]

In addition, the conception of justification-rights is denounced by some theorists for severing wrongly the link between legitimate authority and political obligation. Simmons, for example, argues against Greenawalt's "noncorrelativity thesis" that his argument in fact support only the noncorrelativity of political obligation with the state's *justification*, not with its *legitimacy*.[86] And he suggests that justification-rights are too weak a notion to be profitably employed in evaluating states' morality, even though we do not strictly divide the dimension of institutional evaluation into two, i.e. justification and legitimacy. For it would result in giving premature recognition of legitimacy, which licenses states to encroach on individuals' freedom, to interpret the concept of legitimate authority as a weak, thin notion of justification-rights.

(b) Authority as a Claim-Right

A particularly thick conception of legitimate authority is a right to rule which is a correlative of people's duty owed to it. Simmons terms this kind of rights possessed by authority "legitimacy rights." State legitimacy, according to Simmons, includes not only an exclusive power over subjects to impose duties and enforce them coercively, but also a right to be obeyed which is a correlative of political obligation. To establish, he claims, that any particular state is legitimate is to show that it has the right to rule over persons

---

86) Simmons (1999), p.746 n.20.

within its domain, and that those persons are bound to obey it. Simmons puts it as follows:

> A state's (or government's) legitimacy is the complex moral right it possesses to be the exclusive imposer of binding duties on its subjects, to have its subjects comply with these duties, and to use coercion to enforce the duties. Accordingly, state legitimacy is the logical correlate of various obligations, including subjects' political obligations.[87]

Thus, his notion of legitimacy rights falls under what is termed 'claim-rights' by Joel Feinberg. When rights logically entail other people's duties, Feinberg suggests, such rights can be termed claim-rights.[88] Wolff also stands in with this line, claiming that authority is the right to command, and that the obligation to obey the person who issues the command is a correlative of it.[89]

There is a somewhat modified version of this conception of authority as claim-rights. Edmundson admits that there is no general duty of people to obey the law that is supposed to be a correlative of authority. But, at the same time, he argues that "there is something irreducibly odd about conceiving a state that is justified in

---

87) Simmons (1999), p.746.
88) Joel Feinberg, "The Nature and Value of Rights", Journal of Value Inquiry 4 (1970). Reprinted in Carl Wellman (ed.), *Rights and Duties Vol.1: Conceptual Analyses of Rights and Duties*, Routledge, New York, 2002, p.81. [References are to the reprint.]
89) Wolff (1976), p.9.

enforcing its laws while its citizens have not only no duty to obey the law, but also no duty not to interfere with the *administrative prerogatives* by which law is executed."[90] To put it differently, he claims that there is a general *prima facie* duty of people "not to interfere with" the *bona fide* "administration of the laws" of a just state,[91] and that, in the course of enforcing laws, authorities exercise administrative prerogatives, the word he uses to convey, *inter alia*, the claim of *a right* of noninterference.[92] Therefore his conception also falls under the conception of authority as claim-rights.

Raz criticizes this conception of authority as claim-rights for inaccuracy and lack of perspicuity.[93] First, it is inaccurate since authority is not just a right to rule or to be obeyed, but "can be a right to legislate, to grant permissions, to give authoritative advice, to adjudicate, and so forth." Second, it is not perspicuous since "the notion of right is even more complex and problematic than that of authority." To be free from those flaws, Raz adopts a different definition of authority, i.e. authority as a normative capacity.

---

90) Edmundson (1998), p.55. [Emphasis added.]
91) Edmundson (1998), p.44.
92) Edmundson (1998), p.45.
93) Raz (1983), p.11.

(3) The Normative Capacity to Impose Duties

Raz claims that to have authority over people is to have normative capacity or power, which also ought not to be confused with the Austinian and Hobbesian notion of coercive power or capacity. He defines the notion of normative power as an ability to change a special type of reasons, what he calls protective reasons. In other words, normative power is an ability to change "[a] fact that is both a reason for an action and an (exclusionary) reason for disregarding reasons against it."[94] As regards ways in which authority is exercised, he says as follows:

> There are three ways in which the power holders can change protected reasons that are important to our purpose. The first is by issuing an exclusionary instruction, that is, by using power to tell a person to ϕ, the power-utterance is a reason for that person to ϕ and also a second-order reason for not acting on (all or some) reasons for not ϕ-ing. Exclusionary instructions are, therefore, protected reasons. The second way of exercising power is by making a power-utterance granting permission to perform an action hitherto prohibited by an exclusionary instruction. I shall call such permissions 'cancelling permissions' for they cancel exclusionary reasons. The third form of using power is by conferring power on a person. This does not in itself change protected reasons, but it enables a person to change them. The power a person has can be restricted in many ways — in the way it can be exercised, the persons over

---

94) Raz (1983), p.18.

whom it is held, the actions with respect to which the power-holder can make power-utterances, and so forth.[95]

Shortly, Raz's conception of authority as a normative power is "a power to bind", or "a power or capacity in the authority to issue valid or binding directives",[96] and therefore all authorities claim that people are bound to obey such directives.[97]

It should be noted here that the Razian notion of normative power is not identical to what is generally termed (legal) 'power' by Hohfeld. According to Hohfeld's definition, power is an ability to create or change legal relations through power-holder's *volitional control*.[98] Correlatively to powers to impose a duty on people are the respective *liabilities* of them to have such a duty created,[99] and, therefore, it is unnecessary for subjects of authority to shoulder a *duty* to obey it.[100] However, Raz objects to Hohfeld that not only claim-rights but also "powers can be defined ultimately in

---

95) Raz (1983), p.18.
96) Raz (1990b), p.24.
97) Raz (1990b), p.28.
98) Hohfeld (1913), p.305, p.307. Similarly, a legal power is regarded by Green as "the ability to create or modify obligations", as compared with legal right which is an "interest that warrants holding others under an obligation to protect it." Green (2004), section 1.
99) Hohfeld (1913), pp.308-9.
100) Here, what Christiano calls 'capacity to impose duty' is different from Hohfeld's conception of 'power', since Christiano suggests that legitimate authority as a capacity (to impose duty) is correlated with duties to obey or not to interfere. Christiano (2004), section 1.

terms of duties."[101] He holds that it is not the case that there is no place for a duty to be involved in authority relations, since exercise of authority includes "an appeal to compliance" or "an invocation of the duty to obey."[102] For ignoring this respect Raz criticizes Rolf Sartorius, who regards "a moral and legal capacity to perform certain actions" as one of the constituent parts of authority, while refusing to engage, at any rate, the notion of duty.[103] To sum up, normative power of authority is not an ability *just* to bind, rather a capacity to impose duties on people.[104]

But we have already seen that Raz's notion of protected reasons is not free from flaw: incompatibility of authority with rationality.[105] Then, his notion of normative power is, in turn, also not exempt from the same flaw insofar as Raz defines it as ability to change protective reasons.

---

101) Raz (1978a), p.181; Hart (1983a), p.35. Cf. Raz claims that Hohfeld commits at least four "grave mistakes": "(1) He considered all rights as sets of any number of his four elementary rights, namely claim, privilege, power, and immunity. (2) He thought that every right is a relation between no more than two persons. (3) He thought that all rights are relations between persons. (4) He considered his four elementary rights to be indefinable." Raz (1978a), p.179.
102) Raz (1990b), pp.25-6.
103) Sartorius (1981), pp.144-7. As to Raz's criticism, see Raz (1990b), pp.23-4.
104) Raz claims that there is no general *prima facie* duty or obligation to obey the law even in a just society. Raz (1990b), p.70, p.99 ff; Raz (1983), p.233.
105) See Ⅲ. 1. 1) - (1) - (b) of this book.

2. Two Concepts of Authority

1) Positional Authority: Ability

Whichever conception theorists may pick out of the different basic ideas to unpack the concept of authority, the fact that authority is conceived by them as an 'ability', either normative or positive, to perform certain kinds of action[106] remains unchanged. McBride suggests that authorities have "the *ability* to point to the existence of specific rules within a legal system."[107] And Sartorius thinks that authority imports, *inter alia*, "the *capacity* to issue binding directives" to its subjects.[108] Ladenson also defines power, which is one of the basic elements constituting the notion of authority, as the *ability* to make its subjects do what it wishes.[109] And even theorists who define authority as a claim-right rather than normative power (ability) can be included in this general account. As Feinberg puts it:

> The legal power to claim (performatively) one's right or the things to which one has a right seems to be essential to the very notion of a right. A right to which one could not make claim (i.e. not even for recognition) would be a very "imperfect" right indeed![110]

---

106) Raz (1983), p.7.
107) McBride (1984), p.864. [Emphasis added.]
108) Sartorius (1981), p.145. [Emphasis added.]
109) Ladenson (1980), p.34. [Emphasis added.]

Now, I will call those ability-based theories 'theories of *positional authority*'. I do not use the word 'positional' to indicate what is referred to as being "in authority" by R.S. Peters and R.B. Friedman. According to Peters and Friedman, The notion of being "in authority" must not be confused with that of being "an authority." Friedman writes,

> [T]he basis of the claim to obedience made by a person "in authority" is of a very special kind. This claim does not derive from any special personal characteristics of the person invested with authority, such as superior powers of judgment or special knowledge (as in the case of being "an authority"). His claim to be obeyed is simply that he has been put "in authority" according to established procedure, rather than that his decisions are, on independent grounds, sound, meritorious, or superior decisions.[111]

In the case of being "in authority" the system of authority is logically prior to the person, whereas in the case of being "an authority" the person is prior to the system.[112] As Peters puts it, in the first case "on certain matters certain people are entitled, licensed, commissioned or have a right to be *auctores*. And the right is bestowed by a set pattern of rules",[113] but in the latter case a

---

110) Feinberg (1970), p.83.
111) Friedman (1973), p.79.
112) Friedman (1973), p.81.
113) Peters (1958), p.149. As regards *auctores*, he puts it, "An 'auctor' was, to quote Lewis and Short, 'he that brings about the existence of any

person "does not hold authority according to any system of rules."[114] In this respect, Peters and Friedman make it apparent that
their analyses are under the influence of the Weberian approach in
which legal-rational and traditional authorities are contrasted with
charismatic authority. To simplify their argument, thus, the claim to
obedience is made by a person 'in authority' on the basis of the
occupancy of a *special office*[115] or *official position*.[116]

But I just employ the word 'positional' to indicate that one person, for example, is involved in an authority relationship with others in which that person assumes the *normative* 'relational position'
which is correlated to that others' relational position, and to which
the precedence is given without implicating any official or rule-
systemic post.[117] For instance, right to rule is a correlative of duty

---

object, or promotes the increase or prosperity of it, whether he first ori-
ginates it, or by his efforts gives greater permanence or continuance to
it.'" (p.148.)

114) Peters (1958), p.151.

115) Friedman (1973), p.90 n.49.

116) Wolff, following Weber's notion of *bureaucratic regulations*, suggests that
'[m]ost commonly today, ⋯ authority is granted to those who occupy
official positions.' See Wolff (1976), p.7.

117) For instance in which the word position appears to mean either official
position or relational position: "Many will share Tuck's belief that nobody
has a right to a *position* of (political) authority." Raz (1983), p.6; "[T]he
right to rule over any or all persons within its (claimed) domain (i.e., the
right to occupy the *position* of authority)." Simmons (1999), p.746; "[A]
person who holds a *position* which entitles him to use force to secure
compliance with his decisions⋯" Friedman (1973), p.61; "[T]hey speak
from a certain *position* that gives what they say a character unlike the
mere demand that anyone might make." Edmundson (1998), p.57. Espe-

to obey, and power to change a normative relation is a correlative of liability to recognize the change. And even if we conceive authority, following McBride for example, as a positive *ability*, one's having *ability* resembles his being "an authority" rather than being "in authority" since in the case of the first, says Friedman, "the person claims he should have authority because of his special *capacities*."[118)] It is, then, a matter of course that such a positional authority is of the 'subjective' sort. Two things are worth mentioning. First, even McBride's notion of authority as a *positive* ability to perform certain kinds of actions presumes the *normative* position of authority against its subjects. He admits that authority has its *moral* force only if justified or accepted. And in this respect, as Christiano suggests, there is a similarity between his conception and Ladenson's conception of authority as a justification-right. Second, what I term 'positional authority' is not quite the same as what is termed "possessive conception of authority."[119)] As shall be shown

---

cially, the following two catch our interest because they employ the word 'position' simply in a relational sense: "A person in need, then, is always 'in a *position*' to make a claim, even when there is no one in the corresponding *position* to do anything about it." Feinberg (1970), p.87; "Typically, different perspectives ⋯ are associated with different *positions* within a social relation (such as an authority relation), with different social and political roles (e.g., the judicial, the bureaucrat's and the citizen's perspectives)⋯" S. Lukes, "Perspectives on Authority", in J. Ronald Pennock and John W. Chapman (eds.), *Authority Revisited: NOMOS XXIX*, New York University, New York, 1987. Reprinted in Raz (ed.) *Authority* (1990), pp.204-5. [References are to the reprint. Footnote omitted.]

118) Friedman (1973), p.81.

below, positional authority does not include the authority conferred on a person of respectable properties, whereas possessive conception of authority does.

But such ability is more than mere capacity to foster "feelings of allegiance". As Simmons rightly says, it hardly helps us to ground states' legitimacy to employ the notion of ability which is nothing more than propagandist capacity to encourage the peculiarly emotional attitudes of subjects. Therefore, to evaluate such abilities as constituting positional authority of states, we should frame rather objective standards of legitimacy.

> ··· no plausible theory of state legitimacy could maintain that a state has the rights in which its legitimacy consists—rights to exclusively impose and coercively enforce binding duties on its subjects—simply in virtue of its subjects' feelings of loyalty or its own capacities to generate such feelings. ··· On such accounts states could create or enhance their own legitimacy by indoctrination or mind control; or states might be legitimated solely by virtue of the extraordinary stupidity, immorality, imprudence, or misperceptions of their subjects.[120]

The notion of positional authority in a relational sense is so deeply embedded in the Western tradition that theorists can hardly

---

119) Bong Cheol Lee, "Western Concept of 'Authority' Reconsidered" (in Korean), *Korea and World Politics* 17 (Spring/Summer 2001), The Institute for Far Eastern Studies, p.345 ff.
120) Simmons (1999), p.750.

conceive of the authority of *law* without calling to mind any legal agents who are in a position, both relational and official, to enact or enforce that law. Authority was always the (positional) authority of a *person* or a body of persons involved in an authority relationship with subjects, but not of *law*. Even when Weber stipulates, while explaining legal-rational authority, that "the typical person in authority, the superior, is himself subject to an impersonal order", and that what persons other than the person in authority obey is "only the law", nothing is hinted at with respect to the authority of that order and law.[121]

Raz insists that it is by no means nonsensical to "talk directly of the authority of law" since there are cases in which law is not enacted by an authoritative legislator, and therefore its binding force cannot trace its origin back to a person in authority, such as the case of customary rules.[122] Meanwhile, he preserves the positional characteristic of authority without second-guessing it. He says that he refers interchangeably to the legal agents and the law, and that "[i]t is useful to avail ourselves of the general habit of personifying the law and talking of what it requires, permits, claims, authorizes, etc."[123] Surely, he thinks nothing of it. Of course, I am not calling into question the mere habit of talking in metaphorical

---

121) Max Weber, *Economy and Society: An Outline of Interpretive Sociology*, edited by Guenther Roth and Claus Wittich, University of California Press, Berkeley, 1978 (1956), p.217. [Emphasis omitted.]
122) Raz (1983), p.29.
123) Raz (1990b), p.70.

terms. What matters is that law simply takes the place of legal agents and becomes a party to an authority relationship with people, that is, that law is situated and embedded in a given society as a *member* of it.

Precisely speaking, while habitually personifying the law, Raz and other theorists *illegitimately* confer positional authority on law and, in consequence, the law assumes the relational position which is correlated to that of people's. The whole ethos of personification of the law is reflected in the following passage from Arendt.

> Authority implies an obedience in which men retain their freedom, and Plato hoped to have found such an obedience when, in his old age, he bestowed upon the laws that quality which would make them undisputable rulers over the whole public realm. Men could at least have the illusion of being free because they did not depend upon other men.[124]

2) Dispositional Authority: Properties

What is, then, the basis of an argument for supporting the concept of positional authority as an 'ability' to perform certain kinds of actions? The only detailed explication, known to me, of it is provided by Raz. While criticizing those types of argument which derive substantial knowledge of the nature of authority exclusively from an elucidation of "the conditions under which one has legiti-

---

124) Arendt (1977), p.106.

mate authority", he suggests an analysis which explains "what one has when one has authority" and which concludes that authority is an ability to perform certain actions.

> According to it the concept of authority is to be explained by explaining how claims to authority can be justified. The force of such explanations is clear. They do not presuppose that claims of authority can in fact ever be justified, but merely point out how they are to be justified. On the reasonable assumption that claims to authority are a way of justifying action, it seems almost inevitable that they differ from other justifications of action by the type of justificative arguments involved. In fact this conclusion is far from inevitable. Justifying claims may differ not only in the nature of the justifying argument invoked but also in the nature of the act justified.
>
> There is a considerable plausibility in the idea that authority is to be explained by reference to the kind of act, for example, a claiming, which it justifies. We certainly need authority to perform some actions but not others, and it appears, at least prima facie, that to say that one has a certain authority is to indicate that one could be either justified or capable of doing certain actions, without committing oneself in any way as to the nature of that justification.[125]

What Raz suggests is the fact that the question "how claims to authority can be justified?" is sensitive not only to the justificative arguments but also to the very action that is justified. From this

---

125) Raz (1983), p.6.

fact, he irresistibly indicates that the nature of authority should also be elucidated in terms of the action which is justified by claiming authority. According to him, therefore, authority is always the authority to perform certain kinds of actions. We can rewrite this as follows:

(**S1**) ϕ-ing is justified by reference to claims to authority, rather than other justificative concepts.

(**S2**) ϕ-ing, rather than other actions, is justified by reference to claims to authority.

Such an explication is basically right, I think, but there is a gap between *authority* to perform certain actions and *ability* to perform that. To put it in another way, it seems that Raz logically jumps from the first to the latter.

What, if any, causes him to deviate from the logic? What is the unbridgeable, I claim, gap between authority and ability? To give an answer to these questions, we need reexamine the prior question "how claims to authority can be justified?" As is mentioned above, Raz indicates that this question is sensitive not only to the justificative arguments but also to the very action that is justified. That it is not the whole story is what I want to show here.

The question "how claims to authority can be justified?" is, in fact, also sensitive to the claimant or performer who attempts to justify his own actions, since actions appropriate to be justified by reference to claims to authority can be produced either by the authority or by its subjects. The authority (or a person in authority) appeals to *its own* authority to justify its own actions, whereas its subjects invoke the authority *of a person in authority* to justify their own actions conforming to the law. We can rewrite this as follows:

> **(S3)** ϕ-ing is justified by reference to claims to authority
> laid by X, rather than other persons.

In case claims to authority are laid by the authority (or a person in authority) itself to justify its ϕ-ing, we may well define authority as an *ability* to ϕ. But in case claims to authority are laid by its subjects to justify their ϕ-ing, we can by no means define authority as an *ability* to ϕ. It is indisputable, in case above **(S3)**, that the claimant regards authority as deserving or being entitled to be invoked in order to justify his ϕ-ing. Such a desert or entitlement is not for its ϕ-ing but simply for its being invoked. Moreover, we can say the same thing about attempts to define authority as a *right* or *power* to ϕ. To sum up, all theories of *positional authority* fail to reflect this fact.[126]

---

126) It is noteworthy that Himma writes, in his recent essay, "the head of a crime gang is not properly characterized as an authority despite having the *ability* to tell members what to do and make them do what he demands." Himma believes that any putative authority ought to satisfy what Raz calls the Dependence Thesis, if it is to be a real authority. To put it

Can Raz, or theorists of positional authority at large, respond successfully to this objection? Is this fact nothing more than a minor exception? The answer is clear: no way. In a modern democratic society, to invoke law or to appeal to court is a typical way to settle disputes and to balance private interests among members of it. Claims to the authority of law or judicial authority of court are usually laid by those members to justify their own actions against state or their co-members, and, thus, are in no way exceptional cases.

Finally, we should elaborate a new theory of authority either suitable for all situations or, at least, capable of reflecting the very fact that is missed by theories of positional authority. I will call such a new theory 'the theory of *dis*positional authority'. I use the word 'dispositional' to indicate that a person is *not* presumed to be involved in an authority relationship (with others) in which that person assumes the *relational position*, which is correlated to another's relational position, as well as to convey a sense of favor which the word 'inclinational' lacks. We can find such a distinction between 'disposition' and 'inclination' from Kant. He writes,

---

in another way, any real authority has the conceptual *property* other than the ability to perform certain kinds of actions. According to Raz, however, it is not a matter of concept but a matter of justification whether an authority satisfies the Dependence Thesis. Kenneth Einar Himma, "Revisiting Raz: Inclusive Legal Positivism and Our Concept of Authority" (December 21, 2006), forthcoming in *APA Newsletters on Philosophy and Law* (Available at SSRN: http://ssrn.com/abstract=953392), p.4 n.4. [Emphasis added.]

> What is related to general human *inclinations* and needs has a *market price*; ⋯ Skill and diligence in work have a market price; ⋯ on the other hand, fidelity in promises and benevolence from basic principles (not from instinct) have an *inner worth*. Nature, as well as art, contains nothing that, lacking these, it could put in their place; for their worth does not consist in the effects arising from them, in the advantage and use they provide, but in *dispositions*, that is, in maxims of the will that in this way are ready to manifest themselves through actions, even if success does not favor them. ⋯ And what is it, then, that justifies a morally good *disposition*, or *virtue*, in making such high claims?[127]

It does not presuppose, thus, a vitiated conception of authority as an ability to perform certain kinds of actions, and is aimed at providing a coherent notion of authority. To rewrite this, any coherent concept of authority should fit both the following two descriptions:

(**S4**) ϕ-ing is justified by reference to claims to authority (of a person in authority) laid by that (person in) authority.

(**S5**) ϕ-ing is justified by reference to claims to authority (of a person in authority) laid by its subjects.

I think that such a notion of authority is 'the *property* deserving of public respect in the course of performing certain kinds of actions'. According to this explanation, in the case of being "an au-

---

127) *Groundwork*, 4:434-435, pp.84-5. [Emphasis added.]

thority", a person inherits or acquires respectable properties, and in the case of being "in authority", a person inherits or acquires official position which embodies such properties. And such a notion of authority fits (**S5**) as well as (**S4**):

(**S4***) ϕ-ing is justified by reference to claims to the respectable *properties* (embodied in authority) laid by that (person in) authority.

(**S5***) ϕ-ing is justified by reference to claims to the respectable *properties* (embodied in authority) laid by its subjects.

Moreover, the notion of *dis*positional authority as respectable property frees theorists of awkward expressions. Take the following passages from Hurd, for example.

C1*: "Thus, Knowledge of a condition of incompetence merely makes one a theoretical *authority* about the truth of inferences involving complex sets of premises."[128]

C2*: "His promise thus made him a practical *authority* over his future actions, for it gave him a protected reason to render aid to his mother, however distasteful the task."[129]

---

128) Hurd (1991), p.1623. [Emphasis added.]
129) Hurd (1991), p.1625. [Emphasis added.]

C1* and **C2*** are mentioned by her in the course of refuting Raz's theory of authority. She claims that two main examples employed by Raz to show the exclusionary features of the protected reasons for action which laws are supposed to provide, i.e. **C1** and **C2**, are irrelevant.[130] Her argument is, I admit, very convincing. However, it is decidedly odd to say that in the case of incapacity (**C1**), one who feels exhausted becomes, for that reason, an authority (**C1***). Certainly, authority markedly involved here is not the positional authority of a *person* who is totally exhausted, but the *dis*positional authority of the 'incapability *principle*' (i.e. 'if you are too out of condition to judge the case, you ought not to embark on new businesses.') which is a trustworthy guide for our behavior and is respectable. And we can say the same thing about **C2***: it is very odd to say that in the case of promise (**C2**), one who makes a promise to do something becomes, *simply* for that reason, an authority. The word '*simply*' is, here, added not to mislead attentive readers since one typical way in which a political institution *acquires* as well as exercises its authority is to make promise in the form of law. But even in that case, only the *qualified* political institution can do so and no political institution can acquire authority for the *simple* reason that *it* makes a certain promise.[131] And authority deeply embedded in this context is not the

---

130) See Ⅲ. 1. 1) - (1) - (b) of this book.

131) It makes no difference whether one upholds the theory of the social contract, provided that a political institution is a promisor. When a promisor

positional authority of a *person* who makes that promise, but the *dis*positional authority of the 'promise *principle*' (i.e. 'if you make a promise, you should keep it.') which deserves following.

If Hurd had talked directly of 'the authority of principle', she would not have suffered the disgrace of clumsiness. And it goes without saying that such a notion as the authority of principle is of the *dis*positional and objective sort, rather than positional and subjective.

---

simply, i.e. *without being accepted by the promisee*, expresses his intention to undertake an obligation, this promise is a *pollicitation*, which is denied to be legally binding. Hence, even the theorists of the social contract or those who uphold the view that authority of state is justified when people consent to obey it in general would conclude that the political institution cannot acquire authority for the simple reason that it makes the promise. Cf. A.W.B. Simpson, "Innovation in Nineteenth Century Contract Law", *Law Quarterly Review* 91 (1975), p.257 ff; James Gordley, *The Philosophical Origins of Modern Contract Doctrine*, New York, Oxford University Press, 1991, especially chapter 6 and 7; Reinhard Zimmerman, *The Law of Obligations: Roman Foundations of the Civilian Tradition*, Beck, Juta, 1990, p.546 ff.

IV. The Authority of Law

As Hart describes in the preface of *The Concept of Law*, one of the principal subjects of this book is the normative foundations of a legal system and the concern with "the deficiencies of a simple model of a legal system, constructed along the lines of Austin's imperative theory."[1] Those deficiencies, or the "ways in which the theory failed" are summarized by him as follows:

> First, it became clear that though of all the varieties of law, a criminal statute, forbidding or enjoining certain actions under penalty, most resembles orders backed by threats given by one person to others, such a statute none the less differs from such orders in the important respect that it commonly applies to those who enact it and not merely to others. Secondly, there are other varieties of law, notably those conferring legal powers to adjudicate or legislate (public powers) or to create or vary legal relations (private powers) which cannot, without absurdity, be construed as orders backed by threats. Thirdly, there are legal rules which differ from orders in their mode of origin, because they are not brought into being by anything analogous to explicit prescription. Finally, the analysis of law in terms of the sovereign, habitually obeyed and necessarily exempt from all legal limitation, failed to account for the continuity of legislative authority characteristic of a modern le-

---

1) Hart (1994), p.vi.

gal system, and the sovereign person or persons could not be I-dentified with either the electorate or the legislature of a modern state.[2]

Quite naturally, this itemized list of deficiencies of a simple, re-ductivist model constitutes a major test of validity of any complex model of a legal system. And if it is correct to say that the notion of authority (of law) should be employed in order to render a set of rules systemically organized, and that authority should be con-strued as of a dispositional nature, it follows that the dispositio-nal authority of law should be conducive to validity of the anti-reductivist model of a legal system devised by Kelsen and Hart. And now it will be shown, in this chapter, that not the positional but the dispositional notion of authority (of law) can help the co-herence of their theories of a legal system.

1. Authority and the Salient Features of Law

1) Continuity and Persistence of Law

What Hart calls "two salient features of most legal systems"[3] are the continuity of the authority to make law and the persisten-

---

2) Hart (1994), p.79.
3) Hart (1994), p.51.

ce of law. And a simple model of law as coercive orders comes, in his book, repeatedly under strong criticism to the effect that it fails to reproduce those salient features of a legal system. He casts doubt on a simple model, raising two different but related questions.

> There the question was how, on the basis of the simple scheme of habits of obedience, it could be said that the first law made by a successor to the office of legislator is *already* law before he personally had received habitual obedience. Here the question is: how can law made by an earlier legislator, long dead, *still* be law for a society that cannot be said habitually to obey him?[4]

Hart's strategy for constructive criticism can be summarized as follows:

(1) A simple model, especially the idea of a "habit of obedience", cannot explain the continuity of legislative authority and the persistence of law.

(2) To explain them, the idea of a rule should feature in any models of a legal system.

(3) A socially accepted rule invests past and future, as well as present, legislators with right or authority. ("The social practice, which constitutes the acceptance of a rule", underlies legislative authority.[5])

---

4) Hart (1994), p.62.

Kelsen likewise takes account of a diachronic study of legal phenomena. According to him, the validity of the existing constitution is traced back to the validity of the historically first constitution. But he wrongly assumes that the authors of the existing constitution are eventually authorized by the historically first constitution. As Honoré rightly points out, "[t]he fact that the framers of the original constitution had the right to prescribe how people should behave does not entail that their successors at the present day have the right to make law."[6] There should be the principle that underlies "transmission of title",[7] but Kelsen does not speak of it. Such a principle is nothing else but what Hart calls socially accepted "rules which bridge the transition from one lawgiver to another."[8]

(1) Positional Authority

Now, we turn to the concept of authority. Hart's analysis of Austin's imperative theory, i.e. a simple model of law as coercive orders, shows that deficiencies of the simple model are largely due to the notion of positional authority. Hart's critical analysis of the simple model can be condensed into the following sentences:

---

5) Hart (1994), pp.58-9.
6) Honoré (1987), p.104.
7) Honoré (1987), p.105.
8) Hart (1994), p.54.

(1) The notion of a habit of obedience presupposes the person-to-person relationship between sovereign and each subject as a crucial feature.[9]

(2) A sovereign is considered to be involved in an *authority relationship* with each subject.

(3) The habits of most of subjects are simply convergent.[10] (Note that it is not convergence *in principle* but convergence *in strategy*.[11])

(4) The idea of a rule features in nowhere.

(2) Dispositional Authority

What will happen if dispositional authority replaces its positional counterpart? In that case, we can say that obedience to a sovereign's orders is justified by reference to claims to the dispositional authority (or the respectable properties) of the "principles regulating the proper distribution of human freedom",[12] and therefore that "not only will there be general obedience to his orders, but it will be generally accepted that it is *right* to obey him."[13] A schematic representation of this is as follows:

---

9) Hart (1994), p.52.
10) Hart (1994), p.52.
11) This distinction is borrowed from Ronald Dworkin. See Ronald Dworkin, *Law's Empire*, Harvard University Press, Cambridge, 1986, p.132.
12) Hart (1955), p.4.
13) Hart (1994), p.58.

(1) The notion of a habit of obedience presupposes not the person-to-person but the person-to-principle relationship as a crucial feature.

(2) General obedience to a sovereign's orders is not convertgence *in strategy* but convergence *in principle*.

(3) The notion of rule or its internal aspects have already featured in this alternative model.

2) The Self-binding Force of Legislation

One of the concerns of theorists antagonistic to the Austinian simple model of law as coercive orders is a legal phenomenon called "the self-binding force of legislation."[14] When Austin analyses the concept of law in terms of commands and habits, he regards law as an order backed by threats which is "essentially the expression of a wish that *others* should do or abstain from doing certain things."[15]

Hart says, however, that it is a notable feature of legislation in modern legal systems to take not just other-regarding but also self-regarding form. As a matter of fact, "many a law is now made which imposes legal obligations on the makers of the law."[16] Kelsen also says in a resolute manner that "individuals who create law can undoubtedly themselves be subject to law."[17] After all, the sim-

---

14) Hart (1994), p.43.
15) Hart (1994), p.42.
16) Hart (1994), p.42.

ple model cannot reproduce this feature of a legal system.

To summarize Hart's criticism,

(1) A simple model, especially the idea of an "order backed by threats", cannot explain the self-binding force of legislation.

(2) To explain it, the idea of a rule should feature in all models of a legal system.

(3) A promisor is bound to the promise, of which he is an author, because a rule to the effect that men should keep their word is socially accepted. Similarly, a legislator is bound to the law, of which he is an author, because a rule to the effect that law should be followed by society generally is socially accepted.

(4) Legislation is not an issue of orders but "the introduction or modification of general standards of behaviour to be followed by the society generally."[18] (A legislator is also a member of the society.)

(1) Positional Authority

Hart even criticizes Austin for failing to distinguish between a command and an order (backed by threats). He says that,

---

17) Kelsen (1949), p.198.
18) Hart (1994), p.44.

> To command is characteristically to exercise authority over men, not power to inflict harm, and though it may be combined with threats of harm a command is primarily an appeal not to fear but to respect for authority.
>
> It is obvious that the idea of a command with its very strong connection with authority is much closer to that of law than our gunman's order backed by threats, though the latter is an instance of what Austin, ignoring the distinctions noticed in the last paragraph, misleadingly calls a command.[19]

But Hart admits that the notion of command with its exact meaning can be a false economy. According to him, a command is "too close to law for our purpose; for the element of authority involved in law has always been one of the obstacles in the path of any easy explanation of what law is."[20] In addition, a command is the same as an order in being addressed to *others*, i.e. the speaker's *hearers*.[21]

The reason why Hart distinguishes between two "different forms of imperative"[22] is that he wants to show the deficiencies of the simple model of a legal system without involving himself in a baffling problem of authority. However, the problem whether an imperative appeals to *respect for authority* or to *fear of sanction* is nothing more than the problem whether the authority is construed as

---

19) Hart (1994), p.20.
20) Hart (1994), p.20.
21) Hart (1982b), p.247.
22) Hart (1994), p.20.

a *normative* notion or as a *positive* one. In both cases, the authority is presupposed as a *positional* type. And the deficiencies may
well be imputed to the notion of positional authority:

(1) A sovereign "occupies position of pre-eminence"[23] to
issue an order (or a command) to subjects.

(2) Law is an order (or a command) issued by a sovereign to subjects.

(3) The idea of a rule features in nowhere.

(2) Dispositional Authority

Hart explains the self-binding force of legislation by drawing an
analogy between legislation and promise.[24] And we have already
seen that, in the case of the promise, its self-binding force is justified by reference to claims to the (dispositional) authority of the
'promise principle' (i.e. 'if you make a promise, you should keep
it.') which deserves following irrespective of its legal validity.[25]
So we can say of the legislation that its self-binding force is justified by reference to claims to the (dispositional) authority of the
'universal conformity principle' (i.e. 'the population of a state, including even the authors of law, should be bound to respect its
law.') which is respectable regardless of its legal validity. A sche-

---

23) Hart (1994), p.20.
24) See Ⅳ. 1. 2) of this book.
25) See Ⅲ. 2. 2) of this book.

matic representation of this is as follows:

(1) The authority of 'universal conformity principle' which deserves following is socially recognized.

(2) Law is the socially accepted standards of behaviour.

(3) The notion of rule or its internal aspects has already featured in this alternative model.

2. Authority and the Nature of Law

1) Authority and the Imperative Theory of Law

The imperative theories of law, or "the doctrine that laws are essentially orders and so expressions of the will or intention of a legislator",[26] are upheld by Bentham, Austin and Kelsen, etc. The central thesis against the imperative theory is that there exist various types of rules which cannot be defined in a single form, i.e. as a coercive order.[27] Obviously, the existence of power-conferring rules and customary rules, for instance, is the strong evidence in favour of theorists antagonistic to a simple model of a legal system.[28]

---

26) Hart (1994), p.287.
27) Hart (1994), p.26 ff; Raz (1978a), p.117, p.156.
28) Kelsen's position is somewhat difficult to understand. For, as is shown below, he is an anti-reductivist, while at the same time upholding the imperative theory of law.

However, there remains a problem which is of great importance to do justice to Kelsen and Hart. So far, we have seen that the idea of positional authority embedded in the simple model displays the deficiencies of the simple model, while the idea of dispositional authority can connect coherently to the anti-reductivist model which is supposed to reproduce the salient features of a legal system. But Kelsen and Hart cling to the traditional notion of positional authority *by and large*. I say 'by and large' because there are unusual examples like the following (anti-reductivist) passage from Kelsen:

> "Authority" is usually defined as the *right* or *power* to issue obligating commands. The actual power of forcing others to a certain behavior does not suffice to constitute an authority. The individual who is, or has, authority must have received the right to issue obligating commands, so that other individuals are obliged to obey. Such a right or power can be conferred upon an individual only by a normative order. Authority is thus originally the *characteristic* of a normative order.[29]

It is a virtue of Bentham and Austin's theories, whatever their defects, that three elements of them, i.e. the imperative theory of law, the (simple) reductivist model of a legal system and the idea of positional authority, constitute a coherent set. Now, Kelsen embraces the imperative theory of law and the idea of positional au-

---

29) Kelsen (1949), p.383. [Emphasis added.]

thority (by and large) and rejects the reductivist model of a legal system, while Hart embraces the idea of positional authority and rejects the others. I think Hart is right in rejecting the imperative theory of law, but wrong in embracing the idea of positional authority. For the ideas of a coercive order and positional authority are, I think, analytically interdependent. Strictly speaking, then, Hart does *not* actually reject the imperative theory of law.

Hart says that "certain elements embedded in the notion of command" can give rise to "the idea of an authoritative reason", by which he means the content-independent and peremptory reason for action, although "its introduction into the analysis of the features of law would certainly involve discarding Bentham's imperative theory of law."[30] To put it differently, Hart thinks that Bentham's imperative theory of law should be rejected because it is not a *proper* command-based theory of law.[31] And we have seen that he criticizes Austin for failing to distinguish between a command and an order (backed by threats), i.e. for failing to formulate a *command*-based theory of law.[32] The wholesale renunciation of the imperative theory of law is not Hart's way.

---

30) Hart (1982b), p.243. In this respect, Hart may be thought as upholding the view that the authority of law constitutes a test of validity of any theories of the nature (or concept) of law. But the only that he regards as failing to survive is the reductivist theory of law. Cf. Compare his view with Raz's. See the following Ⅳ. 2. 2) of this book.

31) According to Hart, the *proper* command-based theory of law can be traced back to Hobbes. Hart (1982b), p.253.

32) See Ⅳ. 1. 2) - (1) of this book.

But as we have already seen, the notion of rule or its internal aspects are unlikely to feature in any models of a legal system unless and until the notion of positional authority gives way to the notion of dispositional authority. And Hart would certainly not subscribe to the view that the notion of rule or its internal aspects are not required to reproduce the salient features of a legal system.

2) Theory of Authority: *Thin* or *Thick*

The theories of authority may be divided into two groups: 'thin' and 'thick' ones. The 'thin' theory of authority is called thin because it does not attempt to evaluate the nature (or concept) of law, while the 'thick' theory is called so for the contrary reason. The 'thin' theory regards the authority (of law) simply as necessary for the law to exist as a system. But the 'thick' theory regards it as upholding a particular view on the nature of law. It should be noted that what is 'thin' or 'thick' here is neither 'concept' nor 'conception' of authority. Actually, the modifiers 'thin' and 'thick' have been already used in order to compare two conceptions of authority: claim-rights and justification-rights.[33] But a division between the two conceptions of authority bears little relation to the present distinction between 'thin' and 'thick' theories of authority. Therefore, it is possible to develop the thin *theory* of authority, while allowing the thick *conception* of authority, and *vice versa*.[34]

---

33) See Ⅲ. 1. 2) - (2) of this book.

As has already been mentioned, Raz has it that the authority of law constitutes a test of validity of any theories of the nature (or concept) of law, e.g. the Dworkinian anti-positivism, the exclusive and inclusive forms of legal positivism. As a steadfast defender of *the sources thesis* against *the coherence thesis* and *the incorporation thesis*, Joseph Raz has long argued that we can learn something about the nature of law from the doctrine of authority,[35] and that the sources thesis more accurately captures the nature of law than its competitors.

> The connection between law and authority is used to criticize Dworkin's support of the coherence thesis, as well as the incorporation thesis advocated by Hart and others. The rejection of these views leads to the endorsement of the sources thesis.[36]

But I think that Raz goes too far. Any theories of law can resort to the notion of authority (of law) insofar as it serves them in any way they entertain the idea of (legal) *system*. The next step is, then, to refute his argument that the notion of authority confirms the sources thesis. Raz's main argument, which forms the funda-

---

34) Cf. Himma argues that "*our* concept of authority is too thin to do the work that Raz thinks it does in establishing exclusive legal positivism." But what he calls the Razian "concept" of authority seems exactly the same as what I call the Razian "theory" of authority, the main purpose of which is to establish exclusive legal positivism. Himma (2006), p.18.
35) Raz (1994), p.200.
36) Raz (1994), p.195.

mental part of his entire reasoning, can be summarized as follows:

(1) Though a legal system may not have legitimate authority, or though its legitimate authority may not be as extensive as it claims, every legal system [*necessarily*] claims that it possesses legitimate authority (the authority thesis[37]).[38]

(2) If the claim to authority is part of the nature of law, then whatever else the law is it must be capable of *possessing* authority.[39]

(3) There are two features that must be possessed by anything capable of being authoritatively binding. These are (*a*) it must be, or be presented as, someone's view on what the subjects ought to do, and (*b*) it must be identifiable by means which are independent of the considerations the authority should decide upon.[40]

(4) These two features support the sources thesis [rather than the coherence thesis or the incorporation thesis].[41]

As pointed out by Himma, many attempts have been made to defeat the Razian reasoning by challenging the authority thesis, i.e. the view that law necessarily claims legitimate authority: premise (1).[42] But I doubt whether such attempts are appealing, since these are likely to be carried out by inventing counterexamples which are

---

37) In this naming I follow Kenneth E. Himma. See Himma (2002), p.147; Himma (2006), p.5.
38) Raz (1994), pp.199-200 and p.202.
39) Raz (1994), p.199. [Emphasis added.]
40) Raz (1994), p.205.
41) Raz (1994), p.202.
42) Himma (2002), p.155 ff.

too eccentric to be a reality.

Here, I will try below a somewhat different refutation from those of my predecessors. Straightforwardly speaking, my point is that premise (2) is (also) problematic, and that those who regard it as clear are claiming, at least unconsciously, a metaphysical thesis that "no creature is doomed to pursue what it cannot possess." If premise (2) were clear, it would go as follows:

(2*) If the claim to authority is part of the nature of law, then whatever else the law is it must be capable of *claiming* authority.

If premise (2) fails, then "the fact that law claims authority" is nothing more than "the sheer fact that law makes this claim", and therefore Raz's argument on authority is severed from that of his on the nature of law.

(1) Argument from Falsity

Raz asserts that "if the claim to authority is part of the nature of law, then whatever else the law is it must be capable of *possessing* authority": premise (2). Is it true? He argues as if we could derive premise (2) from premise (1), saying that "even though the law may lack legitimate authority, one can learn a lot about it from the fact that it claims legitimate authority. It must be capable of being authoritative."[43] If (1) is correct, however, the minimum lesson that can be derived from it, and be accepted without controversy, is that every law's claim to authority can be false. But for what exactly? To examine this problem precisely, I suggest here one simple analytic test which I shall call 'the argument from falsity.' It can be summarized as follows:

> **AF**: First, suppose X, who in fact does not succeed, and does not even possess the capability to succeed, in achieving Y, says that she achieved Y by herself. Secondly, suppose the same X says simply that she is capable of achieving Y by herself. Of course, neither of her sayings is true. But these two are different in the light of their inner structure. In the latter case, what X says is false since it does not correspond to only her *properties*, whereas in the first case, what she says is false since it does not correspond to her *experience as well as properties*. In other words, what X in the first case says is false since it does not correspond to her *achievement* in which her capability and practice combine as a whole. But suppose again X^*, who in fact does not succeed, but does possess the capability to succeed, in achieving Y, says the same thing ("I have achieved Y by myself"). In this case, what X^* says is false not because it does not correspond to her *properties*,

---

43) Raz (1994), p.204 ff.

but because it does not correspond to her *experience*. To
sum up, when one claims, contrary to the truth, to have
achieved something, what she says is false either for failing
to correspond to only her experience (the third case), or for
failing to correspond to her properties as well as experience
(the first case).

AF shows that discrepancies between *fact* and statement of it
can exist either (*a*) between *properties* and statement of them, or
(*b*) between *experience* and statement of it, or (*c*) between *achieve-
ment* (as a whole) and statement of it.

Now return to premise (2). Conjoining (2) with (1), Raz argues
that though the law, contrary to its claim, does not have legitimate
authority, or though it claims, contrary to the truth, legitimate authority, it must be capable of possessing authority. To paraphrase
Raz, what the law says is false for failing to correspond to its experience, whenever it claims, contrary to the truth, to possess legitimate authority. In the case of law, Raz excludes the possibility
of the first case mentioned above, i.e. of failing to correspond to
its properties as well as experience.

If **AF** is correct, then can we conclude that Raz is simply
making a mistake here? No, not yet. On the contrary, He actually
anticipates this problem. He says:

But cannot one claim that a person X has authority which it

would make no sense to attribute to X? ⋯ [Comparison between law and "a set of propositions about the behaviour of volcanoes" or "trees"] is enough to show that since the law claims to have authority it is capable of having it.[44]

In brief, Raz thinks that unlike law which is a normative system and is able to communicate with people, "a set of propositions about the behaviour of volcanoes" or "trees", for example, cannot be sincerely claimed to have authority. In comparison with these, he asserts, the law's claim to authority at least makes sense, though can be false, so there is no possibility of law being incapable of possessing authority: premise (2).

However, Raz's explanation is not only insufficient but also inappropriate. For the only basis of his argument is an unfair comparison. What is required is not to compare what may have legitimate authority (*sincere* claimant) with what cannot have any, even *de facto*, authority (*odd* claimant) — for it cannot matter at all to distinguish between them — but to compare two different candidates of the former: *person* and *law*.

(2) The Nature Thesis

Even now, however, it is impossible to conclude that Raz simply makes a mistake. We can only say that Raz makes a mistake unless he presupposes one controversial thesis that I shall call 'the

---

44) Raz (1994), p.201.

nature thesis.' This is because he makes it a proviso that "the claim to authority is part of the nature of law"[45] and it hinders, in turn, the transition from the premise (2) to **AF**. 'The nature thesis' may be formulated as follows:

> **NT**: If the claim to achievement of something — whether being true or not — is part of the *nature* of X, then what X says can be false not because it does not correspond to her properties but because it does not correspond to her experience.

It is an open question whether Raz actually, even implicitly, employs it. In any case, it seems still questionable whether **NT** is true. Accordingly, we can at least say that it demands a further justification to confirm **NT**. But the case is that he has never provided it. Then, we are justified in saying that Raz fails to give *sufficient* support to his argument, and that the theory of authority is therefore severed from the theory of the nature of law *unless and until* **NT** *is confirmed.*

To sum up, Raz's argument that the notion of authority confirms the sources thesis is thus refuted for the present. Not only exclusive but also inclusive and anti-positivism can resort to the authority (of law) in the course of playing around with rules of a legal system.

---

45) See premise (2) in Ⅳ. 2. 2) of this book.

3) Authority and Theory of Legal system

The thesis that "the authority (of law) is necessary for the law to exist as a system"[46] is the central tenet on which this book is based. Here, it may be thought that the truth of that thesis requires, or at least suggests, the truth of the consequent of premise (2), i.e. the statement that "the law must be capable of possessing authority",[47] or *vice versa*. If there exists such a relationship between them, then I am blundering either in affirming that thesis or in denying the consequent of premise (2).

However, there is no such relationship. The authority of law is necessary, although the law is occasionally incapable of possessing it. Actually, owing to capability shortage, two norms belonging to the same legal system come into conflict. Once those norms come into conflict, neither of them possesses authority.[48]

We can say the same thing about the relationship between that thesis and the second half of premise (1), i.e. *the authority thesis* that reads, "every legal system necessarily claims that it possesses legitimate authority."[49] Even if a legal system does not *claim* its authority, the authority (of law) is necessary for the law to exist as a system.

---

46) See Ⅱ. 2. 3) - (1) of this book.
47) See Ⅳ. 2. 2) of this book.
48) See *the thesis (1)* in Ⅱ. 2. 3) - (2) of this book.
49) See Ⅳ. 2. (2) of this book.

These discrepancies are the consequences of the fact that different missions are given to the theory of authority. As I have already mentioned, Raz carries out the analysis of authority in order to provide support for the sources thesis, while I employ it to render a set of rules systemically organized. But it seems possible to reconcile both demands by subscribing to the view that the notion of legal system takes priority over the concept of law. Interestingly, Raz himself is a leading exponent of that view. He puts it that,

> The analysis of the concept of a law depends on the analysis of the concept of a legal system. For the understanding of some types of laws depends on their internal relation with some other laws. They derive their legal relevance from their relations to other laws. The analysis of the structure of legal system is therefore indispensable for the definition of 'a law'.[50]

The gist of the solution is to relate the notion of authority directly to the analysis of the structure of legal system, and therefore to let it influence the theory of law but only indirectly. What constitutes a test of validity of any theories of the nature (or concept) of law is not the authority of law but the system of rules itself. And the authority (of law) is, in turn, necessary for the law to exist as a system of rules.

---

50) Raz (1978a), p.170. [Footnote omitted.]

V. Conclusion

Philosophers have long grappled with the practical problem of obligation to obey the law, either as the problem of the normativity of law or as the problem of the authority of state. The two problems have been dealt with separately, and the issue of relationship between them was until quite recently dismissed. However, considering that law is characterized by its 'so-called' *authoritativeness*, the notion of authority closely relates to the problem of the normativity of law.

Sometimes theorists subscribe to the thesis that the normative foundations of law should be objective and their objectivity, or neutrality, is guaranteed by the possibility of consensus. But it is also the case that the limited human faculty necessitates the entrenchment of authority which can be in conflict with the requirement of consensus. Then, we should take not only neutrality but also authority into account to unravel the puzzle of the normativity of law.

The most remarkable attempts to articulate the grounds of the normativity of law are made by Kelsen and Hart. Kelsen sets forth the basis of the normativity of law by reference to a logical *fiction*, while Hart does the same thing by reference to a *fact*. They

both regard two notions as essential to the explanation of the normativity of law: ultimate rule and systemic validity. According to
them, the ultimate rule is defined as the final reason for, or the
source of the supreme criterion of, validity of all the rules other
than itself that constitute one legal system. And it plays, together
with the systemic notion of validity, a central role in their theories
of the normativity of law.

But even the most remarkable attempts by Kelsen and Hart have
failed for several reasons. First, it remains unclear whether the ultimate rule itself is valid. Second, a valid rule can be in conflict
with another, and even higher, rule which is also valid. Third, a
dynamic principle of 'norm validation' fails to recognize the difference between a norm and a "norm contrary to a norm" insofar as
both of them are valid. Therefore, neither neutrality nor obligatoriness of rules is successfully captured by the ultimate rule and systemic validity. Actually, those problems threatens even the notion
of legal *system*.

The natural lawyers have fixed those problems by upholding a
static principle of 'norm validation', thereby employing the notion
of axiological validity. However, Kelsen and Hart cannot endorse
the solution formulated by natural lawyers without contradicting
themselves. Finally, if they seek to solve those problems, or to invest legal rules with the neutral obligatoriness, without recourse to
the static validation or the axiological validity, they should resort
to the notion of authority of law.

To summarize this solution,

(1) If a norm is legally valid and, at the same time, its content is compatible with the contents of other norms (of the system) which are also legally valid, it has authority to guide people's behaviour.

(2) Even though any norm has authority to guide people's behaviour, it does not follow that the norm is legally valid.

(3) A norm is legally valid when it belongs to a given system of legal norms, while it has authority when people to whom the system applies are bound to respect it in the course of practical reasoning.

(4) The foundations of a legal system do not consist in the validity of the ultimate rule but consist in its authority.

Here, it is necessary for us to examine the notion of authority carefully. For 'authority' has traditionally been construed as the authority of *person*, but not of *law* itself. Actually, there is no consensus among theorists about its nature and function. It has been regarded either (*a*) as providing reason for action or (*b*) as providing reason for belief. And it has been understood either (*a*) as the justified power, or (*b*) as the right—either a liberty or a claim-right—to rule, or (*c*) as the normative capacity to impose duty.

But what really matters is whether it is *positional* or *dispositio-*

nal. Whichever notion above theorists may pick out to unpack the concept of authority, they conceive of it as positional, i.e. as an 'ability' to do something. Authority is, for them, always the positional authority of a *person* or a body of persons involved in an authority relationship with subjects, but not of *law*. However, we should conceive of the concept of authority not as positional but as dispositional, i.e. as respectable properties. For the notion of positional authority is not sensitive enough to reflect a typical way to balance private interests among members of modern societies.

Moreover, the notion of positional authority embedded in a simple reductivist model of a legal system cannot reproduce what Hart calls the salient features of law. It cannot thus explain the continuity of legislative authority, the persistence of law and the self-binding force of legislation. In reality, the notions of coercive orders and positional authority are analytically interdependent. On the contrary, the notion of dispositional authority is conducive to validity of the anti-reductivist model of a legal system devised by Kelsen and Hart. Especially, the notion of rule or its internal aspects are unlikely to feature in any models of a legal system unless and until the notion of positional authority gives way to its dispositional counterpart.

But the authority of law is not construed, in this book, as constituting a test of validity of any theories of the nature (or concept) of law. The theory of authority is, thus, regarded as the "thin" theory which conceives of the authority (of law) simply as necessary for the law to exist as a system. In this respect, I object to Raz's conviction to the effect that the theory of authority provides support for the sources thesis. The critical analysis of Raz's argument done by employing 'the argument from falsity' and 'the nature thesis' shows that he fails to give sufficient support to his argument.

The notion of authority relates directly to the analysis of the structure of legal system, and therefore has an influence on the theory of (the nature of) law but only indirectly. What constitutes a test of validity of any theories of the nature of law is not the authority (of law) but the system of rules itself. And the authority (of law) is necessary for the law to exist as a system of rules. Therefore, not only exclusive but also inclusive and anti-positivism can resort to the authority (of law) in the course of playing around with rules of a legal system.

BIBLIOGRAPHY

(1) Books

Aarnio, Aulis (1997), *Reason and Authority: A Treaties on the Dynamic Paradigm of Legal Dogmatics*, Ashgate / Dartmouth, Aldershot, 1997.

Alexy, Robert (1989), *A Theory of Legal Argumentation: The Theory of Rational Discourse as Theory of Legal Justification*, trans. by Ruth Adler and Neil MacCormick, Clarendon Press, Oxford, 1989 (1978).

_____ (1992), *Begriff und Geltung des Rechts*, Verlag Karl Alber, Freiburg and München, 1992.

Beyleveld, eryck. and Roger Brownsword (1986), *Law as a Moral Judgment*, Sweet & Maxwell, London, 1986.

Bix, Brian (1998). (ed.), *Analyzing Law: New Essays in Legal Theory*, Clarendon Press, Oxford, 1998.

Burton, Steven J. (1985), *An Introduction to Law and Legal Reasoning*, Little, Brown and Company, Toronto, 1985.

Campbell, Tom D. and Adrienne Stone (2003) (eds.), *Law and Democracy*, Ashgate / Dartmouth, Aldershot, 2003.

Chang, Ruth (1997). (ed.), *Incommensurability, Incomparability, and Practical Reason*, Harvard University Press, Cambridge Massachusetts, 1997.

Chemerinsky, Erwin (2002), *Constitutional Law: Principles and Policies*, 2nd Edition, Aspen Publishers, New York, 2002.

Coleman, Jules. and Scott Shapiro (2002) (eds.), *The Oxford Handbook of Jurisprudence and Philosophy of Law*, Oxford University Press, Oxford, 2002.

Cotterrell, Roger (1989), *The Politics of Jurisprudence: A Critical Introduction to Legal Philosophy*, University of Pennsylvania Press, Philadelphia, 1989.

Dworkin, Ronald (1986), *Law's Empire*, Harvard University Press, Cambridge, 1986.

Finnis, John (1991). (ed.), *Natural Law Vol. 2*, New York University Press, New York, 1991

_____ (1980), *Natural Law and Natural Rights*, Clarendon Press, Oxford, 1980.

Forrester, Mary Gore (2002), *Moral Beliefs and Moral Theory*, Kluwer Academic Publishers, Dordrecht, 2002.

Golding, Martin P. and William A. Edmundson (2005). (eds.), *The Blackwell Guide to the Philosophy of Law and Legal Theory*, Blackwell Publishing, Malden, 2005.

Goldman, Alan H (2002), *Practical Rules: When We Need Them and When We Don't*, Cambridge University Press, Cambridge, 2002.

Goodin, Robert E. and Philip Pettit (1993). (eds.), *A Companion to Contemporary Political Philosophy*, Basil Blackwell, Oxford, 1993.

Gordley, James (1991), *The Philosophical Origins of Modern Contract Doctrine*, New York, Oxford University Press, 1991.

Green, Leslie (1990), *The Authority of the State*, Clarendon Press, Oxford, 1990 (1988).

Greenawalt, Kent (1987), *Conflicts of Law and Morality*, Oxford University Press, New York, 1987.

Groarke, Paul (2004), *Dividing the State: Legitimacy, Secession and the Doctrine of Oppression*, Ashgate, Aldershot, 2004.

Hacker, P.M.S. and Joseph Raz (1979). (eds.), *Law, Morality, and Society: Essays in Honour of H.L.A. Hart*, Clarendon Press, Oxford, 1979 (1977).

Haley, John Owen (1991), *Authority without Power*, Oxford University Press, New York, 1991.

Hart, H.L.A. (1994), *The Concept of Law* (2nd Edition), Clarendon Press,

Oxford, 1994 (1961).

Hartogh, Govert den (2002), *Mutual Expectations: A Conventionalist Theory of Law*, Kluwer Law International, The Hague, 2002.

_____ (2000), *The Good Life as a Public Good*, Kluwer Academic Publishers, Dordrecht, 2000.

Hobbes, Thomas (1998), *Elementa Philosophica de Cive* in Tuck, Richard. and Michael Silverthorne (eds.) *Hobbes − On the Citizen*, Cambridge University Press, Cambridge, 1998.

_____ (1996), *Leviathan, or the Matter, Forme, & Power of a Common-wealth Ecclesiasticall and Civill* in Tuck, Richard (ed.) *Hobbes − Leviathan*, Cambridge University Press, Cambridge, 1996.

Kant, I. (1999), *Groundwork of the Metaphysics of Morals*, 4:400 in Gregor, Mary J. (trans. and ed.) *Immanuel Kant − Practical Philosophy*, Cambridge University Press, Cambridge, 1999 (1996).

Kelsen, Hans (1992), *Introduction to the Problems of Legal Theory*, 1st Edition of *The Pure Theory of Law*, translated by Bonnie Litschewski Paulson and Stanley L. Paulson, Clarendon Press, Oxford, 1992 (1934).

_____ (1949), *General Theory of Law and State*, translated by Anders Wedberg, Harvard University Press, Cambridge, 1949.

_____ (1970), *Pure Theory of Law*, trans. by Max Knight from the Second German Edition, University of California Press, Berkeley and Los Angeles, 1970 (1960).

_____ (1991), *General Theory of Norms*, translated by Michael Hartney, Clarendon Press, Oxford, 1991 (1979).

Loveland, Ian D. (2000). (ed.), *Constitutional Law*, Ashgate/Dartmouth, Aldershot, 2000.

MacCormick, Neil (1982), *Legal Right and Social Democracy: Essays in Legal and Political Philosophy*, Clarendon Press, Oxford, 1982.

_____ (1981), *H.L.A. Hart*, Stanford University Press,

Stanford, 1981.

Meyer, Lucas H. et al. (2003). (eds.), *Rights, Culture, and the Law: Themes from the Legal and Political Philosophy of Joseph Raz*, Oxford University Press, New York, 2003.

Park, Hyo Chong (2001), *State and Authority*, Pakyoungsa, Seoul, 2001.

Pattaro, Enrico (2005), *The Law and the Right: A Reappraisal of the Reality that Ought to Be*, Springer, Dordrecht, 2005.

Plato (1961), *Euthyphro*, 10a in Hamilton, Edith. and Huntington Cairns. (eds.) *The Collected Dialogues of Plato Including the Letters*, Princeton University Press, Princeton, 1961.

Postow, B.C. (1999), *Reasons for Action: Toward a Normative Theory and Meta-Level Criteria*, Kluwer Academic Publishers, Dordrecht, 1999.

Rawls, John (2003), *A Theory of Justice*, 2nd Edition, Harvard University Press, Cambridge, 2003 (1971).

Raz, Joseph (2001), *Engaging Reason: On the Theory of Value and Action*, Oxford University Press, New York, 2001 (1999).

_____ (1994), *Ethics in the Public Domain: Essays in the Morality of Law and Politics*, Clarendon Press, Oxford, 1994.

_____ (1990a), *Practical Reason and Norms*, Princeton University Press, Princeton, 1990 (1975).

_____ (1983), *The Authority of Law: Essays on Law and Morality*, Clarendon Press, Oxford, 1983 (1979).

_____ (1978a), *The Concept of a Legal System: An Introduction to the Theory of Legal System*, Clarendon Press, Oxford, 1978 (1970).

_____ (1990b), *The Morality of Freedom*, Clarendon Press, Oxford, 1990 (1986).

_____ (2003), *The Practice of Value*, Clarendon Press, Oxford, 2003.

_____ (2004), *Value, Respect, and Attachment*, Cambridge University Press, Cambridge, 2004 (2001).

Redondo, Cristina (1999), *Reasons for Action and the Law*, Kluwer Academic Publishers, Dordrecht, 1999.

Rottleuthner, Hubert (2005), *Foundations of Law*, Springer, Dordrecht, 2005.

Salmon, Wesley C. (2004), *Logic*, 3rd Edition, translated (into Korean) by Kang Jae Kwak, Pakyoungsa, Seoul, 2004.

Schauer, Frederick (1991), *Playing by the Rules: A Philosophical Examination of Rule-Based Decision-Making in Law and in Life*, Clarendon Press, Oxford, 1991.

Seelmann, Kurt (1994), *Rechtsphilosophie*, C.H. Beck, München, 1994.

Sher, George (1997), *Beyond Neutrality: Perfectionism and Politics*, Cambridge University Press, Cambridge, 1997.

Shim, Hun Sup (1982), *Rechtsphilosophische Untersuchungen I − Recht · Moral · Macht* (in Korean), Bub Moon Sa, Seoul, 1982.

Shiner, Roger A. (2005), *Legal Institutions and the Sources of Law*, Springer, Dordrecht, 2005.

Summers, Robert S. (1971) (ed.), *More Essays in Legal Philosophy: General Assessments of Legal Philosophies*, Basil Blakwell, Oxford, 1971.

Tasioulas, John (1997). (ed.), *Law, Values and Social Practices*, Dartmouth, Aldershot, 1997.

Tuori, Kaarlo (2002), *Critical Legal Positivism*, Ashgate, Aldershot, 2002.

Wacks, Raymond (2005), *Understanding Jurisprudence: An Introduction to Legal Theory*, Oxford University Press, New York, 2005.

Waluchow, Wilfrid (1994), *Inclusive Legal Positivism*, Clarendon Press, Oxford, 1994.

Weber, Max (1978), *Economy and Society: An Outline of Interpretive Sociology*, edited by Roth, Guenther. and Claus Wittich, University of California Press, Berkeley, 1978 (1956).

Wolff, R.P. (1976), *In Defense of Anarchism*, Harper & Row, Publishers, New York, 1976 (1970).

Wróblewski, Jerzy (1992), *The Judicial Application of Law*, Kluwer Academic Publishers, Dordrecht, 1992.

Zimmerman, Reinhard (1990), *The Law of Obligations: Roman Foundations of the Civilian Tradition*, Beck, Juta, 1990.

(2) Articles

Alexander, Larry and Emily Sherwin (2003), "Deception in Morality and Law", *Law and Philosophy* 22 (2003).

Alexy, Robert (2002), "Postscript", *A Theory of Constitutional Rights*, translated by Julian Rivers, Oxford University Press, New York, 2002 (1986).

Anscombe, G.E.M. (1978), "On the Source of the Authority of the State", *Ratio* 20 (1978).

Arendt, Hannah (1977), "What is Authority?", *Between Past and Future: Eight Exercises in Political Thought*, Penguin Books, New York, 1977.

Audi, Robert (2002), "Introduction: A Narrow Survey of Classical and Contemporary Positions in Epistemology", in Michael Huemer (ed.), *Epistemology: Contemporary Readings*, Routledge, London, 2002.

Balsdon, J.P.V.D. (1960), "Auctoritas, Dignitas, Otium", *The Classical Quarterly* 10 (May 1960).

Bix, Brian H. (2002), "Natural law: The Modern Tradition", in Jules Coleman and Scott Shapiro (eds.), *The Oxford Handbook of Jurisprudence and Philosophy of Law*, Oxford University Press, Oxford, 2002.

Bulygin, Eugenio (1998), "An Antinomy in Kelsen's Pure Theory of Law", in Stanley L. Paulson and Bonnie Litschewski Paulson (eds.), *Normativity and Norms: Critical Perspectives on Kelsenian Themes*, Clarendon Press, Oxford, 1998.

_____ (1999), "Valid Law and Law in Force", unpublished proceedings of Alf Ross's 100 Years Birthday Conference, Copenhagen, 1999.

Christiano, Tom (2004), "Authority", *The Stanford Encyclopedia of Philosophy (Fall 2004 Edition)*, Edward N. Zalta (ed.), URL = <http://plato.stanford.edu/archives/fall2004/entries/authority/> [DLV: 2007. 1. 16].

Chung, In-Seop (2004), "Termination of Treaties and Legislative Approval" (in Korean), *Seoul International Law Journal* 11 (2004).

Coyle, Sean (2002), "Hart, Raz and the Concept of a Legal System", *Law and Philosophy* 21 (2002).

Dare, Tim (1999), "Wilfrid Waluchow and the Argument from Authority", in Tom D. Campbell (ed.), *Legal Positivism*, Ashgate / Dartmouth, Aldershot, 1999.

Durning, Patric (2003), "Joseph Raz and the Instrumental Justification of a Duty to Obey the Law", *Law and Philosophy* 22 (2003).

Dworkin, Ronald (1967), "The Model of Rules", *University of Chicago Law Review* 35 (1967).

Edmundson, William A. (2002), "Social Meaning, Compliance Conditions, and Law's Claim to Authority", *Canadian Journal of Law and Jurisprudence* 15 (January 2002).

_____ (2002), "Legitimate Authority without Political Obligation", *Law and Philosophy* 17 (1998).

Feinberg, Joel (1970), "The Nature and Value of Rights", Journal of Value Inquiry 4 (1970).

Feldman, Louis E. (1992), "Originalism through Raz-colored Glasses", *University of Pennsylvania Law Review* 140 (April 1992).

Friedman, R.B. (1973), "On the Concept of Authority in Political Philosophy", in Flathman, R.E. (ed.) *Concepts in Social and Political Philosophy*, Macmillan, New York, 1973.

Gettier, Edmund (1963), "Is Justified True Belief Knowledge?", *Analysis* 23 (1963).

Green, Leslie (1989), "Law, Legitimacy, and Consent", *Southern California Law Review* 62 (March/May 1989).

_____ (2004), "Legal Obligation and Authority", *The Stanford Encyclopedia of Philosophy (Fall 2004 Edition)*, Edward N. Zalta (ed.), URL = <http://plato.stanford.edu/archives/fall2004/entries/legal-obligation/> [DLV: 2007. 1. 16].

Harris, J.W. (1977), "Kelsen's Concept of Authority", *Cambridge Law Journal* 36 (November 1977).

Harris, J.W. (1986), "Kelsen and Normative Consistency", in Richard Tur and William Twining (eds.), *Essays on Kelsen*, Clarendon Press, Oxford, 1986.

Hart, H.L.A. (1955), "Are There Any Natural Rights?", *philosophical Review* 64 (1955).

_____ (1982a), "Legal Duty and Obligation", *Essays on Bentham: Studies in Jurisprudence and Political Theory*, Clarendon Press, Oxford, 1982.

_____ (1982b), "Commands and Authoritative Legal Reasons", *Essays on Bentham: Studies in Jurisprudence and Political Theory* (1982).

_____ (1982c), "Legal Powers", *Essays on Bentham: Studies in Jurisprudence and Political Theory* (1982).

_____ (1983a), "Definition and Theory in Jurisprudence", *Essays in Jurisprudence and Philosophy*, Clarendon Press, Oxford, 1983.

_____ (1983b), "Kelsen's Doctrine of the Unity of Law", *Essays in Jurisprudence and Philosophy*, Clarendon Press, Oxford, 1983.

_____ (1983c), "Scandinavian Realism", *Essays in Jurisprudence and Philosophy*, Clarendon Press, Oxford, 1983.

Himma, Kenneth Einar (2002), "Inclusive Legal Positivism", in Coleman, Jules. and Scott Shapiro (eds.) *The Oxford Handbook of Jurisprudence and Philosophy of Law*, Oxford University Press, Oxford, 2002.

_____ (2006), "Revisiting Raz: Inclusive Legal Positivism and Our Concept of Authority" (December 21, 2006), forthcoming in *APA Newsletters on Philosophy and Law* (Available at SSRN: http://ssrn.com/abstract=953392), p.18. [DLV: 2007. 1. 27].

Hohfeld, Wesley N. (1913), "Some Fundamental Legal Conceptions as Applied in Judicial Reasoning", *The Yale Law Journal* 23 (1913).

Honoré, Tony (1987), "The Basic Norm of a Society", *Making Law Bind: Essays Legal and Philosophical*, Clarendon Press, Oxford, 1987.

Hughes, Graham (1971), "Validity and the Basic Norm", *California Law Review* 59 (1971).

Hurd, Heidi M. (1991), "Challenging Authority", *Yale Law Journal* 100 (April 1991).

Kelsen, Hans (1957a), "Why Should the Law be Obeyed?", *What is Justice?*, University of California Press, Berkeley and Los Angeles, 1957.

_____ (1957b), "A 'Dynamic' Theory of Natural Law", *What is Justice?*, University of California Press, Berkeley and Los Angeles, 1957.

_____ (1991), "Die Grundlage der Naturrechtslehre", translated by Carmen G. Mayer, in John Finnis (ed.), *Natural Law Vol. 1*, New York University Press, New York, 1991.

_____ (1990a), "Die Selbstbestimmung des Recht", translated (in Korean) and edited by Hun Sup Shim, *Schriften zur Rechtstheorie*, Bub Moon Sa, Seoul, 1990.

_____ (1990b), "Der Begriff der Rechtsordnung", *Schriften zur Rechtstheorie* (1990).

_____ (1973a), "Derogation", *Essays in Legal and Moral Philosophy*, translated by Peter Heath, D. Reidel Publishing Company, Dordrecht, 1973.

_____ (1973b), "Law and Logic", *Essays in Legal and Moral Philosophy* (1973).

Ladenson, R. (1980), "In Defense of a Hobbesian Conception of Law", *Philosophy and Public Affairs* 9 (Winter 1980).

Lee, Bong Cheol (2001), "Western Concept of 'Authority' Reconsidered", *Korea and World Politics* 17 (Spring/Summer 2001), The Institute for Far Eastern Studies.

Lukes, S. (1987), "Perspectives on Authority", in Pennock, J. Ronald. and John W. Chapman (eds.) *Authority Revisited: NOMOS XXIX*,

New York University, New York, 1987.

McBride, William (1984), "The Fetishism of Illegality and the Mystifications of 'Authority' and 'Legitimacy'", *Georgia Law Review* 18 (Summer 1984).

Mian, Emran (2002), "The Curious Case of Exclusionary Reasons", *Canadian Journal of Law and Jurisprudence* 15 (January 2002).

Moore, Michael S. (1989), "Authority, Law, and Razian Reasons", *Southern California Law Review* 62 (March/May 1989).

Morigiwa, Yasutomo. (1989), "Authority, Rationality, and Law: Joseph Raz and The Practice of Law", *Southern California Law Review* 62 (March/May 1989).

Nino, Carlos Santiago (1998), "Confusions surrounding Kelsen's Concept of Validity", in Stanley L. Paulson and Bonnie Litschewski Paulson (1998).

Oh, Se-Hyuk (1998), "Hans Kelsens Gedanken über das verfassungswidrige Gesetz: In Bezug auf den Normenkonflikt und Derogation" (in Korean), *Korean Journal of Legal Philosophy* 1 (1998).

_____ (2000), "Normenkonflikte und ihre Lösungsmethoden − unter Einbeziehung von Einheit des Normensystems" (in Korean), unpublished PhD dissertation, Seoul National University, 2000.

Patterson, Dennis, "Explicating the Internal Point of View", *SMU Law Review* 52 (Winter 1999).

Paulson, Stanley L. (1980), "Material and Formal Authorisation in Kelsen's Pure Theory", *Cambridge Law Journal* 39 (April 1980).

Perry, Stephen R. (1989), "Second-order Reasons, Uncertainty and Legal Theory", *Southern California Law Review* 62 (March/May 1989).

Peters, Richard S. (1958), "Authority", *Proceedings of The Aristotelian Society* 32 (1958).

Postema, Gerald J. (1982), "Coordination and Convention at the Foundations of Law", *Journal of Legal Studies* 11 (January

1982).

Raz, Joseph (1978b), "Reasons for Action, Decisions and Norms", in Joseph Raz (ed.), *Practical Reasoning*, Oxford University Press, Oxford, 1978.

_____ (1986), "The Purity of the Pure Theory", in Richard Tur and William Twining (eds.), *Essays on Kelsen* (1986).

_____ (1989), "Facing Up: A Reply", *Southern California Law Review* 62 (March/May 1989).

Regan, Donald H. (1989), "Authority and Value: Reflections on Raz's Morality of Freedom", *Southern California Law Review* 62 (March/May 1989).

Richardson, Henry (2004), "Moral Reasoning", *The Stanford Encyclopedia of Philosophy (Fall 2004 Edition)*, Edward N. Zalta (ed.), URL =< http://plato.stanford.edu/archives/fall2004/entries/reasoning-moral/> [DLV: 2007. 1. 16].

Ross, Alf (1998), "Validity and the Conflict between Positivism and Natural Law", in Stanley L. Paulson and Bonnie Litschewski Paulson (1998).

Ruiter, Dick W.P. (1998), "Legal Powers", in Stanley L. Paulson and Bonnie Litschewski Paulson (1998).

Sartorious, Rolf (1981), "Political Authority and Political Obligation", *Virginia Law Review* 67 (1981).

Shapiro, Scott J. (2002), "Authority" in Coleman, Jules. and Scott Shapiro (eds.) *The Oxford Handbook of Jurisprudence and Philosophy of Law*, Oxford University Press, Oxford, 2002.

Simmons, A. John (1999), "Justification and Legitimacy", *Ethics* 109 (July 1999).

Simpson, A.W.B. (1975), "Innovation in Nineteenth Century Contract Law", *Law Quarterly Review* 91 (1975).

Soper, Philip (1984), "Legal Theory and the Obligation to Obey", *Georgia Law Review* 18 (Summer 1984).

Valdés, Ernesto Garzón (1998), "Two Models of Legal Validity: Hans Kelsen and Francisco Suárez", translated by Ruth

Zimmerling, in Stanley L. Paulson and Bonnie Litschewski Paulson (1998).

Wallace, R. Jay (2004), "Practical Reason", *The Stanford Encyclopedia of Philosophy (Fall 2004 Edition)*, Edward N. Zalta (ed.), URL = <http://plato.stanford.edu/archives/fall2004/entries/practical-reason/> [DLV: 2007. 1. 16].

Weinberger, Ota (1973), "Introduction: Hans Kelsen as Philosopher", in Hans Kelsen, *Essays in Legal and Moral Philosophy* (1973).

_____ (1999), "Legal Validity, Acceptance of Law, Legitimacy. Some Critical Comments and Constructive Proposals", *Ratio Juris* 12 (December 1999).

Weyland, Inés (1986), "Idealism and Realism in Kelsen's Treatment of Norm Conflicts", in Richard Tur and William Twining (eds.), *Essays on Kelsen* (1986).

Williams, Michael (1999), "Skepticism", in John Greco and Ernest Sosa (eds.), *The Blackwell Guide to Epistemology*, Blackwell Publishers, Malden, 1999.

권위의 개념*

I.

1. 정치철학이 다루고자 하는 근본 문제들 중 하나는 '강제력의 행사를 통해 국가가 개인의 자유를 제한하는 것은 정당화될 수 있는가?' 혹은 '국가 권위가 정당화될 수 있다면 그 조건은 무엇인가?'라는 말로 표현될 수 있다. 이를 간단히 **국가의 권위** 문제라고 부를 수 있을 것이다. 한편 법철학이 다루고자 하는 근본 문제들 중 하나는 '강도의 명령과 법의 명령(예컨대 세법상의 조세징수 명령)은 과연 다른가?' 혹은 '법의 명령이 객관적으로 유효한 규범적 명령으로 해석될 수 있다면 그 조건은 무엇인가?'라는 말로 표현될 수 있으며, 이를 간단히 **법의 규범성** 문제라고 일컬을 수 있을 것이다.

최근에는 이러한 정치철학상의 문제와 법철학상의 문제를 연계하여 논의하고자 하는 시도가 속속 등장하고 있으나, 전통적인 논의 지형은 이들 문제를 독립적으로 검토하는 것이었다. 이렇게 된 데는 여러 가지 원인이 있었을 것이나, 한 가지 생각해 볼 수 있는 것은 정치철학자들의 경우 주

---

* 이 글의 일부(Ⅲ)는 필자가 기존에 발표했던 두 편의 논문 내용을 기초로 하고 있다. 그 두 편의 논문 제목은 "조셉 라즈(Joseph Raz)의 권위론에 대한 비판적 고찰"(법철학연구 제10권 1호)과 "권위의 두 개념"(한국법철학회 2007년 춘계학술대회 발표문)이다.

로 국가권위에 대한 **정치적 · 도덕적** 정당화의 문제에 집중한 반면, 법철학자들의 대다수는 주류 이론이라 할 수 있는 법실증주의의 영향에 따라 법과 도덕을 분리하여 생각하고(**분리 테제**, Separation Thesis), 나아가 법의 '존재' 문제와 법에 대한 정치적 · 도덕적 '평가'의 문제를 엄격히 구별하는 경향이 있다는 점이다.

그렇지만 국가의 권위 문제에 대한 정치철학적 접근과 법의 규범성 문제에 대한 법철학적 접근은 사실상 '단일한 대상'을 바라보는 두 개의 시선이라고 볼 수 있다. 여기서 그 '단일한 대상'이 무엇이겠는지를 추론하는 것은 그리 힘든 일이 아니다. 그것은 흔히 **법준수의무**(또는 법복종의무 · 준법의무, Obligation or duty to obey the law)로 일컬어지는 문제이다.

많은 철학자들은 법준수의무의 문제를 국가의 권위 문제의 반면으로 인식하고 있다. 즉 국가의 구성원은 자신이 소속된 국가의 법을 준수해야 한다는 내용의 도덕적 의무가 존재한다면 그것은 곧 (개인의 자유를 제약하는) 법을 제정하는 국가의 권위에 도덕적 정당성을 인정할 수 있는 길을 열어주게 된다는 것이다. 또한 많은 철학자들이 법준수의무의 문제가 법의 규범성 문제와 직결되는 것으로 이해하고 있다. 법이 규범적 효력을 지니고 있다는 것을 보이기 위한 가장 확실한 방법이 바로 법을 준수해야 할 도덕적 의무가 존재한다는 점을 입증하는 것이기 때문이다. 요컨대 법준수의무의 문제는 국가의 권위 문제와 법의 규범성 문제를 연계하여 고찰할 수 있도록 하는 통합의 고리 역할을 한다고 말할 수 있다. 즉 '국가가 제정한 법이기만 하면 이를 모두 준수해야 하는가 아니면 그 법이 일정한 사회 정의의 기준을 충족할 경우에만 그러한가?'하는 질문을 통해 우리는 정치철학적 문제와 법철학적 문제 양자에 관하여 논의를 개시할 수 있는 것이다.

더욱이 위의 두 문제를 연계하여 고찰할 이론적 필요성 또한 존재한다고 볼 수 있다. 그것은 첫째, 종래 정치철학적 논의의 주된 관심사였던 '권위의 (정치적·도덕적) 정당화'는 권위를 둘러싼 많은 문제들 중 하나에 불과하며, 기타 권위의 개념 문제나 기능 문제 등의 논의를 통해 (존재하는) 법의 본질을 이해하는 데 유익한 정보를 얻을 수 있으며(라즈) 둘째, 애초에 법이라는 것은 그것이 가지는 '권위적 성질(authoritativeness)'과 분리하여 생각할 수는 없다고 판단되기 때문이다(켈젠, 하트, 라즈 등).

2. 그렇지만 법의 규범성 문제를 다룸에 있어 법의 권위적 성질을 거론하는 것이 적절한 것인지에 대해서는 한 가지 의문이 있다. 그것은 법의 권위적 성질을 인정하는 것이 과연 법의 규범성의 기초(토대)가 중립적이어야 한다는 요청(**중립성 테제**)과 양립가능한 것인가 하는 의문이다.

주지하듯이 켈젠은 법의 규범성의 기초(토대)가 객관적일 것을 요구하며, 따라서 사람들 간의 합의가 불가능한 도덕적, 정치적 원리들로부터 분리할 것을 주장하고 있다. 여기서 주목해야 하는 점은 법의 규범성의 기초(토대)가 중립적이어야 한다는 켈젠의 테제가 **합의가능성의 기준**으로 구체화되고 있다는 사실이다. 왜냐하면 권위에 기한 판단은 종종 합의에 따른 판단과는 전혀 다른 것으로 묘사되곤 하기 때문이다. 다시 말해서 법의 규범성의 기초(토대)가 중립적이어야 한다는 것을 그러한 기초(토대)에 대해 사람들 간에 합의가 이루어질 수 있어야 한다는 것으로 이해한다면, 합의를 도출하는 것이 불가능한 사항에 관하여 합의를 거치지 않고 권위적으로 제시되거나 혹은 합의를 도출하는 것이 가능한 사항에 관하여 도출된 합의를 깨뜨리고 권위적으로 제시된 것은 법의 규범성의 기초(토대)로서 받아들일 수 없게 되는 문제가 생긴다.

그렇지만 많은 학자들은 인간의 존재론적 한계로 말미암아 합의 원칙 그 자체나 심지어 이미 합의된 사항을 무시할 것이 요구될 수도 있다는 점을 인정하기도 한다. 그리고 합의가능성의 한계 지점에서 종종 권위의 불가피성이 제기되곤 한다는 점도 기억해야 한다.

　권위와 합의의 상호배제적 성질 내지 권위와 합의의 충돌이 실정법의 해석과 관련해서 문제되기도 한다. 다음과 같은 한 사례를 살펴보자. 우리 헌법상 국회 동의로 체결된 조약의 해제 권한은 누가 어떻게 행사하는가? 우리 헌법 제60조 제1항은 "국회는 상호원조 또는 안전보장에 관한 조약, 중요한 국제조직에 관한 조약, 우호통상항해조약, 주권의 제약에 관한 조약, 강화조약, 국가나 국민에게 중대한 재정적 부담을 지우는 조약 또는 입법사항에 관한 조약의 체결·비준에 대한 동의권을 가진다"고 규정하고 있으며, 제73조는 "대통령은 조약을 체결·비준하고, 외교사절을 신임·접수 또는 파견하며, 선전포고와 강화를 한다"고 규정하고 있을 뿐, 조약의 해제 절차나 권한에 대해서는 헌법에 아무런 규정이 없다. 그렇다고 한 번 체결한 조약은 영영 해제할 수 없는 것으로 해석할 수는 없는 노릇이다. 따라서 일단 두 가지 해석론을 상정해 볼 수 있을 것이다. 첫째, 국회의 동의를 거쳐 체결해야 하는 헌법 제60조 제1항의 조약들에 대해서는 그 해제의 경우에도 마찬가지로 국회의 동의를 얻어야 한다고 보거나 둘째, 헌법 제60조 제1항이 국회의 동의를 요구하고 있는 이유는 국민들에게 부담이 될 수 있는 조약의 체결 과정을 국민의 대표기관인 국회가 통제하도록 함으로써 국민들이 불필요한 부담을 떠안지 않도록 신중을 기하자는 데 있으므로, 그러한 부담의 위험으로부터 벗어나도록 하는 행위인 조약 해제의 경우에는 국회가 개입해야 할 필요가 없으며 따라서 체결권자인 대통령이 단독으로 해제할 수 있다고 보는 것이다.

　이 문제는 미국에서도 똑같은 구조로 재판상 다투어진 바 있다. *Goldwater v. Carter* (1979) 사례가 그것인데, 이 사례는 1978년 12월 카

터 대통령이 북경 정부를 중국의 유일한 정부로 승인함에 따라 대만과의
상호방위조약을 종료시킨 결정에 대하여, 골드워터 상원의원 등이 조약
은 상원의 동의하에서만 체결될 수 있으므로, 그 해제도 대통령이 단독으
로 할 수는 없고 상원이 조약 종료에 관한 권한의 일부를 가진다고 주장
함으로써 문제가 되었던 사안이다.

　위의 사례에서 다뤄지고 있는 것은 일차적으로 국회(미국의 사례에서
는 연방 상원)와 대통령이라는 국가기관 간의 불분명한 권한 범위를 확정
하는 문제이다. 하지만 그 (철학적) 배경을 이루고 있는 것은 권위에 기한
판단과 합의에 따른 판단이 본질적으로 상이한 규범적 평가를 받는다는
사실이라고 생각된다. 만일 우리 헌법이 일정한 조약을 체결할 경우 대법
원의 승인을 얻어야 하는 것으로 규정하고 있다고 하자. 그리고 조약의
해제 절차나 권한에 대해서는 역시 아무런 규정이 없다고 하자. 이때 누
군가 그와 같은 조약을 해제하는 것 역시 대법원의 승인이 필요하다는 주
장을 편다면, 과연 그러한 주장이 얼마나 설득력을 지닐 수 있을 것인가?

　원래의 사례에서 살펴본 두 가지 해석론 중에서 첫 번째의 경우는 합
의에 따른 판단을 **의무론적 관점**에서 선호하고 있는 반면, 두 번째의 경
우는 그것을 **결과론적 관점**에서 선호함으로써 각각 다른 결론을 도출하
고 있는 점에서 차이가 있기는 하지만, 두 경우 모두에 있어 국민적 합의
를 대표하는 기관인 국회가 동의하여 체결된 조약을 대통령이 (비록 국가
원수로서 외국에 대하여 국가를 대표하는 지위에 있다 하더라도) 법의 명
시적인 수권 없이 단독으로 파기할 수 있도록 하는 것이 선호되고 있는
것은 아니라는 점을 주목할 필요가 있다. 과연 변경된 사례에서도 그 해
석론에서 (대법원의 승인에 대한) 의무론적 내지는 결과론적 관점에서의
선호를 발견할 수 있을까? 오히려 해제에 관해서는 대법원의 승인을 얻어
야 한다는 규정이 없기 때문에 대통령이 단독으로 파기할 수 있도록 하는

것을 일견 선호하는 전제에서, 대법원의 승인을 요구하는 것이 예외적으로 정당화될 수 있는 경우가 있는지를 모색하는 방향으로 선호 판단이 이루어진다고 봐야 하지 않을까?

Goldwater 사례에서 미연방대법원은 각하 결정을 내림으로써 실체적인 판단으로 나아가지는 않았다. 그리고 각하 결정에 관한 4인의 다수의견은 그것이 **정치문제**에 해당한다는 것이었다. 이러한 사실은 무엇을 시사하는가? 생각건대 그것은 법의 규범성의 기초(토대)를 중립적으로 유지하기 위해서 (법적 수권 없는) 권위에 기한 판단의 문제를 법적인 것의 영역 바깥에 위치지울 수 있다는 점이다. 그렇지만 반드시 그렇게 해야만 하는 것이라고 단정할 수는 없을 듯하다. 중립성 테제가 배제하고자 하는 것은 특정한 정치적·도덕적 입장만을 인정하고 그와 견해를 달리하는 입장을 부정하는 비관용적 태도이지, 인간의 존재론적 한계와 그로 인한 권위의 불가피성 자체는 아니기 때문이다. 결국 법의 규범성의 기초(토대)가 중립적이어야 한다는 것을 그러한 기초(토대)에 대해 사람들 간에 합의가 이루어질 수 있어야 한다는 의미로 좁게 이해할 수는 없는 것이다.

Ⅱ.

1. 앞에서 살펴보았듯이 법준수의무의 문제는 국가의 권위 문제와 법의 규범성 문제를 연계하여 고찰토록 하는 매개항의 역할을 한다고 볼 수 있다. 그리고 두 가지 문제에 대한 연계 고찰이 구체적으로 어떻게 수행될 수 있을 것인지에 대해서는 다양한 가능성이 열려 있다. 이 글에서는 우선 종래 법철학자들의 주된 관심사였던 법의 규범성 문제를 검토하고, 이 문제가 권위 개념의 도입을 통해 새롭게 해석될 수 있음을 논증하는

방식을 따르기로 한다. 이 와중에 전통적인 국가의 권위 문제도 이른바 **법의 권위** 문제로 새롭게 이해되어야 함을 주장하게 될 것이다.

이제 '법의 규범성의 기초(토대)를 이루고 있는 것은 무엇인가?'라는 질문에서 출발하도록 하자. 사실 이 질문은 다음과 같은 두 가지 함의를 내포하고 있는 질문이다. 즉 이것은 한편으로 법의 규범성에 관한 질문임과 동시에 다른 한편으로 법의 규범성 문제를 **토대론적**(foundationa-list) 입장에서 접근하고 있는 질문인 것이다. 법의 규범성 문제를 반드시 토대론적인 입장에서 다루어야 하는 것은 아니다. 예컨대 **정합론적**(coheren-tist) 입장에서 이 문제를 다룰 수도 있는 것이다. 하지만 이러한 인식론적 입장을 모두 검토하는 것은 이 글의 범위를 넘어서는 일이라 생각되며, 여기서는 다만 법의 규범성의 문제를 토대론적 입장에서 다루는 경우에 한정하여 논의를 전개시키고자 한다.

그렇다고 해서 이 글의 가치가 현저히 저하되는 것은 아니라고 본다. 왜냐하면 20세기의 가장 위대한 법철학자라 할 수 있는 켈젠과 하트가 모두 토대론적 입장을 견지하고 있을 뿐만 아니라, 두 학자의 규범체계론은 법(체계)의 규범성 문제를 토대론적 입장에서 접근하는 가장 전형적인 두 가지 방식으로 평가되고 있기 때문에 토대론적 입장을 정리하는 것만으로도 법철학사의 커다란 줄기 하나를 가다듬는 의미를 지니기 때문이다.

켈젠과 하트의 토대론적 규범체계론은 **궁극적 규칙**(ultimate rule)과 **체계상 효력**(systemic validity) 개념을 핵심으로 하면서 특히 **법의 인식** 문제에 관심을 기울이는 특징을 나타낸다는 면에서 상당한 공통점을 지니고 있다. 이하에서는 이 두 개념을 중심으로 켈젠과 하트의 규범체계론을 검토하기로 한다. 이밖에 켈젠의 **"법의 과학의 관점**(point of view of a science of law)"이나 하트의 **"내적 관점**(internal point of view)"도 분명 중요한 이론적 구성요소이기는 하지만, 이들에 대해서는 필요한 경우 그

때그때 언급하는 것으로 한다.

2. 켈젠과 하트는 법의 규범성 문제를 인식론적 토대론과 규범체계론의 결합을 통해 해명하려고 한다. 인식론적 토대론에 관해서는 **뮌히하우젠 트릴레마**(한스 알베르트) 또는 **아그리파의 트릴레마**(마이클 윌리엄스)라고 불리우는 유명한 문제가 있다. 이는 어떠한 믿음이 지식으로 인정받기 위해서는 그러한 믿음의 주체가 그 믿음을 형성하는 과정이 인식적으로 정당화되어야 한다는 점을 전제로, 정당화가 필요한 믿음을 정당화하는 수단으로 제시된 논거 역시 정당화를 시도하는 주체가 보기에는 타당한 것일지 몰라도, 객관적으로 타당한 논거이기 위해서는 여전히 그 자체가 정당화될 필요가 있다는 점에서 아직 주관적인 믿음에 불과하기 때문에 제3의 정당화 논거를 요구하게 되는 상황 때문에 생기는 문제이다. 즉 이같은 상황에서 자신의 주관적 믿음을 정당화하고자 하는 주체에게 주어지는 선택지는 첫째, 끊임없이 새로운 논거를 동원하거나 둘째, 어느 순간 더 이상의 정당화 논거 제시 없이 아직 정당화되지 않은 상태로 남아 있거나 셋째, 최초의 믿음을 정당화하기 위해 제시한 논거를 거듭 정당화하기 위하여 최초의 믿음에 호소하는 순환론에 빠지는 것이다. 이 세 가지 선택 중에 어느 하나도 바람직한 것이 없다는 점에서 이 상황을 트릴레마(trilemma)라고 부르는 것이다.

인식론적 토대론자들은 이른바 '토대적(foundational) 지식'이 존재한다는 점을 보임으로써 이 트릴레마를 벗어날 수 있다고 보는 사람들이다. 여기서 토대적 지식이란 '다른 지식의 (인식적) 정당화 근거로 작용하면서, 동시에 그 스스로의 정당화를 위해서는 다른 지식에 기대지 않아도 되는' 그러한 지식으로 정의된다.

켈젠과 하트는 이와 같은 인식론적 토대론의 전략을 규범체계론과 결합시키고 있다. 그들에 의하면 법체계의 규범성의 토대로서 '당해 법체계에 소속된 여타의 규칙들의 규범성 근거이면서, 동시에 그 스스로의 규범성 확보를 위해서는 다른 규칙에 기대지 않아도 되는' 궁극적 규칙이 존재한다(소위 **법학적 토대론**). 인식론적 토대론에서 단순한 믿음이 '지식'의 지위를 확보하는 과정은 법학적 토대론에서 단순한 의지의 표현이 '법'의 지위를 확보하는 과정으로 응용되고 있다.

주지하듯이 켈젠의 경우는 상하 위계적 구조를 지닌 법체계의 토대를 **근본규범**(basic norm)이라 부르고 있다. 이는 당해 법체계에 속한 여타의 규범들의 최종적 효력 (발생) 근거가 된다. 켈젠의 설명에 의하면 근본규범은 "최초로 정립된 헌법(historically first constitution)"의 직접적 효력 근거가 됨으로써 그 이후에 제·개정된 모든 법의 궁극적인 효력 근거가 된다고 한다. 또한 하트의 경우는 일차적 규칙과 이차적 규칙의 복합적 위계 구조를 지닌 법체계의 토대로서 **승인율**(rule of recognition)을 제시하고 있다. 이는 당해 법체계에 속한 여타의 규칙들에 관한 최고의 효력 (판단) 기준을 제공한다. 하트는 헌법을 준수할 것을 내용으로 하는 별도의 (근본)**규범**을 가정하는 것은 불필요한 반복이며, 하나의 **사실** 문제로서 승인율의 존재를 이야기한다.

켈젠과 하트는 또한 자신들의 토대론적 규범체계론을 구축함에 있어 체계상 효력 개념을 도입하고 있다. 그들은 법이 규칙들의 무질서한 집합이 아니라 긴밀한 내적 관련성을 지닌 체계의 형태로 존재하는 것으로 본다. 따라서 그러한 긴밀함을 **효력의 연쇄**(켈젠) 내지 **법적 추론의 연쇄**(하트)라고 하는 얼개로 구성해냈다. 인식론적 토대론에서 토대와 상층부가 인식적 정당성을 매개 개념으로 하여 결속되는 것과 같이, 법학적 토대론에서는 토대(궁극적 규칙)와 상층부가 체계상 효력 개념을 통하여 결속되는 것이다.

3. 그런데 켈젠이나 하트와 같이 효력(validity) 개념을 체계관련적인 것으로, 즉 이른바 체계상 효력 개념으로 이해하는 것이 타당한 것인지에 대해서는 의론의 여지가 있다. 사실 학자들마다 구사하고 있는 효력 개념이 서로 다르고, 심지어 동일한 학자의 저술 속에서도 교묘하게 서로 다른 의미로 쓰인 효력 개념들을 발견할 수 있다. 불리긴이 이야기한 것처럼 "효력 개념의 의미에 대한 합의는 아직 존재하지 않는다."

따라서 효력 개념에 대하여 제대로 이해하기 위해서는 무엇보다 그 다의적 용례들을 유형화하는 작업이 선행되어야 한다고 말할 수 있다. 학자들도 이러한 사정을 고려하여 몇 가지 형태의 유형화론들을 제시하고 있다. 그들 중 가장 일반적이라 생각되는 것은 알렉시 – 뢰블레브스키 – 불리긴의 효력 개념 **삼분설**로서, 이 견해에 의할 때 효력 개념은 크게 **체계상 효력**(소속성), **사실적 효력**(실효성), **도덕적 효력**(구속성)의 세 가지 의미로 주로 사용되고 있다고 한다.

첫째, 효력 개념은 **소속성**(membership)의 의미로 사용되는 경우가 있다. 이는 앞서 살펴본 바와 같이 켈젠과 하트가 기본적으로 채용하고 있는 의미이다(체계상 효력). 이들에 따르면 특정 규범체계의 궁극적 규칙은 어떠한 규칙들이 당해 규범체계에 속하는지 여부를 판단할 수 있는 기준을 제공하거나, 그 소속성의 근거가 된다. 라즈 또한 비록 일반적으로 규범의 효력이라는 말의 의미는 소속성보다는 넓은 의미를 갖지만, 하나의 법체계를 전제로 하여 법의 효력(legal validity)을 말할 경우에는 소속성 개념으로 파악해도 충분하다고 봄으로써 켈젠과 하트의 견해를 수용하고 있다.

둘째, 효력 개념은 **실효성**(efficacy)의 의미로 쓰이기도 한다. 일부 학자들은 이를 특별히 "사회학적 효력 개념"이라고 부르기도 한다. 그렇지만 켈젠과 하트는 효력 개념과 실효성 개념을 구별해야 한다는 입장을 취하고 있다. 켈젠에 의하면 실효성이란 법 자체의 속성이 아니라 사람들의 사실적 행위의 속성에 불과하다. 하트 또한 법의 사실적 존재를 지칭함에 있어 validity라는 번역어를 사용한 로스의 입장을 비판한 바 있다. 불리긴 또한 실효성은 효력 개념의 한 **의미**인 것이 아니라, 효력 여부를 판단하는 한 가지 **기준**이 된다고 봄으로써 두 개념의 혼동을 비판한다. 그는 제정법의 효력 기준은 제정성으로, 관습법의 효력 기준은 실효성으로 보는데, 결국 이 경우 효력의 의미 자체는 켈젠이나 하트와 같이 소속성으로 파악하고 있다.

셋째, 효력 개념은 **구속성**(binding force)의 의미로 사용되기도 한다. 여기서 반드시 짚고 넘어가야 할 점은 구속성으로서의 효력 개념이 (도덕적 의무인) 법준수의무의 존재를 함축한다는 점이다(로스, 니노, 라즈). 이 부분에 있어 켈젠과 하트의 입장이 무엇인지를 파악하기란 몹시 까다로운 일이다. 우선 켈젠의 경우는 종종 효력 개념을 구속성의 의미로 사용하면서도, 결국 법을 준수해야 한다는 당위를 도덕적 의무가 아닌 (선험)논리적 전제로만 구성해보려 하고 있다. 그리고 하트의 경우는 효력 개념을 구속성의 의미로 사용하기를 거부하면서도, 법을 준수해야 할 도덕적 의무를 논증해보려 하고 있다. 그렇지만 구속성으로서의 효력 개념을 채택하면서도 (도덕적 의무인) 법준수의무를 인정하지 않는 것은 비논리적이며, 법준수의무를 인정하면서도 굳이 구속성을 효력 개념의 의미에서 배제할 이유가 있는지 역시 의문이다. 학자들의 평가도 분분하다. 로스는 켈젠의 이론 중에서 효력 개념을 구속성의 의미로 사용하고 있는 부분들이 제거되어야 한다고 보는 반면, 니노는 그러한 부분들을 켈젠 이론의 본질적 측면이라 강조하고 오히려 효력 개념을 소속성이라는 좁은 의미로만 사용하고 있는 부분들이 재고되어야 한다고 본다.

켈젠과 하트가 토대론적 규범체계론의 구상, 구체적으로는 궁극적 규칙과 체계상 효력 개념을 중심으로 법체계의 규범성을 근거지우려 하는 구상을 공통적으로 가지고 있음에도 불구하고 궁극적 규칙의 속성이나 효력 개념의 내포에 관하여 다르게 파악하고 있는 까닭은 근본적으로 그들이 전제하고 있는 **규범성**(normativity)의 개념이 다르기 때문일 것이다 (라즈). 즉 켈젠은 규범성을 소위 **정당화된 규범성**(justified normativity)으로 이해하고 있으며, 이 견해에 따르면 법이 규범성을 갖는다는 말은 곧 구속성을 갖는다는 말과 같다. 반면 하트의 경우는 규범성을 소위 **사회적 규범성**(social justification)으로 이해함으로써, 법이 규범성을 갖는다는 말은 다만 사회적으로 (구속력 있는 규칙으로서) 승인된다는 말에 지나지 않는다.

켈젠은 소위 사회적 규범성이라는 것은 규범성의 개념일 수 없다고 생각한다. 다시 말해서 사람들에 의해서 승인되었다는 사실만으로는 강제적 행위의 "주관적 의미"가 "객관적 의미"를 얻지 못한다는 것이다. 켈젠의 견해를 따른다면, 하트는 결국 규범성(normativity)을 반복성(regularity)으로 대체하려고 하는 **환원주의**로부터 자신의 이론을 차별화하는 데 실패한 것으로 보게 된다. 이에 대하여 하트는 켈젠이 정당화된 규범성 개념과 구속성으로서의 효력 개념을 고수하는 한, **자연법론**으로부터 자신의 이론을 차별화할 수 없을 것이라 평가할 것이다. 나아가 하트는 "**내적 관점**"에 대한 논의를 통해 환원주의와 다를 바 없다는 비판을 극복하고자 한다. 즉 환원주의자들은 규칙의 내적 측면을 무시한다는 점에서 자신과 확실히 차이가 있다는 것이다. 한편 켈젠도 "**법의 과학의 관점**"에 대한 논의를 통해 자연법론과 다를 바 없다는 비판을 극복하고자 한다. 즉 자연법론자들은 자연법의 절대적 효력을 전제로 하지만, 자신은 어디까지나 "법체계를 규범의 체계로 해석하고자 한다면"이라는 단서를 달고 있는 조건부 해석론을 제시할 따름이며, 따라서 법의 효력은 어디까지나 상대적 효력일 뿐이라고 본다는 점에서 차별화된다는 것이다.

4. 근래의 법철학적 연구에 의하면 법을 다른 규범적 기준(예컨대 에티켓의 규칙)과 구별해주는 본질적 특징 중의 하나는 바로 **법의 체계성**이다 (하트, 라즈). 일찍이 켈젠은 "우리의 관심을 고립된 어느 규칙에만 둔다면, 법의 본질을 파악하는 것은 불가능하다"고 설파한 바 있으며, 라즈는 한 발 더 나아가 "법의 규범성을 해명하는 작업은 법의 개념보다는 법체계의 개념에 기초하며, 법의 개념조차도 법체계의 개념에 의존하고 있다"는 주장을 펴고 있다. 그런데 켈젠과 하트의 이론 속에서 법규범의 체계화의 임무를 맡은 두 개념 즉 궁극적 규칙과 체계상 효력 개념이 과연 그 소임을 다하고 있는 것인지는 매우 의심스럽다. 다음과 같은 몇 가지 문제점들을 살펴보도록 하자.

첫째, 켈젠과 하트의 구상에 따를 때 궁극적 규칙 자체도 효력이 있는 것인가? 주지하듯이 켈젠은 규범의 효력은 오직 상위 규범의 효력에서 나온다고 보기 때문에 개념상 그보다 상위에 있는 규범이 있을 수 없는 근본규범은 결국 효력이 없는 것이며 나아가 효력 없는 근본규범의 하위 규범들도 효력이 없는 것이 된다는 비판을 받고 있다. 이에 대하여 켈젠은 (법의 과학의 관점에서 볼 때) "근본규범은 유효한 것으로 전제"되기 때문에, "근본규범의 효력의 근거는 문제 삼을 수 없다"고 답한다. 하트의 경우 "승인율 그 자체는 효력이 있는 것도 없는 것도 아니"라고 봄으로써 켈젠과 거리를 두려 하지만, 그 역시 "승인율 자체의 효력에 대해서는 문제가 제기될 수 없다"고 주장하고 있는 점에서 비판자들의 문제 제기가 타당치 않다는 켈젠의 (토대론적) 답변에 합류하고 있는 셈이다. 하지만 알렉시 등이 주장하는 바와 같이 궁극적 규칙의 효력에 관한 질문은 종종 제기되고 있으며, 또한 그러한 문제 제기가 부당하다고 볼 이유도 없는 것 같다.

둘째, 토대론적 규범체계론에 의할 때 서로 충돌하는 두 규범이 동시에 유효할 수 있는 것인가? 이것은 이른바 규범충돌의 문제로 알려져 있는 이론적 난제에 관한 물음이다. 이 문제에 관해서는 **켈젠의 트릴레마**(Kelsen's Trilemma)라고 부를 수 있는 선택지를 소개하는 것으로 논의를 시작함이 좋을 듯하다. 이 상황을 트릴레마라고 일컫는 이유는 일련의 세 가지 (바람직한) 목표 중 어느 두 가지를 추구하면, 나머지 한 목표에 대해서는 반드시 부정적인 영향을 미치게 되기 때문이다.

【켈젠의 트릴레마】
(1) 만일 동일한 법체계에 속한 두 규범이 충돌하면, 둘 다 동시에 유효할 수는 없다.
(2) 그 내용이 다른 규범의 내용과 양립불가능한 어느 규범은 그 다른 규범과 충돌하고 있다. 그럼에도 불구하고,
(3) 어느 규범은 비록 그것의 내용과 양립불가능한 내용의 다른 (심지어 상위의) 규범이 있는 경우에도 유효하다.

켈젠의 전기 이론에 의하면 규범충돌은 논리적으로 모순이므로 불가능하다. 켈젠은 이를 상하위 규범들 간의 충돌과 동위 규범들 간의 충돌의 경우로 나누어 설명한다. 우선 **상하위 규범들 간의 충돌**은 불가능하다. 켈젠은 이를 입증하기 위해 다음과 같은 **후건부정식**(modus tollens)을 사용하는 것으로 분석된다.

1. 만일 동일한 법체계에 속한 두 규범이 충돌하면, 둘 다 동시에 유효할 수는 없다[(1) 긍정].

2. 그런데, 어느 규범은 비록 그것의 내용과 양립불가능한 내용의 상위 규범이 있는 경우에도 유효하다[(3) 긍정 즉 (1)의 후건 부정].
3. 따라서, 그 내용이 상위 규범의 내용과 양립불가능한 어느 규범은 상위 규범과 충돌하는 것이 아니다[(2) 부정 즉 (1)의 전건 부정].

또한 **동위 규범들 간의 충돌**은 항상 즉시 해소되므로 충돌 상태의 존속은 불가능하다. 이를 입증하기 위하여 켈젠은 다음과 같은 **전건긍정식**(modus ponens)을 사용하는 것으로 분석된다.

1. 만일 동일한 법체계에 속한 두 규범이 충돌하면, 둘 다 동시에 유효할 수는 없다[(1) 긍정].
2. 그런데, 그 내용이 그와 동위에 있는 다른 규범의 내용과 양립불가능한 어느 규범은 그 동위 규범과 충돌하는 것이 된다[(2) 잠정적 긍정 즉 (1)의 전건 긍정].
3. 따라서, 서로 양립불가능한 내용을 갖는 복수의 동위 규범이 있을 경우에는 최소한 그 중 하나는 효력이 없는 것으로 해석되고 더 이상 충돌은 문제되지 않는다[(3) 부정 즉 (1)의 후건 긍정].

이상의 분석을 통하여 켈젠의 전기 이론이 논리적인 오류를 범하고 있음을 알 수 있다. 하나의 조건명제에서 출발하여 동시에 전건긍정식과 후건부정식을 사용할 수는 없음에도 불구하고 켈젠은 그렇게 하고 있는 것이다. (물론 예컨대 하나의 조건명제에서 전건긍정식을 사용함과 동시에 그 조건명제의 대우명제에서 후건부정식을 사용하는 것은 가능하다. 이는 논리적으로 동일한 작업을 두 차례 행한 것에 불과하기 때문이다.) 그 결과 상하위 규범들 간의 충돌을 논함에 있어서는 명제 (2)를 부정하면서 명제 (3)을 긍정하는 반면, 동위 규범들 간의 충돌을 논함에 있어서는 명제 (2)를 긍정하면서 명제 (3)을 부정하는 자의적인 결론에 이르고 있다.

켈젠은 후기의 이론에서 이러한 논리적 오류를 시정하고 있다. 그는 자신의 전기 이론상의 논리적 오류가 명제 (1)을 긍정하고 있기 때문에 생겨난 것임을 직시하고 이제 명제 (1)의 부정으로 나아간다. 즉 하나의 법체계 안에서 충돌하는 두 규범이 동시에 유효할 수도 있다는 것이다. 이는 그의 이론이 하트의 규범충돌 이론과 유사하게 됨을 의미한다. 하트는 규범의 충돌을 "동시충족의 **논리적** 불가능성"으로 정의하는 한편, 이러한 정의는 충돌하는 규범들이 동일한 규범체계 내에 "동시에 **유효하게** 존재할 수 있는지" 여부에 관해서는 열려 있다고 보기 때문이다.

이러한 켈젠과 하트의 규범충돌 이론이 정작 그들의 토대론적 규범체계론에 부합하는 것인지에 대해서는 의문이 남는다. 해리스의 지적처럼 규범적 일관성(normative consistency)은 토대론적 규범체계론 자체 혹은 좁게는 체계상 효력 개념에 전제되어 있는 것일 수 있기 때문이다. 또한 법실증주의의 입장을 취하는 한 '불법적 판결'이나 '위헌적 법률'의 효력을 긍정하기 위해서는 '정의롭지 못한 법'의 효력을 긍정할 때와는 차별화된 논리가 필요할 것인데, 효력 개념의 본질을 해치지 않으면서 그러한 논리를 제시하는 것도 쉽지 않은 일이다.

셋째, 사실 위의 문제는 **정태적 규범체계**(static normative system)와 **동태적 규범체계**(dynamic normative system)를 구별하는 켈젠의 규범체계론과도 관계가 있다. 켈젠은 법체계를 동태적 규범체계로 보며, 어떠한 법규범이 유효한 까닭은 그것의 **내용**이 근본규범으로부터 **연역**되기(de-duced) 때문이 아니라, 그것이 근본규범이 정하고 있는 **방식**, 즉 합헌적 방식에 따라 **창설**되기(created) 때문이라고 설명한다. 마찬가지로 어떠한 규범이 효력을 상실하게 되는 까닭도 그것이 합헌적 방식에 따라 **폐지**되기(annulled) 때문이라고 한다.

그런데 켈젠이 규범충돌에 관한 자신의 전기 이론에서 "동위규범들 간의 충돌은 항상 즉시 해소된다"는 주장을 뒷받침하기 위한 예로 들고 있는 것은 신·구법의 충돌시 구법은 **내용**적으로 신법과 양립할 수 없기 때문에 신법에 의해서 즉시 효력을 상실한다는 것이다. 이같은 설명은 켈젠의 전기 이론이 정태적 규범체계와 동태적 규범체계의 구별이라는 관점과도 엇갈리고 있음을 드러낸다. 이 때문인지 켈젠은 규범충돌에 관한 후기 이론을 전개함에 있어서는 정태적 규범체계와 동태적 규범체계의 구별이라는 관점에 더욱 충실해지고 있다. 앞에서 언급한 바와 같이 켈젠의 후기 이론에서는 트릴레마의 한 축이던 명제 (1)이 부정되는데, 이와 함께 남은 명제 (2), (3)이 각각 정태적 의미와 동태적 의미를 지니고 있음을 분명히 하고 있는 것이다. 요컨대 명제 (2)는 규범충돌의 판정에 관한 정태적 기준 즉 하트가 이야기한 "동시충족의 논리적 불가능성"을 의미하는 것으로 보며, 명제 (3)은 규범의 효력 득실에 관한 동태적 기준으로서 특히 규범충돌과 관련해서는 그 해소에 관한 동태적 기준이 된다고 본다. 따라서 규범충돌의 사실만으로 당연히 (어느 한 규범의) 효력이 상실되는 것은 아니며 "합헌적 방식에 따른 폐지"가 있어야 비로소 효력이 상실되는 것이다. 명제 (3)은 당연히 동태적 규범체계의 경우에만 적용되는 것이나, 명제 (2)는 모든 규범체계에 적용되는 것으로 파악된다.

그렇지만 명제 (3)은 통상의 규범과 '상위 규범에 반하는 규범'을 구별하지 못한다. 왜냐하면 양자 모두 (합헌적 방식에 따라 창설된 이상) 유효한 규범이 되기 때문이다. 통상의 규범은 완전한 효력을 지니나 '상위 규범에 반하는 규범'은 불완전한 효력을 지닌다고 보기도 힘들다. 둘 다 당해 규범체계에 속하는 것으로 보는 순간, 둘 다 완전한 의미의 체계상 효력을 지니는 것이기 때문이다.

5. 이상에서 살펴본 바와 같이 켈젠과 하트가 법을 하나의 체계 개념으로 인식하는 과정에서 궁극적 규칙과 체계상 효력 개념은 큰 한계를 드러

내고 있다. 이 글은 바로 이러한 한계에 주목하고 있다. 그리고 이러한 한계를 보완하기 위하여 '권위'의 개념을 또 하나의 중심 개념으로 도입해야 한다고 주장한다.

　사실 효력 개념과 권위 개념은 매우 긴밀하게 연관되어 있는 개념이다. 발데스는 이 점을 법준수의무 개념과 효력 개념이 (특히 켈젠에 있어) 동의어처럼 사용되고 있다는 말로써 표현하고 있다. 하지만 정확히 말해서 양자가 동의어인 것은 아니라고 생각된다. 다만 효력 개념을 체계에 대한 규범의 소속성이라는 의미로 이해할 경우, 권위 개념은 규범의 구속성을 의미하는 것으로 새길 수 있을 것이다. 왜냐하면 첫째, 이러한 해석이 권위 개념을 법준수의무 개념의 반면으로 이해하는 전통적인 입장에 부합하고 둘째, 켈젠이 글의 명확성을 희생시키면서까지 '효력'이라는 말을 소속성이라는 일차적 의미 외에 (군데군데) 구속성이라는 의미로 사용할 수밖에 없었던 점에 비추어, 효력 개념을 소속성의 의미로 한정할 경우 구속성의 의미로 사용할 수 있는 새로운 개념이 필요하다는 사정에도 부응하는 것이기 때문이다.

　이 글에서 권위 개념을 통해 토대론적 규범체계론을 보완하는 논리를 간단히 정리해보면 다음과 같다.

　첫째, 하트가 말하는 내적 진술(internal statement)의 차원과는 별도로 법적 추론(legal reasoning)의 차원을 상정함으로써, 내적 진술을 통해 특정 규범의 법적 효력이 인정되는지 여부와 법적 추론의 과정에서 그 규범이 권위를 보유하고 있는지 여부를 구분한다. 그리고 법적 효력이 인정되는 규범이라 하더라도 같은 체계 내의 법적으로 유효한 다른 규범과 충돌한다면 권위를 보유하지 못하는 것으로 본다. 그러한 경우에는 당해 규범이 수범자의 행위 내용을 '구속할' 수 없기 때문이다.

둘째, 법적 추론의 과정에서 권위를 보유하는 규범이라고 해서 반드시 내적 진술을 통해 법적 효력이 인정될 필요는 없다. 따라서 하트가 "승인율 그 자체는 효력이 있는 것도 없는 것도 아니"라고 한 점에 대하여, 그럼에도 불구하고 승인율은 권위 있는 규칙이라고 말할 수 있는 것이다. 이러한 맥락에서 법체계의 기초(토대)는 궁극적 규칙의 효력이 아니라 그 권위에 달려 있다고 말할 수도 있을 것이다(**법의 권위**).

셋째, 법적 추론의 과정에서 권위를 보유하는 규범이라 하더라도 그것이 도덕규범에 불과하다면 법적 효력이 인정되지 않는 점도 권위 개념과 효력 개념의 구분을 통해 간단히 설명할 수 있다.

Ⅲ.

1. 이제 본격적으로 권위 개념에 대하여 논의할 때가 된 것 같다. 그런데 권위 개념에 대한 탐구는 그 출발부터 매우 험난하다. 학자들마다 권위 개념을 구성해내는 방식이 다른 것은 물론이고, 애초에 '권위'라는 말이 가리키는 바가 무엇인지를 감수하는 태도마저 다르기 때문이다.

첨예한 대립이 시작되는 부분은 정치와 법의 영역에서 말하는 '권위'가 과연 **행위의 근거**(reason for action)가 되는가 아니면 단지 **믿음의 근거** (reason for belief)에 불과한가 하는 점이다. 권위가 행위의 근거가 된다고 보는 견해는 **실천적 권위**(practical authority) 개념에서 출발하는 반면, 권위가 단지 믿음의 근거에 불과하다고 보는 견해는 **이론적 권위**(theoretical authority) 개념에서 출발하게 된다.

이와 같은 견해 대립은 이른바 철학적 무정부주의(philosophical anarchism)의 도전에 대한 이론적 대응 방식의 차이로 나타나게 된다. 철학적

무정부주의자들에 따르면 실천적 권위 개념은 인간의 도덕적 자율성
(autonomy) 및 합리성(rationality) 개념과 양립할 수 없기 때문에 어떠한
경우에도 정당화될 수 없다(권위의 역설). 이러한 비판에 대하여 어떤 학
자들은 권위의 역설을 피하면서도 실천적 권위 개념의 이론적 지위를 유
지할 수 있는 방법을 모색하는가 하면, 다른 학자들은 기본적으로 철학적
무정부주의자들의 비판을 수용하면서 이론적 권위 개념을 그 대안으로
제시하려고 한다.

　권위 개념의 탐구를 위한 출발점을 제대로 설정하는 일은 위와 같은
견해 대립에 대하여 면밀히 검토를 거친 후에야 가능할 것으로 보인다.
따라서 이하에서는 철학적 무정부주의의 주장과 그에 대한 학설들의 상
이한 이론적 대응 과정을 볼프, 라즈 그리고 허드의 이론을 중심으로 자
세히 살펴보기로 한다.

　2. 볼프는 자신의 칸트에 대한 해석을 통해 인간은 자유 의지와 이성을
지닌 존재로서 자신의 행위에 대하여 책임을 질 의무(the obligation to
take responsibility for one's action)를 지닌다는 전제하에, 도덕적 자율성
은 자유와 책임의 결합물이며, 이는 곧 스스로 그 자신에 대해 제정한 법
칙에 복종함이라고 말한다. 따라서 자율적인 인간은 그가 자율적인 한,
타인의 의지에 종속되지 않는다는 것이다.

　그는 이와 같은 자율성을 포기하지 않는 것이 바로 인간의 일차적인
의무(primary obligation)라고 말한다. 이 말은 인간에게는 타인의 지배를
거부할 의무가 있음을 의미한다. 문제는 소위 지배할 권리(right to rule)
로 해석되는 권위가 — 이는 볼프의 견해일 뿐 모든 학자가 이렇게 해석
하는 것은 아님을 유의할 필요가 있다. 권위 개념을 구성해내는 다양한
방식들에 대해서는 뒤에서 자세히 소개할 것이다. — 국가의 본질적 요

소를 이룬다는 점에 있다. 즉 국가는 본질적으로 개인들에 대해 지배할 권리가 있음을 주장하는 데 반해, 개인들은 국가를 포함한 타인의 지배를 거부할 의무가 있는 것이 되어 양자 간에는 해결할 수 없는 모순이 발생한다는 것이다.

한 가지 주의해야 할 점은 타인의 지배 혹은 명령에 복종한다는 것이 무엇을 뜻하는가 하는 것이다. 타인이 명령한 바에 단순히 외적으로 부합하는(conforming) 행위를 했다고 해서 그의 명령에 복종한 것이라고 말할 수는 없다. 명령을 받았다 하더라도 그 명령이 지시하는 내용에 대한 자신의 숙고의 결과, 그 내용을 실현시키는 것이 좋겠다고 판단하여 당해 행위로 나아갈 수도 있기 때문이다. 명령에 복종하는 것이 되기 위해서는, 명령한 바에 따르는(complying, 순응하는) 행위가 있어야 하며, 다시 말해 명령의 내용이 옳기 때문이 아니라 "명령이기 때문에" 지시된 행위로 나아갈 것이 요구된다(내용독립성). 주지하듯이 부합(conformity)과 순응(compliance)을 구분하는 인식은 칸트에게서 찾아볼 수 있다. 그의 취지에 따르자면, 부합과 달리 순응에는 소위 '동기의 지배'라고 부를 수 있는 사태가 결부되는 것이라 말할 수 있을 것 같다.

볼프의 결론은 권위는 자율성의 의무와 충돌을 일으킨다는 전제하에, 자율성의 덕과 조화를 이룰 수 있는 유일한 정치적 교설은 무정부주의라는 것이다. 즉 정당성을 갖춘 국가라는 개념은 공허하며, 계몽된 인간을 위한 유일 타당한 정치적 신념은 철학적 무정부주의라는 것이다.

3. 볼프 식의 철학적 무정부주의를 극복하고자 했던 많은 노력들 중 단연 돋보이는 시도는 라즈에 의해 이루어졌다. 그는 볼프가 "배제적 근거(exclusionary reason)"라는 유형의 행위 근거가 존재하지 않는다고 잘못 전제한 나머지 "일차적 근거(first-order reason)"들을 저울질했을 때 해야

할 것이라 판단되는 바를 행하지 않는 것은 절대로 정당화될 수 없다고 결론짓는 실수를 범하고 있다고 한다. 요컨대 배제적 근거라는 유형의 행위 근거를 고려할 때, 권위의 명령을 따르는 데는 이성의 포기도, 자율성의 상실도 수반되지 않으며, 철학적 무정부주의자들이 주장하는 역설이 실은 착오에 불과하다는 것이다. 이러한 라즈의 논변을 이해하기 위해서는 그의 실천적 추론에 관한 이론 특히 근거 충돌의 해소 방식에 관한 이론을 살펴보아야 한다.

라즈에 의하면 행위 근거는 "강도(strength)"와 "위상(level)"이라는 두 가지 상이한 차원을 가진다. 우선, 어떤 행위 근거는 다른 것들보다 논리적으로 강하고 비중이 커서, 그와 상충하는 약한 행위 근거를 "압도한다 (override or outweigh)." 다시 말해 어떠한 행위를 지지하는 근거와 반대하는 근거간의 충돌은 당해 근거들의 상대적인 강도나 비중에 의해 해소되는 것이다. 다음으로, 어떠한 행위 근거는 다른 것들보다 위상이 높고, 위상이 높은 근거와 낮은 근거가 충돌할 경우에는 언제나 전자가 우세하다(prevail over). 여기서 라즈는 하트가 "일차적 규칙"과 "이차적 규칙"을 구분한 점에 착안하여, 행위 근거는 그 위상에 따라 "일차적 근거(first-order reason)"와 "이차적 근거(second-order reason)"로 구분할 수 있으며, 후자가 전자보다 위상이 높다고 설명한다. 따라서 양자가 상충하는 경우에는 그들의 상대적인 강도나 비중에 의하는 것이 아니라 종류(kind) 혹은 위계(rank)에 의해 그 충돌이 해소된다. 그는 이차적 근거를 "어떠한 근거에 입각하여 행위할 근거 혹은 어떠한 근거에 입각하여 행위하지 않을 근거"라고 정의하고, 전자를 "이차적 적극 근거(positive second-order reason)", 후자를 "이차적 소극 근거(negative second-order reason)"로 각각 명명한다. 이 이차적 소극 근거가 바로 배제적 근거이다. 즉, 일차적 근거와 배제적 근거간의 충돌은 항상 후자가 전자를 "배제함으로써

(exclude)" 해소된다는 것이다.

　그런데 어떤 경우, 일차적 행위 근거가 또한 동시에 "그 근거와 충돌하는 다른 근거에 입각하여 행위하지 않을" 배제적 근거이기도 한 때가 있는데 이러한 복합적 성격의 근거를 라즈는 "보호된 근거(protected reason)"라고 부른다. 이 보호된 근거라는 개념을 통해 그는 실천적 권위로서 정치적 및 법적 권위가 갖는 본질적 특성을 설명하는 작업에 이른다. 그는 실천적 권위가 일종의 "규범적 권한(normative power)"을 갖는 것으로 파악하는데, 여기서 규범적 권한이란 바로 "보호된 근거를 변경할 수 있는 능력"이라고 정의함으로써 철학적 무정부주의에 대한 반론의 물꼬를 튼다. 보호된 근거 P를 변경하는 방법 중 하나가 바로 새로운 보호된 근거 P*를 제공하여 그 구성 부분인 배제적 근거 P*e로 하여금 이전의 보호된 근거(P)를 구성하는 배제적 근거 Pe를 무력화하는(defeat) 것이기 때문이다.

　이제 실천적 권위의 전형적인 행사 양식인 명령의 경우를 생각해 보자. 앞에서 명령이 내용독립적 근거(content-independent reason)의 특징을 지닌다는 점을 살펴보았다. 라즈는 이에 더해 명령이 보호된 근거로 취급될 것을 의도하며 발하여진다고 말한다. 다시 말해서 명령은 단지 일차적 근거의 저울을 기울이는 것뿐만 아니라 그러한 저울질을 통해 판단된 특정한 행위를 배제하는 것 또한 목표로 하여 발하는 것이다. 그리고 만일 어떤 사람이 명령할 자격이 있는 사람이라면, 즉 예컨대 보호된 근거를 제공하여 기존의 다른 보호된 근거를 변경할 자격이 있다면, 그 사람은 수명자에 대하여 실천적 권위를 갖는다고 말할 수 있다. 그리고 수명자는 일차적 근거를 저울질한 결과대로 행위하지 않고 달리 행위를 하는 것이 정당화된다. 왜냐하면 그보다 우세한 '그렇게 행위하지 않을 근거'가 주어져 있기 때문이다. 결국 실천적 권위의 명령을 따르는 것은 이성의 포기도, 자율성의 상실도 아니며, 사람들의 실천적 추론 속에 합리적으로 편입될 수 있는 지극히 정상적인 삶의 양식이라는 것이 라즈의 주장이다.

4. 이상과 같은 라즈의 논증이 소개되었을 때 학자들은 즉각 열렬한 환호로 답하였다. 이제 철학적 무정부주의는 '논리적으로' 극복되었고 더 이상 국가 권위의 정당성이라는 개념을 수용할 수 있는지에 대한 의문은 필요치 않은 것 같았다. 하지만 정말로 라즈의 논증이 철학적 무정부주의에 대한 타당한 반론을 제공하고 있는가? 아래에서는 이와 같은 의문을 매우 강력한 논증으로 설득력 있게 다루고 있는 허드의 이론을 살펴보고자 한다. 그녀의 전반적인 이론 자체에는 몇 가지 문제점이 있지만, 여기서는 그러한 문제점에도 불구하고 여전히 의미가 있다고 생각되는 논증 부분만을 간단히 소개하기로 한다.

허드는 라즈가 시도한 실천적 권위 개념과 자율성 내지 합리성 개념간의 양립화 논증이 실패했다고 주장한다. 여기에는 두 가지 이유를 들 수 있는데, 하나는 라즈가 제시하고 있는 사례들이 모두 부적절하거나 불충분하다는 점이고, 다른 하나는 그의 '보호된 근거' 개념이 근본적으로 비정합적이라는 점이다. 즉 허드에 따르면 라즈는 단지 구체적인 사례를 들어 자신의 논변을 지지하는 데 실패한 것일 뿐 아니라, 애초에 논리적인 문제를 안고 있는 논변을 전개했던 것이어서 당연히 설득력 있는 사례를 동원할 수 없었다는 것이다.

보호된 근거의 구성 부분을 이루는 배제적 근거가 존재함을 보이기 위해 라즈가 제시하고 있는 사례는 크게 두 가지 종류이다. 하나는 무능력 사례 C1, 다른 하나는 약속 사례 C2라고 부를 수 있는데, 이들을 요약하여 제시하면 다음과 같다.

C1: 앤은 온종일 비정상적으로 극심한 격무에 시달린 후 퇴근하였다. 그

날 밤 그녀의 친구는 그녀가 평소 알아보고 있던 '투자할 만한 건수'를 알려주려 그녀에게 전화를 걸었다. 이 투자 제안에는 한 가지 조건이 있었는데, 그것은 그날 자정까지 투자 여부를 확답해줘야 한다는 것이다. 그녀는 너무도 피곤한 나머지 제대로 된 판단을 할 수 없을 것 같다고 생각했다. 그래서 그 제안을 검토하지 않고, 투자를 하지 않기로 했다.

C2: 콜린은 그의 아내에게 아이들의 교육 문제에 관한 한 아이들 본인의 이익만을 고려하고 다른 모든 사유들은 고려치 않겠노라고 약속했다. 이제 그는 아들을 명문 사립 고등학교에 보낼 것인지를 결정해야 한다. 그는 결국 자신이 약속을 했기 때문에 다른 문제들 예컨대 재정적인 형편, 이웃들의 눈총 등에 개의치 않고 아들을 명문 사립 고등학교에 보내기로 했다.

허드는 C1에 대해 녹초가 되었다는 사실은 일차적 근거를 저울질한 결과대로 행동하지 않을 근거가 아니며, 사실 '행위 근거(reason for action)' 자체가 아니라고 한다. 그것은 다만 현재로서는 파악되고 있지 않지만, 만일 파악된다면 당해 투자 제안을 거부할 이유가 될 근거들이 있을 것이라고 '믿을 근거(reason for belief)'에 불과하다는 것이다. 또한 C2의 경우 라즈는 콜린의 약속이 그의 아들의 이익을 고려할 일차적 근거와 동시에 그에 반하는 다른 근거들을 고려하지 않을 배제적 근거를 제공한다고, 다시 말해 보호적 근거를 제공한다고 말하지만, 허드에 따르면 이 사례는 불충분하다. 왜냐하면 궁극적으로 라즈가 설명해야 할 바는 (일차적) 근거의 저울질을 토대로 결정한 바에 어긋나는 행위를 요구하는 법을 따르는 것이 언뜻 불합리해 보이지만 실은 그렇지 않다는 것인데, 이 점을 보이기 위해 약속의 경우를 예로 든다는 것은 동일한 논란('약속을 지키는 것이 과연 합리적인가?')에 노출되어 있는, 잘 알려진 다른 사례를 보여줄 뿐, 그러한 논란을 종식시키는 사례를 제시하는 것이 아니기 때문이다.

허드는 라즈의 논증이 안고 있는 근본적인 문제는 바로 보호적 근거의 개념 자체가 "개념적으로 비정합적(conceptually incoherent)"이라는 점이라고 주장한다. 라즈가 부적합한 사례를 제시하는 데 그칠 수밖에 없었던 이유도 바로 개념상의 문제를 안고 이론을 구성하려 했기 때문이라는 것이다. 그녀는 이러한 자신의 주장을 다음과 같이 정식화하여 제시하고 있다.

1. 만일 명령이 제공하는 배제적 근거가 명령의 내용을 이루는 행위를 하지 않을 일차적 근거에 기초한 '행위'를 금지한다면, 그것은 실질적으로(pragmatically) 그러한 (일차적) 근거의 '고려'를 금지하는 결과를 초래한다.

2. 만일 명령이 제공하는 배제적 근거가 명령의 내용을 이루는 행위를 하지 않을 (일차적) 근거의 '고려'를 실질적으로 금지하는 결과를 초래한다면, 그것은 '명령이 발하여졌다'는 사실 이외의 것으로서 당해 행위를 지지하는 (일차적) 근거의 '고려'도 실질적으로 금지하는 결과를 초래한다.

3. 그러므로 명령을 받게 되면, 수명자가 '고려'해야 할 유일한 행위 근거는 어떤 행위를 하도록 명령을 받았다는 사실뿐이다.

4. 그러나 만일 어떠한 행위가 단지 명령되었기 때문에 그것을 이행하는 것이 합리적이라면, 명령된 것이기만 하면 어떠한 행위를 하더라도 합리적인 것이 된다.

5. 달리, 어떠한 행위를 하는 것이 다른 요건에 부합할 경우에만 합리적이라고 한다면, 단순히 명령을 받았다는 사실만으로는 그 행위의 수행을 정당화할 수 없다.

6. 전제 4의 후건이 거짓이므로, 전제 4의 전건은 거짓임이 분명하다.

7. 전제 4의 전건이 거짓임이 분명하므로, 전제 5의 전건은 참임이 분명하다.

8. 만일 전제 5가 참이라면, 합리적인 사람은 어떤 행위를 할 때 그렇게 하도록 명령을 받았다는 사실 이외의 행위 근거에 따라 행동해야 한다.

9. 그러므로 배제적 근거에 기초하여 행위를 수행하는 것은 비합리적이다.

그녀는 이어 이와 같은 비판을 극복하기 위한 다양한 시도들이 라즈 자신과 그의 지지자들에 의해 이루어졌지만 모두 실패로 돌아갔음을 보이고 있다. 여기서는 이러한 내용을 자세히 소개할 수는 없기 때문에, 그 핵심적인 대목만 소개하자면 다음과 같다. 라즈 자신과 그 지지자들은 전제 4를 수정함으로써 위의 논리 흐름에서 빠져나갈 수 있기를 기대한다. 즉 전제 4에서 말하는 명령에는 어떠한 명령이든 모두 해당되는 것이 아니라, 정당성을 지닌 권위(legitimate authority)가 그의 관할 범위 내에서 (within its jurisdiction) 내린 명령만이 이에 해당된다는 것이다.

하지만 이에 대한 허드의 재반박은 매우 설득력 있어 보인다. 그녀는 다음과 같이 말한다. '그렇다면 과연 그 권위가 정당성을 지니고 있는지 그리고 그의 관할 범위 내에서 명령을 내린 것인지를 어떻게 알 수 있는가?' 즉 수명자의 입장에서 그러한 믿음에 이르기 위해서는 스스로 판단을 내릴 수 있어야 하며, 그러한 판단(고려)이 금지되지 않아야 한다고 그녀는 말한다. 그런데 이는 바로 실천적 권위의 개념 자체가 "실질적으로" 금하고 있는 바이다.

혹자는 여기서 실천적 권위는 행위만을 요구할 뿐, 어떠한 동기로 행위하는지 여부 혹은 요구된 행위에 대해 이러저러하게 생각하고 판단하는 것 자체에 대해서는 규정하는 바가 없다는 말로써 반박을 시도할 것이다. 그러나 이러한 주장은 그 문제가 이미 전제 1, 2를 구성하는 과정에서 고려되었고, '실질적으로(pragmatically)'라는 단서를 닮으로써 논의의 차원이 의미론이 아닌 화용론으로 변화하였음을 간과한 것이라고 말할 수 있다. 실제로 당사자인 라즈 자신도 단순히 실천적 권위와 이론적 권위를 구별하지 못한 초보적인 착오라는 식의 형식적인 반박에 그치는 것이 아니라, 일정 정도 타당한 비판일 수 있음을 명시적으로 인정하면서 끊임없이 새로운 표현을 써가며 반박을 시도하고 있음을 알 수 있다.

그럼에도 불구하고 정치와 법의 영역에서 권위 개념이 문제된다면 그것은 실천적 권위로서 그러할 것이라고 생각된다. 설령 실천적 권위 개념이 합리성의 개념과 양립불가능하다고 하더라도 이 점이 '권위'라는 말이 가리키는 바가 무엇인지를 감수하는 태도를 바꿔야 한다는 결론으로 이어지지는 않는다. (물론 권위 개념을 구성해내는 방식을 달리 할 수는 있을 것이다.) 합리성의 관점에서 권위 개념이 정당화되거나 되지 않거나가 문제되고 있는 상황에서, 정당화가 되지 않는다고 하여 그 개념을 굽히는 것은 딜레마의 한 쪽 뿔을 임의로 자르는 것과 같기 때문이다.

5. 이제 권위 개념을 실천적 권위로 이해하는 입장을 전제로 하여, 이하에서는 권위 개념을 구성해내는 다양한 방식들에 대해 검토해보고자 한다. 학설들은 (정당성 있는) 권위 개념을 다양한 기초적 관념으로 환원시켜 이해하고 있다. 그 중 가장 친숙하게 제시되고 있는 것이 바로 정당화된 힘, 지배할 권리 그리고 규범적 권능이라는 관념이다. 이들 관념에 관하여 순차적으로 살펴보자.

첫째, 정당화된 힘. 맥브라이드는 권위가 '강제할 수 있는 능력 내지 힘을 보유하고 행사함'을 뜻할 뿐이라고 한다. 그에 의하면 권위와 단순한 강제의 개념적 차이는 다만 사람들이 그러한 강제를 사회적으로 수용하고 있느냐에 달려 있다고 한다. 홉스와 오스틴도 종종 이러한 견해를 취하고 있는 것으로 여겨진다. 주의할 점은 홉스에 대해서는 평가가 일치하지 않는다는 점이다. 래든슨은 하트가 홉스와 오스틴의 주권 개념을 단지 "신뢰할 만한 위협으로 뒷받침되는 명령을 발할 수 있는 지위에 있음"을 의미하는 것으로 평가하고 있으며, 이러한 하트의 지적은 오스틴에 대해서는 옳지만 홉스에 대해서는 옳지 않다고 주장한다. 그에 따르면 홉스는 권력(힘)과 권위의 개념을 구분하고 있다.

홉스의 견해가 정확히 무엇이었는지를 밝히는 것은 이 글의 과제가 아니다. 이 글은 다만 (정당성 있는) 권위를 정당화된 힘 또는 영향력으로 이해하는 견해에 대한 평가에 일차적인 관심을 두고 있기 때문이다. 이러한 견해는 첫째, 정당화된 권위와 정당화된 힘을 구분하지 못하고 있다는 비판을 받고 있다. 라즈는 "정당하게 힘을 사용하는 것과 권위를 갖는 것은 별개의 문제"이며, "사실상의(de facto) 권위를 보유하기 위해서는 힘(또는 영향력) 이상의 무엇이 필요하다"고 말한다. 그 '무엇'이 무엇을 의미하는지에 대해 학자들은 "권위의 상대방은 이에 순응해야 한다고 하는 호소" 또는 "두려움이 아닌 존경에의 호소" 또는 (단순한) "위협을 넘어선 (규범적) 요구" 등의 설명을 덧붙이고 있다. 둘째, 설혹 사실상의 권위는 결국 힘과 동일한 것이라 할지라도, (정당성 있는) 권위를 정당화된 힘으로 보는 견해는 "주객이 전도된 견해"라는 비판에 노출되어 있다. 라즈에 의하면 정당성 있는 권위는 정당화된 사실상의 권위로 정의될 수 없는데, 그것은 "사실상의 권위라는 관념이 정당성 있는 권위의 관념을 전제하고 있기 때문이다."

둘째, **지배할 권리**. 권위를 일종의 권리 개념으로 파악하는 견해는 다시 권위의 상대방이 그에 상응하는 의무를 부담하는지 여부에 따라 두 가지 유형으로 나뉘는데, 이는 대체로 호펠드가 특권(privilege)과 청구권(claim)이라고 각각 명명했던 규범적 지위와 유사한 것으로 이해할 수 있을 것이다.

래튼슨은 권위와 힘의 개념을 구분하는 전제에서 통치적 권위 개념은 통치력과 **정당화권**(justification-right)이라는 두 요소로 구성된다고 주장한다. 그가 주장하는 정당화권의 개념은 권리 상대방의 의무를 전제로 하지는 않는 개념으로, 다만 (정당성 있는) 권위의 보유자의 지위를 강도의 그것으로부터 구별해 주는 정당한 이유(warrant)를 함축하고 있을 뿐이다. 그리너발트도 래든슨의 정당화권 개념을 원용하며 정치적 권위 개념과 시민들의 법준수의무를 규범적 상관 개념(correlatives)으로 파악하는 통설적 견해를 비판한다.

이에 대해 크리스티아노는 정당화권으로 파악된 권위는 정당화된 강제 개념과 크게 다를 바가 없다고 본다. 이러한 평가는 래든슨과 맥브라이드의 견해를 비교해 보면 상당히 적절한 지적임을 알 수 있다. 그들은 모두 권위가 통치력 내지 강제력의 요소와 상대방에 의한 사회적 수용(social acceptance)의 요소로 이루어진다고 보는 점에서 실질적으로 동일한 구성을 보이고 있는 것이다. 그렇다면 정당화권으로 파악된 권위 개념에 대해서는 우선 정당화된 힘으로 파악된 권위 개념의 경우와 마찬가지의 비판("주객의 전도")을 가할 수 있을 것이다.

한편 시몬즈는 정당화권의 개념이 정당성 있는 권위와 정치적 의무(political obligation) 사이의 연결고리를 부당하게 단절시키고 있다고 비판한다. 시몬즈에 의하면 그리너발트의 논증은 정치적 의무와 국가의 정당화(justification) 간의 상관성을 부정한 것일 뿐, 정치적 의무와 국가의 정당성(legitimacy) 간의 상관성을 부정하지는 못하고 있다. 시몬즈는 (정당성 있는) 권위가 보유하게 되는 권리를 정당화권과 구별하여 특히 **정당성의 권리**(legitimacy right)라 명명한다. 시몬즈에 의하면 국가의 정당성은 시민들에게 의무를 부과하고 이를 강제할 수 있는 힘뿐만 아니라 시민들의 정치적 의무에 상응하는 복종 받을 권리(right to be obeyed) 또한 포함하는 것이라고 한다. 이 견해에 따르면 권위는 파인버그가 청구권(claim-right)이라고 불렀던 유형의 권리 개념에 속하는 것이 된다. 권위를 명령권(right to command)이라 부르고 있는 볼프도 상대방의 복종 의무를 전제로 하는 청구권의 일종으로 권위 개념을 이해하고 있다. 한편

에드먼슨의 견해도 세부적으로는 이러한 견해들과 차이가 있지만 근본적으로 동일한 학설 구조를 나타낸다고 볼 수 있다. 에드먼슨은 정당성 있는 권위가 갖는 권리를 **집행적 우선권**(administrative prerogatives)이라 보고, 이에 대한 상관 개념은 '법준수의무'가 아니라 '(선의의) 법집행을 방해하지 않을 의무(duty not to interfere with administration of the laws)'로 보고 있다.

라즈는 권위를 일종의 청구권으로 이해하는 개념은 부정확하고 명료하지 못하다며 비판한다. 즉 첫째, 권위는 단지 지배할 권리 내지 복종받을 권리가 아니라, "입법, 허가, 유권적 조언, 사법 판단 등을 할 수 있는 권리로 볼 수 있는" 어떤 것이라는 점에서 부정확하며 둘째, "권리 개념이 권위 개념보다 더 복잡하고 미심쩍은" 것이라는 점에서 명료하지 못하다고 한다.

셋째, (의무를 부과할 수 있는) **규범적 권능**. 라즈는 권리 개념을 통한 권위의 이해가 갖는 문제점들을 피하기 위해 규범적 권능의 개념을 끌어들인다. 앞에서 살펴보았듯이 그는 규범적 권능을 그가 보호된 근거라고 부르는 특수한 유형의 행위 근거를 변경시킬 수 있는 능력으로 정의한다. 요컨대 라즈가 주장하는 규범적 권능으로 설정된 권위 개념은 (규범적) "구속력" 내지 "유효하고 구속력 있는 지시를 발할 수 있는 권능"을 의미하는 것으로, 권위의 상대방은 그러한 지시에 복종해야만 하는 것으로 이해된다.

여기서 라즈의 규범적 권능 개념은 호펠드의 권능(power) 개념과 같지 않다는 점에 주목할 필요가 있다. 권능의 상관 개념을 의무(duty)가 아니라 책임(liability)으로 보는 호펠드와 달리, 라즈는 청구권뿐 아니라 권능도 궁극적으로 의무 개념을 통해 정의될 수 있다고 본다. 이는 권위의 행사라는 현상이 단순한 힘의 사용을 넘어 "순응에의 호소" 또는 "복종 의무에의 의탁"을 내포하는 것으로 보는 그의 입장을 통해서도 추측할 수 있는 바이다. 권위 개념을 설명함에 있어 의무 개념과 무관한 권능 개념을 채택하고 있는 사르토리우스의 견해를 라즈가 비판하는 취지도 여기에 있다. 결국 (정당성 있는) 권위의 규범적 권능이란 상대방에게 의무를 부과할 수 있는 능력을 의미한다고 볼 수 있다.

그러나 라즈의 견해 또한 심각한 비판에 직면해 있다. 예컨대, 이미 언급한 바와 같이 라즈는 규범적 권능을 정의함에 있어 보호된 근거의 개념을 사용하고 있지만, 보호된 근거의 개념이 (라즈의 바람과는 달리) 합리성의 개념과 양립할 수 없기 때문에 (정당성 있는) 권위 개념을 설명하는 데 원용할 수 없다는 취지의 비판이 있다(허드).

6. 위에서 살펴 본 세 가지 관념들 중 어느 것을 취하든지 간에, 학자들은 모두 다음과 같은 한 가지 인식을 공유하고 있다. 즉 권위는 일정한 종류의 행위를 할 수 있는 (규범적 또는 실증적) 능력(ability or capacity)이라는 인식이 바로 그것이다. 이제 이렇듯 능력에 기초한 권위 개념을 **'포지셔널 오쏘리티**(positional authority)'라고 부르기로 하자.

한 가지 주의할 점은 포지셔널 오쏘리티가 피터스나 프리드먼의 **직무상 권위**[being in authority] 개념을 의미하지는 않는다는 점이다. 피터스와 프리드먼은 베버의 연장선상에서 직무상 권위 개념과 **인격적 권위**[being an authority] 개념을 대비시키며, 전자의 경우는 권위를 갖는 사람보다 권위의(혹은 권위의 승인에 대한 규칙의) 체계가 논리적으로 우선한 반면, 후자의 경우는 그 반대라고 한다. 즉 피터스와 프리드먼이 말하는 직무상 권위 개념은 공적 직위(official position)를 점하는 사람에게 권위를 인정함을 의미하는 것이다.

그렇지만 이 글에서 포지셔널(positional)이라는 말은 이와는 다른 의미로 사용되고 있다. 예컨대 어떤 사람이 다른 사람과의 관계에서 일정한 규범관계 상의 위치를 점하고, 그 다른 사람의 규범관계 상의 위치가 이에 상응할 때, 그리고 문제의 규범관계가 특히 권위관계(authority relationship)일 때, 관계 내의 두 위치 중 상대적으로 우월한 위치를 나타내는 개념이 바로 포지셔널 오쏘리티이며, 여기에는 반드시 공적 직위의 개념이 전제될 필요가 없다.

이러한 포지셔널 오쏘리티의 개념은 비단 위에서 언급한 몇몇 학자들의 인식뿐 아니라, 서구의 사고 전통에 깊이 뿌리를 내리고 있는 하나의 배경적 개념이라고 생각한다. 그리하여 '법의 권위'를 이야기할 때마다 그들은 법을 집행할 수 있는 우월한 위치의 점유자를 상기할 수밖에 없는 것이다. 다시 말해 서구의 사고 전통에 기반한 '법의 권위' 개념은 언제나 어떤 사람 내지 사람의 집단의 포지셔널 오쏘리티이며, 법 그 자체의 권위는 아닌 것이다. 요컨대 관습적으로 법을 의인화하는 와중에 대다수의 학자들은 부당하게도 포지셔널 오쏘리티를 법에 부여하였고, 그 결과 법이 사람들과의 권위관계 속에서 서로 상응하는 규범적 위치를 분점하고 있는 것으로 곡해하고 있다.

그렇다면 권위를 (주체의) 능력의 일종으로 보는 포지셔널 오쏘리티 개념을 취해야 할 이유가 있는 것일까? 달리 말해 포지셔널 오쏘리티 개념에 대한 지지 논거를 이론적으로 제시할 수 있을까? 현재까지 이러한 논거 제시를 시도하고 있는 학자는 라즈가 유일한 것 같다. 라즈는 권위를 '일정한 행위를 할 수 있는 능력(ability to perform certain actions)'으로 규정할 수 있다고 한다. 그가 제시하고 있는 논거를 압축적으로 표현하면 다음과 같다.

"권위를 주장하는 것이 어떻게 정당화될 수 있는가?"하는 질문은 (권위 논변이라고 부를 수 있는 유형의) 정당화 논변에 대해서만이 아니라 정당화되는 대상 행위에 대해서도 민감한 질문이다. 즉 이 질문은 어느 맥락에서 보면 권위 논변의 본질에 대한 질문일 수도 있지만, 다른 맥락에서 보면 그러한 논변에 어울리는 대상 행위의 본질에 대한 질문일 수도 있다. 따라서 권위의 개념은 권위 논변이 독특한 정당화 논변이라는 측면에서 얻어지는 부분도 있지만, 그와 특별히 어울리는 정당화 대상 행위가 있다는 측면에서 얻어지는 부분도 있다.

여기서 라즈는 권위가 항상 특정한 행위를 할 수 있는 능력이라는 결론을 도출한다. 즉 권위 논변에 기대어 정당화할 수 있는 대상 행위란 결국 권위의 수행 능력 범위 내의 행위이어야 하며, 아무 행위나 다 권위의 이름으로 정당화할 수는 없다는 것이다.

7. 위에서 라즈가 포지셔널 오쏘리티 즉 능력과 위치적 우월성에 터잡은 권위 개념의 근거로 제시하고 있는 논거를 상기해 보면, 그는 "권위를 주장하는 것이 어떻게 정당화될 수 있는가?"라는 질문으로부터 출발하고 있다. 이제 이 질문에 대한 답으로 라즈가 생각하는 바를 맥락적으로 제시해 보면 다음과 같다.

(S1) Ø는 다른 정당화적 개념을 주장함으로써가 아니라, 바로 **권위를 주장함으로써** 정당화된다.

(S2) 다른 행위가 아닌, 바로 **Ø가** 권위를 주장함으로써 정당화된다.

이러한 설명은 기본적으로 옳다고 볼 수 있다. 그렇지만 주의 깊게 살펴보면 여기서 라즈가 놓치고 있는 또 다른 맥락이 존재함을 알 수 있다. 즉 "권위를 주장하는 것이 어떻게 정당화될 수 있는가?"라는 질문은 정당화 논변과 정당화 대상 행위뿐 아니라 정당화 시도 주체에 대해서도 민감한 질문인 것이다. 자신의 행위를 정당화하기 위해 권위 논변에 기대고자 하는 주체는 권위 자신일 수도 있고, 일반 시민일 수도 있는 것이다. 다시 말해 권위는 예컨대 논란의 여지가 있는 자신의 사법 판단을 정당화하기 위해 사법 판단의 최종적 권위성을 내세울 수 있으며, 일반 시민도 예컨대 자신의 철거 행위를 정당화하기 위해 (철거를 인용한) 사법 판단의 권위를 주장할 수 있는 것이다. 따라서 최초의 질문에 대한 세 번째 답을 맥락적으로 제시할 수 있게 된다.

> (S3) Ø는 다른 사람이 아닌, 바로 **X가** (누군가의) 권위를 주장함으로써 정당화된다.

여기서 X가 권위 자신일 경우, 즉 권위가 자신이 행한 Ø를 정당화하기 위해 (자신의) 권위를 내세울 경우에는 권위를 'Ø를 행할 수 있는 능력'으로 정의할 수 있다. 그러나 X가 일반 시민일 경우, 즉 일반 시민이 자신이 행한 Ø를 정당화하기 위해 (예컨대 사법기관의) 권위를 내세울 경우에는 권위를 'Ø를 행할 수 있는 능력'으로 정의하는 것은 불가능하다.

요컨대 라즈가 놓치고 있는 맥락을 포함시켜 생각한다면 권위를 '일정한 행위를 할 수 있는 능력'으로만 규정할 수는 없는 셈이다. 따라서 포지셔널 오쏘리티의 개념을 이론적으로 근거지우려는 라즈의 시도는 불충분한 것으로서 받아들일 수 없다.

위와 같은 비판은 결코 주변적인 것으로 치부될 수 없다. 왜냐하면 이미 살펴보았듯이 (S3)는 한마디로 현대의 법치주의 국가에서 이루어지고 있는 사법 기능의 본질적 구조(즉 일반 시민이 자신의 행위를 정당화하기 위해 사법기관의 권위를 내세우는 분쟁해결 구조)를 반영하고 있기 때문이다.

따라서 우리는 적어도 위의 세 가지 맥락을 모두 반영할 수 있는 새로운 권위 개념이 필요함을 알 수 있다. 그리고 그러한 개념은 좀 더 객관적인 시각에서 권위를 '의지·존중할 만한 자질이나 속성(properties)'으로 이해할 때 얻어질 수 있는 것 같다. 속성과 객관적 임무에 적합한 자질에 터잡은 대안적 권위 개념은 첫째, 그것이 능력과 위치적 우월성에 터잡은 개념이 아니라는 점에서 둘째, (칸트의 경우에서와 같이) 경향성(inclination)이라는 말에는 없는 호감을 담아내기 위해서 **디스－포지셔널 오쏘리티**(dis-positional authority)라고 부를 수 있을 것이다. 요컨대 디스－포지셔널 오쏘리티의 개념은 '특정한 행위의 수행과 관련하여 공중의 신뢰와 존중을 누리기에 적합한 자질이나 속성'을 의미한다고 말할 수 있다.

Ⅳ.

1. 이상의 논의에서 드러난 바와 같이, 이 글은 법체계의 규범성의 기초(토대)에 관한 문제가 **"법의 권위"**라는 개념의 도입을 통해 보다 적절히 논의될 수 있다는 주장을 펴고 있다. 아울러 이 글은 권위 개념의 구성을 시도하는 기존의 다양한 방식들이 법의 권위 개념을 제대로 구성해내지 못하고 있음을 논증하고, 그에 대한 대안으로 디스－포지셔널 오쏘리티의 개념을 제안하고 있다.

그렇다면 앞으로의 논의는 과연 이 글의 제안이 얼마나 실효성이 있는지, 다시 말해 이 글의 제안을 수용할 경우 토대론적 규범체계론의 기획이 얼마나 정교해지는지를 살펴보는 것이어야 할 터이다. 따라서 이하에서는 하트가 법체계에 대한 **단순 모델**이라 지칭하며 극복하고자 한 오스틴의 환원주의적 이론의 문제점들을 놓고, 포지셔널 오쏘리티와 디스－포지셔널 오쏘리티 중 어느 개념을 취할 때 하트의 의도가 더 잘 살아나는지를 살펴보고자 한다. (오스틴과 하트는 모두 포지셔널 오쏘리티 개념을 전제하고 있다.) 구체적으로는 첫째, 오스틴의 단순 모델에 전제되어 있는 포지셔널 오쏘리티 개념을 디스－포지셔널 오쏘리티 개념으로 바꾸었을 때 하트가 지적하고 있는 문제점들에 어떤 변화가 생길 수 있는지를 살펴보고 둘째, 하트의 대안적 모델 속에서 권위 개념이 갖는 의미에 관하여 숙고해 볼 것이다.

논의의 순서상 먼저 하트가 단순 모델의 문제점으로 지적하고 있는 점들을 간단히 언급하고 넘어가자. 하트에 따르면 법체계는 다음과 같은 현저한 특징들을 지니고 있는데, 오스틴의 단순 모델은 이러한 특징들을 이론적으로 재현해낼 수 없다고 한다. 그러한 특징들로서는 첫째, 입법적 권위의 계속성 및 법의 지속성 둘째, 입법의 자기구속력 셋째, 강제적 명령의 개념으로 환원될 수 없는 **"권한수여율**(power-conferring rules)"이나 "관습법"의 존재 등을 들 수 있다. 요컨대 이러한 특징들을 이론적으로 재현해낼 수 있는지 여부가 법체계에 대한 이론적 모델들의 성공 여부를 가늠하는 기준이 될 수 있다는 것이 바로 하트의 제안이다. 이제 이들 각각의 특징에 비추어 새로운 권위 개념의 적절성 여부를 검증해 보도록 한다.

첫째, 입법적 권위의 계속성 및 법의 지속성. 이 점에 관한 하트의 단순 모델 비판 전략은 다음과 같이 정리할 수 있다.

1. 단순 모델(특히 **"복종의 습관"** 개념)은 입법적 권위의 계속성과 법의 지속성을 설명할 수 없다.
2. 그러한 특징들을 설명할 수 있으려면 **규칙**의 관념을 도입해야 한다.
3. 사회적으로 수락된 **규칙**이 현재뿐 아니라 과거, 미래의 입법자에게도 권리 내지 권위를 부여하는 것이다.

사실 켈젠도 이 문제를 다루었으나 그의 설명에는 중대한 오류가 있음이 지적되고 있다. 즉 그는 현행 헌법의 기초자들이 최초로 정립된 헌법으로부터 **수권**되고 있는 것으로 설명하고 있지만, 이러한 설명은 '어떻게 현재의 입법자가 (미처 "복종의 습관"을 얻어낼 겨를도 없이) 자신의 첫 작품으로 제정한 법도 법이 되는 것인가? 또한 어떻게 과거에 제정된 법이 현재의 사람들을 구속하는가?'라는 문제에 대한 답변이 아니라 문제 그 자체라고 할 수 있다(오노레). 반면 하트는 이 문제에 대해 입법적 권위의 계속성과 법의 지속성을 정하고 있는 규칙이 사회적으로 수락되어 있기 때문에 켈젠이 설명하고자 한 그러한 수권이 가능하다는 답변을 제시하고 있는 것이다.

이제 단순 모델에 대한 하트의 묘사를 포지셔널 오쏘리티 개념을 중심으로 재구성하면 다음과 같다.

> 1*. 단순 모델 속의 복종의 습관 개념은, 주권자와 시민들 각자 간에는 **개인 대 개인**의 관계가 있음을 전제하고 있다.
> 2*. 즉 주권자는 각 시민들과 권위관계를 이루고 있다고 판단된다.
> 3*. 시민들의 복종은 단순히 수렴되는 것으로 파악된다. (**원리적 수렴**이 아닌 **전략적 수렴**.)
> 4*. 요컨대 단순 모델에서는 주권자와 시민들 사이의 관계를 규정하는 규칙과 같은 것은 등장하지 않는다.

그런데 이와 같이 재구성된 단순 모델에서 (주권자의) 포지셔널 오쏘리티 개념을 (법의) 디스-포지셔널 오쏘리티 개념으로 바꾸면 (주권자와 시민들 사이의 관계를 규정하는) 규칙의 부재라고 하는 단순 모델의 문제점이 사라지게 된다. 이 점을 도식적으로 나타내면 다음과 같이 정리해 볼 수 있을 것이다.

1**. 시민들의 복종은 이제 개인 대 개인의 관계가 아니라 **개인 대 규칙(원리)의 관계**를 전제하게 된다.

2**. 즉 주권자의 명령에 대한 일반적인 복종은 전략적 수렴이 아니라 원리적 수렴으로 파악된다.

3**. 이 경우 규칙의 관념 내지 규칙의 내적 측면이 이미 등장하고 있다.

둘째, 입법의 자기구속력. 이 점에 관한 하트의 단순 모델 비판 전략은 다음과 같이 정리할 수 있다.

1. 단순 모델(특히 **"제재의 위협이 따르는 명령"** 개념)은 입법의 자기구속력을 설명할 수 없다.
2. 그러한 특징을 설명할 수 있으려면 **규칙**의 관념을 도입해야 한다.
3. 마치 약속자가 자신의 약속에 구속되는 것이 "약속준수의 규칙"으로 정당화되는 것과 같이, 입법자가 자신의 입법에 구속되는 것은 "일반적 법준수의 규칙"으로 정당화된다(약속과 입법의 유추).
4. 입법은 일방이 타방에 대해 발하는 명령이 아니라, (입법자를 포함한) 사회 일반이 준수해야 할 행위 기준의 도입 혹은 수정이다.

사실 법을 주권자의 명령으로 보고, 복종을 강제하기 위해 주권자는 제재의 위협이라는 수단을 사용한다고 설명하는 단순 모델 속에서, 법을 정립하는 주권자가 스스로에게 명령을 내리거나 위협을 가하는 상황은 가히 정신분열적이라고 할 수 있다. 따라서 입법자 자신은 법에 구속되는 것으로 볼 수 없다. 그렇지만 현대 국가에서 입법자가 자신이 제정한 법에 구속되는 것은 너무도 현저한 현상이다. 그리고 이러한 현상은 현대 국가의 구성원들이 지위고하를 막론하고 국가의 구성원 모두는 자국의 법을 준수해야 한다는 원리(규칙)를 승인하고 있는 점에서 그 규범적 계기를 찾아볼 수 있다는 것이 하트의 설명이다.

다시 단순 모델에 대한 하트의 묘사를 포지셔널 오쏘리티 개념을 중심으로 재구성해 보자.

> 1*. 단순 모델 속의 주권자는 시민들에게 명령을 발하고 그에 대한 복
>   종을 제재의 위협이라는 수단으로 강제할 수 있는 **탁월한 지위**를
>   점하고 있다.
> 2*. 따라서 법은 주권자가 시민들에게 발하는 (제재의 위협에 의해 뒷
>   받침되는) 명령으로 정의된다(명령설).
> 3*. 요컨대 단순 모델에서는 주권자도 자신이 제정한 법에 구속되도록
>   하는 **규범적 계기**는 발견되지 않는다. 다만 사실상 주권자 자신이
>   법을 어기지 않음으로써 단순히 시민들의 복종과 수렴될 수 있을
>   뿐이다.

그런데 앞에서와 마찬가지로 재구성된 단순 모델에서 (주권자의) 포지
셔널 오소리티 개념을 (법의) 디스－포지셔널 오소리티 개념으로 바꾸게
되면, 다시 말해서 입법적 권위의 탁월함 대신에 '공중의 신뢰와 존중을
누리기에 적합한' 규범적 계기를 고려하게 되면 단순 모델의 문제점은 사
라지게 된다. 이 점 역시 도식적으로 나타내면 다음과 같이 정리해 볼 수
있을 것이다.

> 1**. 제재의 위협 때문이 아니라 준수할 만한 가치가 있기 때문에 지지
>   되는 "일반적 법준수의 규칙"이 사회적으로 승인되어 있다.
> 2**. 이제 법은 **사회적으로 수락된 행위의 기준**으로 정의된다.
> 3**. 이 경우 규칙의 관념 내지 규칙의 내적 측면이 이미 등장하고 있다.

　　셋째, 권한수여율 및 관습법의 존재. 하트는 오스틴의 단순 모델이 법
을 "주권자가 시민에게 발하는 (제재의 위협에 의해 뒷받침되는) 명령"으
로 정의함으로써 그러한 강제적 명령의 개념으로 환원될 수 없는 권한수
여율이나 관습법 등도 법이 되는 이유를 설명하지 못하게 됨을 비판한다.

사실 이같은 비판에 대해서는 새삼 설명을 덧붙일 필요조차 없을 것이다. 따라서 여기서는 이와 관련하여 보다 중요하지만 자주 간과되었던 문제 한 가지를 제기하고자 한다.

위에서 살펴본 바와 같이 단순 모델의 문제점들 속에는 포지셔널 오쏘리티 개념이 내재해 있고, 하트의 대안적 모델의 설명력과 궤를 같이하는 것은 디스-포지셔널 오쏘리티 개념임에도 불구하고 정작 하트 자신은 포지셔널 오쏘리티 개념을 취하고 있다. (이 점은 켈젠도 마찬가지이다.) 그렇다면 순전히 이론적 정합성이라는 측면에서 오스틴, 켈젠 그리고 하트를 평가한다면 어떨지가 사뭇 궁금해진다.

먼저 오스틴(그리고 벤담)의 법이론에 대해서 평가한다면, 그의 이론은 이미 지적된 여러 가지 단점들에도 불구하고 다음의 세 가지 이론적 요소들이 매우 정합적으로 결합되어 있다고 말할 수 있을 것 같다.

> (1) 법의 개념에 관한 명령설
> (2) 법체계에 대한 (환원주의적) 단순 모델
> (3) 포지셔널 오쏘리티 개념

그런데 켈젠과 하트의 경우는 위 세 가지 요소들 중의 일부만을 선택적으로 취하고 있는 것으로 보인다. 우선 켈젠의 경우에는 (1)과 (3)은 수용하고 있지만, (2)는 거부하고 있으며, 하트는 (3)만을 수용하고 (1)과 (2)는 거부하고 있는 모습이다. 하지만 위에서 살펴보았듯이 최소한 (1)과 (3)은 분석적으로 상호의존적인 성격이 매우 강하다. 따라서 하트와 같이 둘 중 어느 하나만 수용하는 것은 그다지 합당한 태도는 아닌 듯싶다. 켈젠의 경우는 이들 양자를 다 수용하고 있다는 점에서는 옳지만, 다같이 중대한 한계를 안고 있는 (1)과 (2) 중에서 하나는 계속 고수하고 다른 하나는 거부하고 있어 문제가 된다. 요컨대 켈젠과 하트의 경우 최소한 이론적 정합성의 측면에서는 오스틴이나 벤담의 경우보다 나을 것이 없지 않는가 하는 생각이다.

나아가 하트가 진정 (1) 즉 법의 개념에 관한 명령설을 거부하고 있는 것인지에 대해서도 의문의 여지가 있다. 하트는 먼저 사령(command)이라는 관념에 내장되어 있는 어떤 요소가 **"권위적 근거**(authoritative reason)"라는 관념을 낳는다고 말한다. 여기서 권위적 근거라는 것은 **내용독립적**(contend-independent)이고 **확정적인**(peremptory) 행위 근거를 의미하는데, 그는 법이 이처럼 특수한 행위 근거의 성격을 갖는다는 점을 강조하고 있다. 그런데 여기에 하트가 덧붙이고 있는 다음과 같은 말에 주목할 필요가 있다. "법의 특징들을 분석하는 데 사령이라는 관념을 도입하게 되면 필연적으로 벤담의 명령설(imperative theory)을 포기하게 된다." 그렇다면 하트는 벤담의 명령설이 사령이라는 관념에 제대로 기초한 법이론이 아니기 때문에 받아들일 수 없다고 말하고 있는 듯하다. 게다가 **법의 개념**(*The Concept of Law*)에서 하트가 오스틴의 환원주의를 비판하는 논거 중의 하나는 오스틴이 규범적 개념인 사령과 순전히 사실적 개념인 명령(order)의 차이를 간과하지 못함으로써 종종 '사령'이라는 말을 단순한 '명령'의 의미로 사용하고 있다는 일상언어분석적 고찰이었다. 따라서 이 모든 점들을 고려해 보면 하트가 명령설을 전적으로 거부하고 있는 것이 아니라, 오히려 제대로 된 명령설을 고대하고 있는 것이라는 해석이 가능할 듯하다. 이는 곧 하트도 켈젠과 마찬가지로 (1)과 (3)을 수용하고 있는 것으로 이해될 수 있음을 의미한다. (참고로 하트는 자신이 명령설을 'imperative theory'라고 부르는 이유에 대하여, '사령(command)'과 '명령(order)'을 아우를 수 있는 중립적 개념이 필요하기 때문이라고 밝힌 바 있다. 따라서 사령의 개념을 전제로 하는 것은 진정한 명령설이 아니라고 간단히 반박하려는 시도는 적절치 못하다.)

2. 이로써 이 글의 전체적인 테마, 즉 법의 권위 개념이 법체계의 규범성의 기초(토대)에 관한 문제 해명에 기여할 수 있다는 주장의 타당성을 확인해 볼 수 있었다. 이제 부수적인 문제 한 가지만 더 논의한 뒤 글을 마무리하고자 한다. 그것은 (법의) 권위에 관한 분석이 법체계의 규범성의 기초(토대) 문제를 해명하는 데 기여하는 외에 어떤 (전통적인) 법철학적 문제들의 논의에 적용될 수 있을 것인지에 관한 문제이다. 이 문제를 검토하고자 하는 이유는 바로 이 문제가 현재 주장되고 있는 (법의) 권위에 관한 교설들이 미묘한 입장차를 드러내는 지점이기 때문이다. 다시 말해서 현재 주장되고 있는 (법의) 권위에 관한 교설들은 그 이론적 함의의 폭을 기준으로 약한(thin) 이론과 강한(thick) 이론으로 나누어 볼 수 있다. 전자는 권위에 관한 분석으로부터 "법의 개념" 내지 "법과 도덕의 관계"와 같은 전통적인 법철학적 주제들에 대한 함의를 이끌어 내려 하지는 않는 반면, 후자는 그러한 함의 도출이 가능하다고 본다.

강한 이론을 제시하고 있는 대표적인 학자인 라즈는 권위에 관한 분석으로부터 특히 법의 본질(nature of law)에 관한 특정 견해(구체적으로는 자신의 견해인 배제적 법실증주의)를 지지하는 결론을 이끌어 내고 있다. 다시 말해서 그는 권위 교설로부터 법의 본질에 관한 유익한 시사를 얻을 수 있을 뿐만 아니라, 그렇게 얻어진 법의 본질에 관한 내용을 보다 정확하게 파악할 수 있는 법이론적 명제는 자신의 원천 테제(sources thesis)이지, 드워킨의 정합성 테제(coherence thesis)나 하트의 포용 테제(incorporation thesis)가 아니라고 강조한다. 이하에서는 라즈의 이러한 논변을 중심으로 법의 권위 개념이 불러일으킬 수 있는 이론적 반향의 폭이 어느 정도일지를 가늠해 보고자 한다.

결론을 먼저 이야기하자면, 라즈의 논증에는 오류가 있는 것으로 보인다. 따라서 권위의 개념은 단지 법체계의 규범성의 기초(토대)를 해명하고, 일련의 규칙들의 집합을 하나의 체계로 볼 수 있도록 구성하는 데 기여할 뿐, 법의 본질에 관한 특정 견해를 직접적으로 지지하는 관계에 있지는 않는 것 같다(약한 이론). 이제 권위 개념과 법의 본질 간의 관계에 대한 라즈의 논증을 검토함으로써, 이와 같이 결론 내리게 된 이유를 살펴보도록 보자. 먼저 라즈의 관련 논변을 요약해 보면 다음과 같다.

(1) 비록 법체계가 정당성 있는 권위를 갖지 못할지라도, 또는 정당성 있는 권위를 가지기는 하지만 그가 주장하는 것만큼 광범위한 것이 아닐지라도, 모든 법체계는 필요적으로(necessarily) 자신이 정당성 있는 권위를 갖는다고 주장한다.

(2) 만일 권위에 대한 주장이 법의 본질의 일부라면, 법이 다른 무엇이라 정의되건 간에 그것은 (정당성 있는) 권위를 가질 능력이 있어야만 한다[권위를 가질 능력이 있음이 분명하다].

(3) 권위를 가질 수 있는 주체라면 다음의 두 가지 특성을 가져야만 한다[가질 게 분명하다]. ① 그것은 그를 따르는 자들이 행해야 할 바에 관한 누군가의 견해이어야 하거나 혹은 그러한 견해로서 제시되어야 한다. ② 그것은 권위가 반영해야 하는 고려사항들과는 독립적인 수단을 통해 확인 가능해야 한다.

(4) 이러한 두 가지 특성은 정합성 테제나 포용 테제가 아니라 원천 테제를 지지한다.

힘마의 지적에 따르면, 많은 학자들은 전제 (1)(권위 테제), 즉 법이 필요적으로 정당성 있는 권위를 주장한다는 라즈의 견해를 논박함으로써 라즈의 논증을 무력화시키고자 한다. 하지만 극히 비일상적인 관념적 반례를 만들어냄으로써 수행되고 있는 이러한 시도들이 만족스러운지에 대해서는 의문이 있다. 따라서 이하에서는 그와 같은 선행 시도들과는 조금 다른 각도에서 라즈의 논증을 검토해보고자 한다. 단도직입적으로 말해서, 필자의 견해는 전제 (1)이 아니라 전제 (2)를 문제 삼는 것이다. 전제

(2)에서 아무런 문제도 발견할 수 없다는 사람들은 부지불식간에 한 가지 억측, 즉 '어떠한 것도 자신이 가지지 못할 것을 본질적으로 추구하도록 만들어지지는 않았다'는 형이상학을 전제하고 있다. 그러나 만일 아무런 문제가 없도록 하려면 전제 (2)는 다음과 같이 수정되어야 할 것이다.

> (2)* 만일 권위에 대한 주장이 법의 본질의 일부라면, 법이 다른 무엇이라 정의되건 간에 그것은 (정당성 있는) 권위를 **주장할** 능력이 있어야만 한다[권위를 **주장할** 능력이 있음이 분명하다].

전제 (2)를 검토한 결과 그것이 성립하지 않는다고 밝혀질 경우, '법은 권위를 주장한다'는 언명은 단순히 '법이 사실상 그런 주장을 한다'는 **현상**에 대한 언명에 지나지 않게 되고, 따라서 라즈의 권위 교설은 법의 **개념** 내지 **본질**에 대한 이론과 단절되게 될 것이다.

이제 본격적으로 라즈의 논증을 검토하기에 앞서, 논의의 편의를 위해 라즈의 전제 (1), (2)만을 따로 다시 한 번 적어보자.

> (1) 비록 법체계가 정당성 있는 권위를 갖지 못할지라도, 또는 정당성 있는 권위를 가지기는 하지만 그가 주장하는 것만큼 광범위한 것이 아닐지라도, 모든 법체계는 필요적으로(necessarily) 자신이 정당성 있는 권위를 갖는다고 주장한다.
> (2) 만일 권위에 대한 주장이 법의 본질의 일부라면, 법이 다른 무엇이라 정의되건 간에 그것은 (정당성 있는) 권위를 가질 능력이 있어야만 한다[권위를 가질 능력이 있음이 분명하다].

여기서 전제 (2)는 참인가? 그는 마치 전제 (1)로부터 전제 (2)가 도출되는 것처럼 말하고 있다. 그리고 에드먼슨과 마찬가지로, 법이 주장하고 있는 권위를 실제로는 갖고 있지 않은 경우 즉 권위 주장의 진리값이 거짓인 경우에도 문제될 것은 없다는 입장을 취하고 있다. 그러나 만일 전제 (1)이 옳다고 하더라도 그로부터 논쟁의 여지없이 도출할 수 있는 최소치라고 생각되는 '법의 권위 주장은 그 진리값이 거짓일 수 있다'는 언명에 먼저 주목해 보자. 이 언명을 구체적으로 다시 표현하자면 '모든 법은 권위를 보유하고 있다는 취지의 진술을 하며, 그 진술은 사실에 반하는 것일 수도 있다' 정도가 될 것이다. 문제는 거짓 진술이 되는 경우에 당해 진술에서 정확히 어떤 부분이 사실에 반하기 때문에 거짓 진술이 되고 있는가 하는 점이다. 이를 다음과 같은 예를 중심으로 생각해 보자.

첫째, 어떤 사람 X는 사실 어떤 일 a를 할 수 있는 능력도 없고, 실제로도 하지 않았음에도 불구하고 "나는 a를 했다"고 진술하였다. 둘째, 동일한 사람인 X는 이제 단순히 "나는 a를 할 수 있다"고 진술하였다. 물론 두 진술 모두 거짓인 진술이다. 그러나 양자는 그들의 내적 구조가 상이하다. 두 번째 진술의 경우 X는 오로지 자신의 속성에 대해서만 사실에 반하는 진술을 한 것이고, 첫 번째 진술의 경우 그는 자신의 속성에 대해서뿐만 아니라 자신의 경험에 대해서도 사실에 반하는 진술을 한 것이다. 다시 말해서, 첫 번째 진술에서 X는 능력(속성)과 실천(경험)이 복합적으로 작용하여 나타나는 결과물이라고 할 수 있는 업적 혹은 성취 전체에 대해 사실에 반하는 진술을 한 것이다. 셋째, 다른 사람 Y는 사실 어떤 일 a를 할 수 있는 능력은 있었지만, 실제로는 그 일을 하지 않았음에도 불구하고 "나는 a를 했다"고 진술하였다. 이 경우 Y는 자신의 속성에 대해서는 사실에 반하는 진술을 한 것이 아니며 다만 자신의 경험적 실천에 대해서만 사실에 반하는 진술을 한 것이다. 이상으로부터 다음과 같은 일반화에 이를 수 있다. 누군가가 사실에 반하여 자신의 업적(성취)에 대한 진술을 하는 경우에는, 단순히 자신의 경험(실천)이 사실에 반하는 것이거나[셋째 경우] 아니면 경험(실천)과 속성(능력) 모두에 있어서 사실에 반하는 것일 수 있다[첫째 경우].

이제 라즈의 전제 (2)로 돌아가 보자. 전제 (2)를 전제 (1)에 결합하면 라즈는 "비록 법이 자신의 주장과 달리 실제로는 정당성 있는 권위를 갖지 못하는 경우에도" 혹은 바꾸어 말해서 "비록 법이 사실에 반하여 자신이 정당성 있는 권위를 갖고 있다고 주장하는 경우에도" 언제나 "법은 (정당성 있는) 권위를 가질 능력이 있어야만 한다[권위를 가질 능력이 있음이 분명하다]"고 말하고 있는 것이다. 즉 라즈에 따르면, 법이 사실에 반하여 자신이 "정당성 있는 권위를 갖고 있다"고 진술하는 경우에, 법은 언제나 자신의 경험(실천)에 대해서만 사실에 반하는 진술을 하고 있을 뿐이다. 요컨대 라즈는 법이 자신의 경험(실천)에 대해서뿐만 아니라 자신의 속성(능력)에 대해서도 사실에 반하는 진술을 할 가능성은 배제시키고 있다.

그렇다면 라즈는 단순한 실수를 범하고 있는 것일까? 그렇지는 않다. 반대로 그는 이 문제를 정확히 예견하고 있던 것 같다. 그는 권위 보유의 주장과 권위 귀속을 위한 자질이 전혀 무관할 수는 없겠는가 하고 스스로 질문을 던진다. 그리고 몇 가지 예들을 검토하는 일련의 논변을 통하여 법이 자신의 속성(능력)에 대해 사실에 반하는 진술을 할 가능성은 전혀 없다는 취지로 자답하고 있다.

> "하지만 어떤 사람 X가 이치상 그에게로는 권위를 귀속시킬 수 없음에도 불구하고 누군가가 X가 그 권위를 보유하고 있다고 주장하는 것일 수는 없는가? … (중략) … 이상의 논의로부터 법이 권위를 갖는다고 주장하기 때문에 법은 권위를 가질 능력이 있다는 점은 충분히 증명된다."

라즈가 자칭 '충분한 증명'으로서 제시한 예들은 법과 달리 ① 규범적 체계성과 ② 사람들과의 (직간접적) 의사소통 가능성을 구비하지 못한 '화산 활동에 관한 명제들의 집합'이라든가 '나무들'로서 이들이 권위를 보유하고 있다고는 누구도 진지하게 주장할 수 없는 경우이다. 그의 취지는 이런 예들과 대조적으로 법이 권위를 보유하고 있다는 주장은, 비록 사실에 반할 수는 있어도, 최소한 말은 되지 않느냐는 것이다. 그리고 이러한 차이를 보임으로써 법이 권위를 보유할 능력이 없을 가능성은 없다는 점(전제 (2))을 충분히 입증한 셈이라는 것이다.

　그러나 라즈의 소위 증명은 충분하지도 않고 적절하지도 않아 보인다. 라즈는 대조의 대상을 부적절하게 선정함으로써 그 대조 자체가 아무런 의미를 갖지 못하고 있다. 그가 했어야 하는 일은 정당성 있는(legitimate) 권위를 가질 가능성이 있는 것(eg. 법)과 어떠한 권위도, 즉 사실상의(de facto) 권위조차 가질 가능성이 없는 것(eg. 나무들)을 무의미하게 대조하는 것이 아니라 ─ 왜냐하면 그 둘간의 분별이 문제될 일 자체가 없을 것이므로 ─ 정당성 있는 권위를 가질 가능성이 있는 두 후보 즉 거짓 진술을 하는 것인지도 모르는 사람과 거짓 진술을 하는 것인지도 모르는 법을 대조하는 것이다. (왜냐하면 라즈가 전자의 경우에는 자신의 경험(실천)에 대해서뿐만 아니라 자신의 속성(능력)에 대해서도 사실에 반하는 진술을 할 가능성이 있는데, 후자의 경우에는 그러한 가능성이 없다고 주장하고 있기 때문이다. 왜 이러한 차이가 있는 것인가를 그는 보여야 했다.) 우리가 피해야만 하는 것은 명백히 부적절한 대상(eg. 나무들)에 권위를 귀속시키는 '터무니없는' 오류가 아니라 세심한 자격 심사 없이 권위에 정당성을 인정하는 '충분히 가능한' 오류이기 때문이다. 사실에 반하는 진술이 정교할수록 그 진술이 참인 것으로 잘못 받아들여질 가능성이 높아지듯이, 법의 이름으로 행해지는 불법일수록 그 실체적 악에 대한 인간의 감수성은 떨어지게 된다는 점을 상기할 필요가 있다.

　그러나 아직까지도 라즈가 단순한 실수를 범하고 있는 것이라고 결론지을 수는 없다. 다만 필자가 이제 '본질 테제(nature thesis)'라고 부르려하는 (논쟁적) 가정을 그가 전제하고 있는 것이 아니라야만, 비로소 그가 실수를 범하고 있다고 말할 수 있다. 왜냐하면 그는 전제 (2)에서 "만일 권위에 대한 주장이 법의 본질(nature)의 일부라면…"이라는 단서를 닮으로써 전제 (2)를 위에 소개한 거짓 진술 사례에 등장하는 단순한 상황들과 다소 상이하게 만들고 있기 때문이다. 소위 '라즈의' 본질 테제는 다음과 같이 정식화할 수 있을 것이다.

> NT: 만일 어떤 일 a의 성취를 주장하는 것이 – 그것이 사실이건 사실이 아니건 – X의 본질의 일부라면, X는 자신의 속성(능력)에 대해서가 아니라 경험(실천)에 대해서만 사실에 반하는 진술을 할 수 있다.

확실히 이 가정은 추가적인 정당화를 필요로 하는 것 같다. 그리고 비록 라즈가 정말로 이 가정을 전제하고 있는 것인지는 알 수 없지만, 어느 경우이든지 라즈가 그 자신의 논증을 지지할 충분한 근거를 제시하는 데 실패하고 있다고 말할 수는 있는 것 같다. 만일 라즈가 NT를 전제하지 않고 있다면, 그가 단순한 실수를 범하고 있는 것이고(이는 거짓 진술 사례를 통해 입증된다), 만일 그가 NT를 전제하고 있다면, 그는 '본질'의 의미에 대한 '형이상학적'(달리 말하여 '정당화 되지 않은') 가설에 의존하는 셈이기 때문이다. 따라서 앞서 언급한 바와 같이 그의 권위 교설은 법의 본질론과 단절되고, 원천 테제와 정합성 테제 및 포용 테제간의 치열한 경합은 아직 승부가 나지 않은 것으로 보인다.

V.

이상의 논의를 요약해 보자. 학자들은 법준수의무(obligation to obey

the law)의 문제를 법의 규범성(normativity) 문제 혹은 국가의 권위(authority) 문제로서 다루어 왔다. 그들은 이 두 문제를 각각 따로 논하였으며, 양자간의 관계에 대해서는 비교적 최근까지도 크게 관심을 기울이지 않았다. 그러나 법은 그것의 '이른바' 권위적인 성질(authoritativeness)로 특징지을 수 있다고 보는 것이 전통적인 인식이라는 점에서, 권위의 개념은 법의 규범성 문제와 긴밀하게 연관되어 있음을 알 수 있다.

학자들은 종종 법의 규범적 기초(토대 foundations)가 객관적이어야 하며, 그 객관성 내지 중립성은 합의가능성에 의해 보장된다고 하는 견해를 취한다. 그러나 인간의 존재론적 한계로 말미암아 모종의 권위를 확립시키는 것 또한 불가피한데, 그 경우 권위와 합의의 요청은 서로 충돌할 수도 있다. 그렇다면, 법의 규범성 문제를 해명하기 위해서는 그 합의가능성뿐만 아니라 권위도 함께 고려되어야 할 것이다.

법의 규범성의 근거를 밝히고자 했던 시도들 중 가장 주목할 만한 것은 한스 켈젠과 허버트 하트에 의해 이루어졌다. 켈젠은 법의 규범성의 기초(토대)를 논리적 의제(logical fiction)를 통해 설명하고자 했고, 하트는 이를 하나의 사실(fact)로 보고자 했다. 두 사람은 모두 궁극적 규칙(ultimate rule)과 체계상 효력(systemic validity) 개념을 법의 규범성을 설명하는 데 필수적인 것으로 여겼다. 그들에 따르면, 궁극적 규칙은 법체계를 구성하는 모든 규칙들 중 그 자신만을 제외한 나머지 전부의 효력에 관한 '최종적 근거' 내지 '최고의 준거를 제공하는 원천'이라고 정의된다. 이러한 궁극적 규칙은 체계상 효력 개념과 더불어 켈젠과 하트의 법의 규범성 이론에서 중심적인 역할을 담당한다.

그러나 켈젠과 하트의 주목할 만한 시도들도 여러 가지 이유에서 다른 시도들과 마찬가지로 한계를 안고 있다고 평가할 수 있다. 그러한 한계가 뚜렷해지는 대목으로는 가령 첫째, 궁극적 규칙 자체도 효력을 갖는지 여부가 여전히 불분명하다. 둘째, 유효한 규칙이 유효한 다른 규칙 혹은 심지어 상위의 규칙과도 충돌할 수 있다. 셋째, 규범의 효력 득실에 관한 동태적 기준(a dynamic principle of "norm validation")에 관하여 본다면, 이는 다른 규범 나아가 상위규범에 반하는 규범과 통상의 여느 규범들의 차이를 인식하지 못한다. 따라서 규칙의 중립성과 의무부과성(obligatoriness) 중 어느 하나도 궁극적 규칙과 체계상 효력 개념으로 파악할 수 없다. 사실 위와 같은 문제점들은 법체계의 개념 자체를 위태롭게 한다.

자연법론자들은 규범의 효력 득실에 관한 정태적 기준(a static principle of "norm validation") 및 나아가 도덕적 효력(axiological validity) 개념을 취함으로써 그러한 문제점들을 해소하고 있다. 그러나 켈젠과 하트가 자연법론자들에 의해 제시되고 있는 이러한 해법을 받아들인다면, 스스로 모순을 범하는 셈이 된다. 결국 그들이 정태적 규범 유효화 원리 혹은 도덕적 효력에 의하지 않고서 그러한 문제점들을 해소하고, 법적 규칙들에 중립적 의무부과력을 부여코자 한다면, 반드시 법의 권위라는 개념에 호소해야만 한다.

이 해법은 다음과 같이 요약 정리해 볼 수 있다.

(1) 만일 어떤 규범이 법적으로 유효하고, 동시에 그 내용이 동일한 법체계에 속한 다른 유효한 규범의 내용과 양립가능하다면, 그 규범은 사람들의 행동을 지도할 수 있는 권위를 갖는다.

(2) 어떠한 규범이 사람들의 행동을 지도할 수 있는 권위를 갖는다고 해서, 그것이 법적으로 유효하다고 말할 수는 없다.

(3) 규범은 일정한 법적 규범들의 체계에 속할 경우에 법적으로 유효하지만, 당해 법체계의 적용을 받는 사람들이 실천적 추론(practical reasoning)의 과정에서 그것을 존중해야만 할 때 권위를 갖는다.

(4) 법체계의 규범적 기초(토대)는 궁극적 규칙의 효력이 아니라 그것의 권위에 달려 있다.

여기서 반드시 검토되어야 할 점은 바로 권위의 개념이라고 할 수 있다. 왜냐하면 권위는 전통적으로 어떠한 사람의 권위로 이해되었고 법 그 자체의 권위로 이해되지 않았기 때문이다. 사실 학자들도 권위의 본질과 기능에 대한 합의에 이르지 못하고 있다. 한편으로 권위는 (a) 행위의 근거(reason for action)를 제공하는 것으로 여겨지거나 혹은 (b) 단지 믿음의 근거(reason for belief)만을 제공하는 것으로 여겨져 왔 다. 권위는 다른 한편으로 (a) 정당화된 힘(justified power), (b) 지배할 권리(right to rule: 자유권 liberty 또는 청구권 claim-right) 또는 (c) 의무를 부과할 수 있는 규범적 능력(normative capacity)으로 이해되어 왔다.

그러나 정작 중요한 문제는 권위가 포지셔널 오쏘리티(positional authority)인지 아니면 디스－포지셔널 오쏘리티(dis-positional authority)인지 하는 것이다. 학자들이 위의 개념들 중 어느 것을 통해 권위의 개념을 풀어내더라도, 그들은 권위를 포지셔널 오쏘리티인 것으로 즉 무엇인가를 할 수 있는 '능력(ability)'으로 본다. 그들에게 있어 권위란 법의 권위인 것이 아니라, 어디까지나 권위 관계 속에서 그에 복종하는 사람들과 마주하고 있는 사람 혹은 사람의 집단이 처한 규범적 위치에 따른 권위일 뿐이다. 그러나 권위의 개념은 포지셔널 오쏘리티 즉 무엇인가를 할 수 있는 능력으로서가 아니라 디스－포지셔널 오쏘리티로, 즉 존중할 만한 속성(respectable properties)으로서 이해되어야 한다. 왜냐하면 포지셔널 오쏘리티의 개념은 현대 사회에서 그 구성원들 간에 사적 이익의 균형을 도모하는 데 이용되고 있는 전형적인 방식 즉 재판에 의한 분쟁해결 방식을 반영할 수 없기 때문이다.

더욱이, 포지셔널 오쏘리티 개념은 법체계에 관한 환원주의적(reductivist) 단순 모델과 불가분의 일체를 이루면서, 이 모델로 하여금 하트가 말하는 법의 현저한 특징들(salient features of law)을 재현해낼 수 없도록 하는 데 기여한다. 즉 그 개념으로는 입법적 권위의 계속성(continuity), 법의 지속성(persistence) 그리고 입법의 자기구속력(self-binding force)을 설명할 수 없다. 실로, 강제적 명령(coercive orders)의 개념과 포지셔널 오쏘리티의 개념은 상호 분석적으로 의존하고 있는 것이다. 반면에 디스-포지셔널 오쏘리티의 개념은 켈젠과 하트에 의해 고안된 법체계에 관한 비환원주의적(anti-reductivist) 모델의 타당성을 높이는 데 기여한다. 특히 규칙의 관념 또는 규칙의 내적 측면(internal aspects)이라는 관념은 포지셔널 오쏘리티 개념을 디스-포지셔널 오쏘리티 개념으로 대체하지 않으면 어떠한 법체계의 모델에도 반영되기 어렵다.

그러나 이 글에서 법의 권위는 법의 본질에 관한 이론들의 타당성을 판정하는 함의를 갖는 것으로 해석되지는 않는다. 즉 권위에 관한 이론은 (법의) 권위를 단지 법이 하나의 체계를 이루면서 존재한다는 점을 보이기 위해 필요한 것으로 보는 '약한(thin)' 이론으로 간주되고 있다. 이 점에서 본 논문은 권위에 관한 이론이 자신의 원천 테제(the sources thesis)를 지지한다고 보는 조셉 라즈의 '강한(thick)' 이론에는 반대하고 있다. 나아가 이 글에서는 '거짓 진술 논변(the argument from falsity)' 및 '본질 테제(the nature thesis)'라는 분석적 수단을 도입하여 라즈의 논변에 대한 비판적 분석을 수행하고, 이를 통해 그가 자신의 논변을 충분히 근거짓지 못하고 있음을 보이고 있다.

권위의 개념은 법체계의 구조 분석과 직접적으로 연관되며, 따라서 법본질론 내지 법개념론에 대해서는 단지 간접적으로만 영향을 줄 수 있다. 특정한 법본질론의 타당성을 판정하는 기준이 되는 것은 (법의) 권위가 아니라 규칙들의 체계 그 자체이다. 그리고 (법의) 권위는 법이 규칙들의 체계로서 존재한다는 점을 보다 적절하게 인식하기 위해 필요한 것이다. 따라서 배제적 법실증주의(exclusive positivism)뿐만 아니라 포용적 법실중주의(inclusive positivism) 및 비실중주의적(anti-positivist) 견해를 취할 경우에도, 법체계의 규칙들을 상대로 씨름하는 와중에 (법의) 권위 개념에 호소할 수 있는 가능성은 여전히 열려 있다.

하트(H.L.A. Hart)와 라즈(Joseph Raz)의 법철학*

1. 들어가며

하트(H.L.A. Hart)와 그의 제자 라즈(Joseph Raz)의 만남에 대해서는 잘 알려진 일화가 있다. 예루살렘에 있는 히브루(Hebrew University)에서 법학을 공부하고 있던 라즈가 학회차 이스라엘을 방문한 하트에게 깊은 인상을 심어주었고, 결국 하트의 권유에 따라 영국으로 건너와 옥스퍼드의 베일리얼(Balliol) 칼리지에서 수학하게 되었다는 이야기이다.[1] 이후 라즈는 하트와 마찬가지로 '분석적 법실증주의'의 입장에서 활발한 저술 활동을 전개함으로써 세계적인 명성을 얻게 된다.

하지만 우리는 비교적 잘 알려지지 않은 부분에 대해 이야기하고자 한다. 그것은 하트의 이론 중 구체적으로 어떠한 측면이 라즈에게 이어지고 있고, 또 어떠한 측면이 거부되고 있는지, 어떠한 발전적 변용이 있었는지 등에 대한 이야기이다.[2] 하트의 존재가 라즈의 학문적 삶에 있어 결정

---

* 이화여자대학교 <법학논집> 11권 2호에 수록된 논문임.

1) http://en.wikipedia.org/wiki/Joseph Raz 참조.

2) 이와 관련하여 한 가지 눈길을 끄는 점은 하트가 1983년에 출판된 그의 논문집 (*Essays in Jurisprudence and Philosophy*)의 서문에서 자신의 비평자들 중에서도 특히 그의 저작을 "주요 타겟(principal target)"으로 삼았던 학자들로서 풀러(Lon Fuller), 드워킨(R. Dworkin), 피니스(J. Finnis) 등과 함께 라즈를 언급하고 있다는 사실이

적인 영향을 미쳤음에도 불구하고 이 주제에 대하여 아직 본격적으로 다루어지지는 않은 듯하다.

우리는 먼저 하트의 법이론을 구성하고 있는 몇 가지 특징들에 대해 언급하고, 그에 관하여 라즈가 어떠한 입장을 취하고 있는지를 검토해 보고자 한다. 주의할 점은 여기서 언급하게 될 하트 법이론의 특징들은 그의 이론의 정수를 압축적으로 보여줄 수 있는가 하는 기준에 따라 선정된 것이 아니라, 다만 라즈의 이론과의 관계에서 어떠한 단절이나 연속성을 드러내 보이기에 적합한가 하는 기준에 따라 선정된 것이라는 점이다. 그러한 비교점들을 요약하면 다음과 같다.

> (1) 언어철학적 방법론
> (2) 규칙의 본질에 관한 관행 이론(practice theory)
> (3) 반환원주의적(anti-reductivist) 규범관
> (4) 규칙의 체계로서의 법
> (5) 법의 본질적 징표로서의 권위
> (6) 법 준수 의무(obligation to obey the law)의 긍정
> (7) 포용적 법실증주의(inclusive legal positivism)

2. 방법론과 규칙의 본질에 관하여

대체로 하트는 그의 논문 "Definition and Theory in Jurisprudence" 이래 일상 언어의 분석을 중시하는 언어철학적 방법론을 법철학의 영역에 응용하고 있는 것으로 평가받고 있으며, 그 주요한 징표가 되는 것은 단어가 아니라 문장을 분석의 기본 단위로 삼는 의미론적 접근 방법이라고 할 수 있다.[3]

다. H.L.A. Hart, *Essays in Jurisprudence and Philosophy*, Clarendon Press, 1983, 1면.
3) 일상언어철학과 기술적 사회학이라는 하트 법이론의 방법론상의 문제에 대한 상세

그런데 하트의 제자인 라즈가 과연 방법론적 차원에서 하트로부터 어떠한 영향을 받았는지에 대해서는 그다지 연구된 바가 없는 것 같다. 다만 라즈가 '권위'의 문제를 다루고 있는 방식을 살펴보면, '권위'라는 단어 자체에 대한 해명 내지 '권위란 무엇인가?'라는 형태의 문제 제기에서 출발하고 있는 것이 아니라 'X는 π에 관하여 Y에 대해 권위를 갖는다'는 말의 의미를 이해하려는 데서 출발하고 있음을 알 수 있는데,[4] 이는 적어도 의미론적 접근의 기초를 깔고 있는 것 아닌가 하는 생각이 든다.

하지만 라즈는 "일상 언어가 그 자체로써 문제를 해결하는 것은 아니며, 이론적 고찰의 여지를 남겨두고 있다"고 말한다.[5] 즉 라즈는 자신이 궁극적으로 도달하고자 하는 "실천이성의 일반이론(general theory of practical reason)"을 언어철학적 방법론을 통해 온전히 구축하는 것은 불가능하다고 생각한 것 같다. 일례로 그는 행위 근거(reason for action)를 일차적 근거(first-order reason)와 이차적 근거(second-order reason)로 구별하는 자신의 이론에 대한 설명에서, 이러한 구별이 일상 언어적 표현 중에 직접적으로 반영되지 않는 까닭에 기존의 철학자들이 그와 같은 구별을 인식하지 못한 것이라고 말하고 있다.[6]

규칙의 본질을 일종의 관행으로 설명하는 하트의 견해[7]에 대해서도 라즈는 유사한 태도를 보인다. 즉 사회적 규칙(social rule) 또는 법적 규칙(legal rule) 등은 그것이 실행될(practiced) 때에 비로소 규칙이 되는 것이라고 봄으로써[8] 부분적으로는 하트의 설명을 긍정하는 듯하면서도, 규칙

한 논의는 김현철, "하트 법이론의 철학적 의의에 대한 비판적 고찰", 이화여자대학교 <법학논집> 11권 2호, 2007 참조.

4) Joseph Raz, *Practical Reason and Norms*, Princeton University Press, 1990 (1975), 62면.

5) Joseph Raz, 앞의 책, 70면.

6) Joseph Raz, 앞의 책, 36면.

7) H.L.A. Hart, *The Concept of Law*, Clarendon Press, 1994 (1961) 참조.

자체 또는 규칙 일반에 대한 설명으로서는 관행설(practice theory)이 적절하지 않다고 한다.[9]

이와 관련하여 라즈는 규칙 또는 규칙이 존재한다는 사실의 규범적 의미도 소위 "실천이성의 일반이론" 속에서 논의되는 것이 옳다고 본다.[10] 따라서 그에게 규칙(이 존재한다는 사실)은 일종의 행위 근거이며, 규칙을 이해한다는 것은 무엇보다 "그것이 어떠한 종류의 (행위) 근거이며, 여타의 (행위) 근거들과는 어떻게 다른지를 살펴보는 것"[11]을 의미한다. 이러한 측면에서 보았을 때, 하트의 이론은 규칙이 실행되고 있다는 점 내지 규칙의 '관행적 존재 양상'이 바로 그러한 차이점이라고 설명하는 것이 된다. 그렇지만 라즈는 관행설이 다음과 같은 "세 가지 치명적인 결함"을 안고 있음을 지적한다.

> "첫째, 관행설은 실행되지 않는 규칙들을 설명하지 못한다.
> 둘째, 관행설은 또한 사회적 규칙과 널리 받아들여진 근거(widely accepted reason)를 구별하지 못한다.
> 셋째, 규칙의 본질을 관행으로 보게 됨으로써 규칙의 규범적 성격(normative character)을 소거하게 된다."[12]

특히 첫 번째와 세 번째의 결함은 드워킨 또한 하트 법이론의 문제점

---

8) Joseph Raz, 앞의 책, 53면.
9) Joseph Raz, 앞의 책, 51-8면.
10) 하트는 이같은 라즈의 견해에 대하여 반대의 의사를 분명히 하고 있다. 즉 그는 객관적 (행위) 근거라는 용어로써 법적 의무를 인식주의적(cognitive)으로 해석하는 입장을 취해야 할 이유가 없을 뿐 아니라, 규범적 법명제에 대한 라즈의 인식주의적 설명 자체도 잘못되었으며, 심지어 그러한 견해는 은근히 자연법론적인 구석이 있다고 비판한다. H.L.A. Hart, "Legal Duty and Obligation", *Essays on Bentham: Studies in Jurisprudence and Political Theory*, Clarendon Press, 1982, 155-60면.
11) Joseph Raz, 앞의 책, 51면.
12) Joseph Raz, 앞의 책, 53면.

으로 지적하고 있는 바이고, 하트 스스로도 **법의 개념**(*The Concept of Law*) 의 후기에서 그러한 비판을 받아들이고 있다.

다만 드워킨이 아닌 라즈가 세 번째의 결함을 지적하는 것과 관련해서 는 약간의 의문이 있다. 그것은 라즈가 규범성(normativity)에 대하여 설 명하는 글을 통해 규범성이라는 개념 자체에 관하여 두 가지의 경쟁적 관 점이 존재한다는 점을 인정하고 있기 때문이다. 그것은 "정당화된 규범성 (justified normativity)"과 "사회적 규범성(social normativity)"이다.13) 이 글에서 라즈는 하트가 "사회적 규범성"의 관점에서 법의 규범성을 (비교 적 성공적으로) 논하고 있는 반면, 켈젠(Hans Kelsen)은 "정당화된 규범 성"의 관점에서 논의를 전개하고 있다고 평가하고 있으며, 궁극적으로 어 떠한 관점이 더 적합한 것인지에 대해서는 직접적인 판단을 유보하고 있 다. 그것은 "사회적 규범성"의 관점이 환원주의로 흐를 수 있다는 비판에 노출되어 있는 것과 마찬가지로, "정당화된 규범성"의 관점도 자연법론 과 다를 바 없다는 비판에 노출되어 있기 때문일 것이다.

그렇다면 라즈가 관행설을 규범성의 소거라는 측면에서 비판하는 논거 는 과연 무엇일까? 라즈는 관행의 존재 그 자체가 필연적으로 행위 근거 가 되지는 않는다는 점에 주목한다. 다시 말해 이러이러한 관행이 존재한 다는 점 또는 많은 사람들이 (일정한 상황에서) 이러이러하게 행동한다는 점만을 근거로 자신의 그러한 행동을 정당화할 수 있는 것도, 그와 다르 게 행동하는 타인에 대한 사회적 비난을 정당화할 수 있는 것도 아니라는 것이다. 그렇다면 이러한 정당화 기능을 수행할 수 있기 위해서는 관행이 존재한다는 점 외에 그러한 사실이 행위 근거가 되도록 하는 정보가 추가 로 제시되어야 한다.14)

---

13) Joseph Raz, *The Authority of Law: Essays on Law and Morality*, Clarendon Press, 1983 (1979), 134면.

14) 하트에 의하면, 이와 같은 정당화 기능의 수행은 사회적 규칙이 존재하기 위한 필

라즈가 보기에 그러한 추가적 정보 제시는 '규칙'이라는 말의 사용으로 충분히 달성될 수 있는데, 그것은 규칙(이 존재한다는 사실)이 일종의 행위 근거이기 때문이다. 따라서 'X는 ϕ를 해야 한다는 것이 규칙이다(it is a rule that X ought to ϕ)'는 말 속에는 'X는 ϕ를 해야 한다(X ought to ϕ)'는 내용 외에 '그러한 행위는 규칙에 따른 행위이므로 정당하다'는 함의가 실려 있다. 그러나 하트의 경우 규칙의 본질을 관행으로 이해하기 때문에 'X는 ϕ를 해야 한다는 것이 규칙이다'는 말은 곧 'X는 ϕ를 해야 한다는 것이 관행이다'는 말이 되는데, 후자의 표현 속에는 'X는 ϕ를 해야 한다'는 내용 외에 그러한 행위가 정당한 것이라는 함의는 존재하지 않는다. 앞서 언급했듯이 관행이 존재한다는 점만으로는 행위를 정당화할 수 없기 때문이다. 라즈의 지적에 따르면, 이상의 분석을 반영이라도 하듯이 하트는 'X는 ϕ를 해야 한다는 것이 규칙이다'는 말과 'X는 ϕ를 해야 한다'는 말을 동일한 의미로 사용하고 있다.[15]

요컨대 관행설을 따를 경우, 규칙이 존재한다는 사실을 언급하는 것은 미묘한 수사적 장치(rhetorical device)를 사용하는 것에 불과하며 실천적 추론(practical reasoning)과는 무관한 것으로 강등된다는 점이 라즈의 주장이다.

요충분조건의 일부를 이루고 있다. 이에 대한 지적으로는 Joseph Raz, 앞의 책(각주 4), 53면. 라즈의 정리에 따르면, 사회적 규칙이 존재하기 위한 필요충분조건의 구성요소로 하트는 다음의 네 가지를 들고 있다. (1) 당해 규칙이 그 수범자인 사회 구성원에 의해 규칙적으로 준수될 것. (2) 당해 규칙을 준수하지 않을 경우 (다른 구성원의) 비판적 반응이 있을 것. (3) 그러한 비판적 반응 자체에 대해서는 더 이상 (다른 구성원의) 비판적 반응이 일어나지 않을 것. (4) 사회 구성원은 'X는 ϕ를 해야 한다'는 표현 및 'X는 ϕ를 해야 한다는 것이 규칙이다'는 표현을 사용함으로써 자신의 그러한 행동을 정당화하고, 다른 사람으로 하여금 그렇게 행동하도록 요구하는 것 또는 그와 다르게 행동하는 것을 비난하는 것을 정당화한다.

15) Joseph Raz, 앞의 책(각주 4), 205면 미주 6) 참조.

3. 규범, 법체계, 권위

하지만 라즈가 하트의 법이론을 환원주의적인(reductivist) 것으로 평가하는 것은 아니다. 사실 하트는 벤담(J. Bentham)과 오스틴(J. Austin)의 견해로 대표되는 환원주의적 규범관에 대하여 법규범은 "복종의 습관(habit of obedience)"이나 "(제재의) 위협에 의해 뒷받침되는 명령(order backed by threat)"과 같은 사실적 언어로 기술되지 않는 측면을 포함하고 있음을 주장한다.16) 라즈 또한 이러한 하트의 견해를 거의 전적으로 수용함으로써 반환원주의적(anti-reductivist) 규범관을 따르고 있다.17)

그렇다면 위에서 언급한 관행설 비판의 세 번째 논거 즉 규칙의 본질을 관행으로 보게 됨으로써 규칙의 규범적 성격을 소거하게 된다는 라즈의 주장은 규칙 일반을 염두에 둔 것이며, 사회적 규칙 내지 법적 규칙이라는 특수한 유형의 규칙에 한정하여 말한다면 너무 과도한 것이라고 말할 수 있을 것 같다. 현재로서는 이러한 해석이 (법적 규칙의) "사회적 규범성" 관념과 (규칙 일반의) 규범성 소거 비판을 정합적으로 이해할 수 있는 유일한 길이 아닌가 생각된다.

한편 하트가 법을 규칙의 체계로 설명한다는 점은 주지하는 바이다. 이점은 라즈도 마찬가지이다. 그렇지만, 하트의 법이론에서 중심이 되는 것은 어디까지나 '규칙'이며, 그가 이야기하는 '법체계(legal system)'의 의미에 대해서는 뚜렷한 설명이 없다. 말하자면 복수의 규칙들로 하여금 하나의 체계를 이루도록 만들어 주는 것도 또한 (승인의) 규칙일 뿐, 법체계의 개념이 규칙 개념에 선재하거나 규칙 개념을 인도하는 것으로 파악되

---

16) H.L.A. Hart, 앞의 책(각주 7), 50면 이하.

17) Joseph Raz, *The Concept of a Legal System: An Introduction to the Theory of Legal System*, Clarendon Press, 1978 (1970) 및 앞의 책(각주 13) 참조.

지는 않는다.

그렇지만 라즈에 의하면 (1) "법의 규범성에 대한 설명은 법의 개념보다는 법체계의 개념에 달려 있고", (2) "법의 개념에 대한 분석은 법체계의 개념에 대한 분석에 달려 있다"고 봄으로써,[18] '규칙'이 아닌 '법체계'가 그의 법이론에서 중심적인 역할을 담당한다. 그는 또한 어떠한 규칙이 특정한 법체계의 일부로 존재하는지 여부를 판단하기 위하여 굳이 승인의 규칙(rule of recognition)과 같은 궁극적 규칙(ultimate rule)을 전제할 필요는 없다고 말한다.[19] 이러한 그의 주장은 관행설을 거부하는 기본 입장과도 일맥상통하는 것으로 보인다. 요컨대 하트는 법을 규칙의 체계로 보지만, 라즈는 법을 규칙의 체계로 보는 것이라고 말할 수 있을 것이다.

하트의 법이론과 라즈의 그것 사이에서 가장 뚜렷한 연속성을 보이는 대목은 바로 권위의 분석에 관한 부분일 것이다. 하트가 권위를 법의 본질적 징표로 인식하고 있었다는 사실은 다음과 같은 그의 말에서도 잘 나타나 있다.

> "사령(command)이라는 관념은 권위와 강한 연관성이 있어서, 위협에 의해 뒷받침되는 권총강도의 명령(order)에 비해 법의 관념에 훨씬 가깝다. … 그렇지만 사령은 법과 너무나 가까운 것이어서 [그것을 분석의 기초로 삼는 것은] 우리의 목적 달성에 적합하지 않다. 왜냐하면 법에 포함된 권위의 요소는 항상 법이 과연 무엇인가 하는 점을 쉽게 설명하는 데 하나의 걸림돌이 되어 왔기 때문이다. 따라서 우리는 법을 해명함에 있어 사령이라는 관념을 사용해서 유익할 것이 없다. 그 관념 또한 권위의 요소를 포함하고 있기 때문이다."[20]

---

18) Joseph Raz, 앞의 책(각주 17), 169-70면.
19) Joseph Raz, 앞의 책(각주 17), 200면.
20) H.L.A. Hart, 앞의 책(각주 7), 20면.

하트는 권위의 특성을 설명함에 있어 그것이 "내용독립적 근거(content-independent reason)"임과 동시에 "확정적 근거(peremptory reason)"의 성격을 갖는다고 말한다.[21] 즉 '이러이러한 행위를 해야 한다'는 지시를 권위적 근거(authoritative reason)라 평가할 수 있는 경우란, 지시의 상대방이 생각하기에 지시된 행위가 바람직한 내용을 담고 있어서 그 지시를 따르기로 하는 경우가 아니라, 단지 지시자로부터 지시가 있었다는 이유만으로 지시된 행위를 수행하는 경우이어야 한다(내용독립적 근거). 뿐만아니라 그러한 지시가 내려지기 전까지는 논란의 여지가 있었음에도 불구하고, 일단 그러한 지시가 내려진 이상 논의는 마감이 되고(cut off), 지시된 행위를 수행해야 한다는 점은 종국적으로 긍정되는 경우이어야 한다(확정적 근거).

라즈는 하트의 분석을 보다 발전시켜, 권위가 (지시 상대방의) 실천적 추론의 과정에서 "내용독립적 근거", "배제적 근거(exclusionary reason)" 그리고 "선취적 근거(preemptive reason)"로 작용한다고 말한다. 즉, 지시가 있었다는 사실이 지시의 상대방으로 하여금 '스스로의 판단에 근거하여 저울질하지 않을' 근거가 된다는 점에서 "이차적 근거"의 하나인 "배제적 근거"로서의 성격을 지니며, 나아가 단순히 지시 상대방의 사적인 행위 근거를 '배제'할 뿐 아니라 이를 '대체(replace)'함으로써, 일단 지시가 주어지면 더 이상 이전의 사적인 근거를 행위 근거로 삼을 수는 없도록 한다는 의미에서 "선취적 근거"가 된다는 것이다.[22]

나아가 라즈는 권위를 법의 본질적 징표로 보는 하트의 통찰을 받아들이고, 권위 개념을 매개로 하여 자신이 추구하던 "실천이성의 일반이론"과 전통적 법철학의 주제들을 통합하기에 이른다. 그 대표적인 예가 바로

---

21) H.L.A. Hart, "Commands and Authoritative Legal Reasons", 앞의 책(각주 10), 243면.

22) Joseph Raz, *The Morality of Freedom*, Clarendon Press, 1990 (1986), 38면 이하.

권위 개념의 분석을 통해 '배제적 법실증주의(exclusive legal positivism)'
를 설파하고자 하는 시도이다. 그는 이 문제에 관한 자신의 기본 입장을
다음과 같은 말로 정리하고 있다.

> "법과 권위의 관련성을 이용하여 드워킨의 정합성 테제(coherence the-
> sis)와 하트 등의 포용 테제(incorporation thesis)를 비판할 수 있다. 이러한
> 견해들을 거부함으로써 원천 테제(sources thesis)를 받아들이게 된다."[23]

4. 법 준수 의무와 법의 본질에 관하여

법 준수 의무(obligation to obey the law)의 문제란, 간단히 말해서, '법
은 단지 그것이 법이기 때문에 준수되어야 한다고 말할 수 있는가?' 하는
문제이다. 하트는 법을 준수할 도덕적 의무를 긍정할 수 있기 위한 유일
한 토대는 공정성(fairness)일 것이라고 한다.[24] 이러한 하트의 입장은 종
종 '페어플레이(fair play) 이론'이라는 말로 표현된다. 하트에 의하면 사
회 구성원들 사이에서 자유의 제한이라는 부담을 평등하게 배분토록 하
는 공정성의 가치는 구성원들이 (자신이 직·간접적으로 동의한 적이 없
는) 사회의 자유제한적 규칙을 준수할 근거로 삼기에 충분하다.

---

23) Joseph Raz, Ethics in the Public Domain: *Essays in the Morality of Law and Politics*,
Clarendon Press, 1994, 195면. 이러한 라즈의 견해는 이 글의 말미에서 검토하기
로 하고, 여기서는 다만 그가 권위 개념에 관한 하트의 통찰을 발전시켜, 그것을 법
철학의 근본 문제들에 관한 이른바 '열쇠 개념'으로 삼고 있다는 사실만을 지적하
고자 한다.

24) H.L.A. Hart, "Are There Any Natural Rights?", *philosophical Review* 64 (1955).
Reprinted in Carl Wellman (ed.), *Rights and Duties vol. 4: Human Rights and Universal Duties*, Routledge, 2002, 17면. [면수는 재수록 면수임.]

"많은 사람들이 규칙에 따라 공동의 업무를 수행하며 이로 말미암아 자신들의 자유를 제한할 때, 필요시 그와 같은 제한을 감수하고 있는 사람들은 그들의 감수로 말미암아 수혜를 입고 있는 자들로 하여금 그들과 마찬가지로 제한을 감수하도록 할 권리를 가진다."[25)

주의할 점은 하트가 법 준수 의무를 인정함에 있어 그러한 법을 제정할 수 있는 정치적 권위의 개념을 필요로 하는 것은 아니라는 점이다. 하트에 따르면 법 준수 의무는 정치적 권위의 지배권과 규범적 상관 관계에 있는 것이 아니라, 협력 관계에 있는(co-operating) 사회의 구성원들에 대한 도덕적 의무인 것이며, 그러한 의무와 규범적 상관 관계에 있는 것도 바로 구성원들이 가지게 되는, 규칙 준수에 대한 도덕적 권리(moral right to obedience)인 것이다.

라즈는 이러한 하트의 견해를 수용하지 않는다. 그는 우선 법 준수 의무가 사회의 구성원들에 대하여 부담하는 도덕적 의무라는 설명에 동의하지 않고, 정당성 있는(legitimate) 정치적 권위의 지배권과 규범적 상관 관계에 있는 도덕적 의무로 받아들인다. 따라서 국가의 (정치적) 권위가 정당성을 갖는다면 그 권위의 상대방인 일반시민들은 법을 준수할 의무를 지니게 되는 것으로 본다. 그렇다고 해서 라즈가 전통적인 의미의 법 준수 의무가 존재한다고 결론짓는 것은 아니다.[26) 그에 따르면 어떠한 국가도 스스로 주장하는 만큼의 정당성을 확보할 수는 없기 때문에[27) 전통적인 의미의 법 준수 의무는 존재하지 않는다고 한다.

국가 권위의 정당성을 옹호하고자 하는 많은 학자들의 우려에도 불구하고, 라즈가 현대 사회의 이른바 '정당성의 위기'를 조장하고 있는 것은 아니다. 오히려 라즈는 법을 '의무'의 객체가 아니라 '존경(respect)'의 대

---

25) H.L.A. Hart, 앞의 글(각주 24), 11면.
26) Joseph Raz, 앞의 책(각주 13), 237면.
27) Joseph Raz, 앞의 책(각주 22) 70면 이하.

상으로 바라봄으로써 그러한 위기의 원천을 제대로 파악할 수 있다고 보는 것이다.[28] 요컨대 그가 말하고자 하는 바는 사회 구성원들의 법에 대한 태도의 문제는 객관화된 도덕적 의무의 측면이 아닌, 일종의 시민적 덕성(civic virtue)의 측면에서 접근해야 할 문제라는 점이다.

마지막으로 하트가 **법의 개념**의 후기에서 밝힌 실증주의관에 대하여 살펴보고자 한다. 하트는 자신의 법이론에 대한 드워킨의 비판을 재비판하는 과정에서, 자신의 실증주의는 이른바 "연성 실증주의(soft positivism)"이며, 실정법의 효력에 대한 판단 기준(criteria of validity)으로서 도덕적 원리에 부합할 것을 이미 요구하고 있다는 사실을 드워킨이 간과하고 있다고 말한다.[29]

이러한 하트의 견해에 의하면 실정법의 효력에 대한 판단 기준이 일정한 도덕적 원리들을 포함할 수 있을 뿐만 아니라, 그러한 가능성을 인정하는 것이 실증주의적 법체계 개념에 모순되는 것도 아니다(포용 테제 incorporation thesis).

라즈는 이와 같은 하트의 포용 테제가 일견 드워킨의 정합성 테제(coherence thesis)[30]보다는 합당한 것으로 평가한다. 왜냐하면 드워킨의 견해는 "사회적 사실만에 의하여 그 존재와 내용이 파악되는 법과 그 법이 본질적으로 주장하게 되는 [정당성 있는] '권위' 사이의 특수한 연관성을 파악하지 못하고"[31] 있기 때문이다. 드워킨에 대한 라즈의 비판은 '실증주의 논쟁'의 배턴(baton)이 하트로부터 라즈에게로 이어지고 있음을 그대로 보여주고 있는 것이라 할 수 있다.

---

28) Joseph Raz, 앞의 책(각주 13), 250면 이하.
29) H.L.A. Hart, 앞의 책(각주 7), 후기 참조.
30) 라즈의 표현에 따르면 "법은 사회적 사실만에 의하여 그 존재와 내용이 파악되는 법과 그러한 법에 대한 도덕적으로 가장 건전한 정당화(the morally soundest justification)로 구성된다"는 명제를 의미함. Joseph Raz, 앞의 책(각주 23), 195면.
31) Joseph Raz, 앞의 책(각주 23), 210면. [필자의 강조 및 보충.]

그렇지만 라즈는 하트의 포용 테제에 대해서도 반론을 제기한다. 라즈의 반론은 인식론적이라고 할 수 있다. 그것은 마치 노직(R. Nozick)의 "논리적 함축 하에서의 지식의 폐쇄성 원리(principle of closure of knowledge under entailment)"에 관한 논의[32]를 법의 인식 또는 확인(cognition or identification of law)의 문제에 응용하고 있는 것과 같은 인상을 준다. 여기에는 그럴 만한 이유가 있다. 그것은 라즈가 포용 테제 그 자체를 위에서 언급한 일반적으로 제시되는 형태와는 달리 규정함으로써, '논리적 함축'의 문제가 전면에 부각될 수 있는 여건을 조성하고 있기 때문이다. 라즈가 규정하는 바에 따르면, 포용 테제는 법체계를 구성하는 유효한 규칙들에는 이른바 "사회적 사실(social facts)만에 의하여 그 존재와 내용이 파악되는 규칙[source-based rules]" 외에도 "그러한 규칙으로부터 논리적으로 함축되는 규칙[rules entailed by source-based rules]"도 포함된다는 내용을 담고 있다.[33] 그리고 이렇게 규정된 포용 테제는 "지식의 폐쇄성 원리"가 거부되는 것과 동일한 이유에서 거부되는 것이다. 다시 말해서 특정한 법체계 내에 사회적 사실만에 의하여 그 존재와 내용이 파악되는 규칙이 주어져 있고, 그러한 규칙이 특정한 규범적 명제를 논리적으로 함축하고 있다고 하더라도, 그러한 규범적 명제의 존재와 내용이 또한 사회적 사실만에 의하여 파악되지 않는 한, 당연히 그것이 당해 법체계에 소속된 규칙이라고 말할 수는 없다는 것이다. 이를 간단한 식으로 표현하면 다음과 같을 것이다.

---

32) R. Nozick, *Philosophical Explanations*, Cambridge University Press, 1981 참조. 노직은 다음과 같은 내용을 담고 있는 원리를 "논리적 함축 하에서의 지식의 폐쇄성 원리"라고 부르면서 그것을 합당한 인식론 상의 원리로 받아들일 수 없다고 한다: $[p \Rightarrow q] \Rightarrow [K(p) \Rightarrow K(q)]$ (여기서 K는 '지식' 연산자.)

33) Joseph Raz, 앞의 책(각주 23), 194면 이하. 그러나 이 글에서 포용 테제의 내용을 이렇게 규정하는 이유에 대해서는 함구하고 있다. 따라서 과연 라즈의 규정이 합당한 것인지 여부에 대해 우선 생각해 봐야 할 것이다.

$$[p \Rightarrow q] \not\Rightarrow [L(p) \Rightarrow L(q)]$$ (여기서 L은 '법' 연산자.)[34]

결국 라즈는 하트의 이론과 달리, "모든 법은 사회적 사실만에 의하여 그 존재와 내용이 파악된다"고 하는 "경성 실증주의(hard positivism)" 또는 "배제적 법실증주의(exclusive legal positivism)"의 길을 가게 된다. 그리고 하트로부터 물려받은 '권위'에 대한 통찰을 확장하여 배제적 법실증주의야말로 법의 개념 내지 본질을 제대로 반영하고 있는 입장임을 입증하려는 것이다.

5. 맺음말

이상과 같이 우리는 하트의 법이론을 구성하고 있는 몇 가지 특징들에 관하여 라즈가 어떠한 입장을 취하고 있는지를 검토하였다. 즉 하트의 이론 중 구체적으로 어떠한 측면이 라즈에게 이어지고 있고, 또 어떠한 측면이 거부되고 있는지, 어떠한 발전적 변용이 있었는지 등을 살펴봄으로써 '분석적 법실증주의' 진영의 내부에서 들려오는 다양한 목소리를 만날 수 있었다. 본문의 검토 내용을 요약하면 다음과 같다.

첫째, 라즈는 하트의 언어철학적 방법론이나 관행 이론으로부터 큰 영향을 받지는 않은 것 같다. (특히 "실천이성의 일반이론"을 구축하려는 기획 하에서는 이러한 하트의 유산을 거부할 수밖에 없었지만, 그렇다고 해서 일종의 '특수이론'으로서의 가능성도 부인하고 있는 것은 아니다.)

둘째, 라즈는 하트의 반환원주의적 규범관, 법을 규칙의 체계로 파악하는 관점, 그리고 권위를 법의 본질적 징표로 파악하는 견해를 계승·발전시켰다.

---

34) 이를 '법의 개방성 원리'라고 부를 수 있을까?

셋째, 라즈는 법 준수 의무를 긍정하는 하트의 견해 및 그의 포용적 법 실증주의에 대해서는 정면으로 반대한다.

결국 라즈는 벤담과 오스틴의 법이론에 대한 하트의 비판을 계승함과 동시에, 법과 도덕의 개념적 분리라는 실증주의적 전제를 극단적으로 옹호하고 있다고 말할 수 있다. 그러나 이 모든 세부적인 견해의 표명이 "실천이성의 일반이론"이라는 그의 야심찬 기획의 일부인 점을 고려한다면, 라즈의 법이론에 대한 제대로 된 평가는 아마도 그러한 밑그림부터 파악한 후에라야 가능할 것 같다.

Index

박 준 석 Joon Seok Park

학력 및 경력
서울대학교 법과대학
동 대학원 법학과(법학박사)
이화여자대학교 생명윤리법정책연구소 박사후과정연구원
현 전북대학교 법과대학 전임강사

The Concept of Authority　　　　　　　　　값 13,000원

2007년 10월 18일　초판 인쇄
2007년 10월 28일　초판 발행

저　　자 : 박 준 석
발 행 인 : 한 정 희
발 행 처 : 경인문화사
편　　집 : 한 정 주
　　　　　서울특별시 마포구 마포동 324-3
　　　　　전화 : 718-4831～2, 팩스 : 703-9711
　　　　　e-mail : kyunginp@chol.com
　　　　　homepage : http://www.kyunginp.co.kr
　　　　　　　　　　한국학서적.kr
등록번호 : 제10-18호(1973. 11. 8)

ISBN : 978-89-499-0529-7 94360